MALADJUSTED YOUTH

This research is dedicated by the researchers to the memory of

FRAN MILČINSKI (1867–1932)

pioneer of Slovene criminology for juveniles

No child who gets stuck in mud chose the place by himself, but was pushed into it! It is wrong, of course that the child has muddy spots, but there is no logic and no justice in a human society which wants to punish the child for these reasons ...

Fran Milčinski, 1909

Maladjusted Youth

An experiment in rehabilitation

Edited by   KATJA VODOPIVEC

In collaboration with   MILICA BERGANT
MILOŠ KOBAL
FRANC MLINARIČ
BRONISLAV SKABERNE
VINKO SKALAR

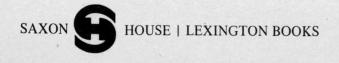

SAXON HOUSE | LEXINGTON BOOKS

Published by

SAXON HOUSE, D.C. Heath Ltd.

Westmead, Farnborough, Hants., England.

Jointly with

LEXINGTON BOOKS, D.C. Heath & Co.

Lexington, Mass. U.S.A.

ISBN 0 347 01046 6
Library of Congress Catalog Card Number 74-3919
Printed in Great Britain by Robert MacLehose & Co. Ltd
The University Press, Glasgow

Contents

PART IV   RESULTS

Researchers and consultants

Dr Milica BERGANT Ph.D.: Pedagogue, Professor at the Faculty of Philosophy.

Andrej CASERMAN: Graduate in psychology, Researcher at the Institute of sociology and philosophy, University of Ljubljana.

Dr Miloš KOBAL MD: Psychiatrist, graduate in law, Professor at the Faculty of Medicine, University of Ljubljana, and Director of the Psychiatric Clinic.

Franc MLINARIČ: Graduate in psychology, Counsellor for clinical treatment of convicted offenders, Department for Justice, Republic of Slovenia.

Dr Bronislav SKABERNE LL.D.: Scientific Counsellor at the Institute of Criminology at the Faculty of Law, University of Ljubljana.

Vinko SKALAR: Graduate in psychology, Higher Professional Collaborator at the Institute of Criminology at the Faculty of Law, University of Ljubljana.

Dr Katja VODOPIVEC LL.D.: Professor of Criminology at the Faculty of Law and Scientific Counsellor at the Institute of Criminology, University of Ljubljana.

Principal Investigator and Editor of the final report: Katja VODOPIVEC

The staff of the institution included in the experiment

Bogo AJDIČ, director's assistant
Rozalija AJDIČ-ROŽEN, nurse
Branko BAVEC, educator
Janez BEČAJ, psychologist
Anton BREJC, psychologist
Ernest DEMŠAR, educator
Ivan GUČEK, instructor (shopmaster)
Aljoša GUTNIK, instructor (shopmaster)
Ivan IVANUŠA, educator
Nadja IVANUŠA-LUBEJ, educator
Janez JELOVŠEK, instructor (shopmaster)
Marjan KERPAN, instructor (shopmaster)
Jože KLOPČIČ, educator
Vinko KRALJ, instructor (shopmaster)
Andrej LOGAR, educator
Božena PEKAROVIČ-PAVŠIČ, socialworker
Metod RESMAN, educator
Janez RUPNIK, educator
Franc ŠEMROV, instructor (shopmaster)
Ivan ŠKOFLEK, director
Jože ŠKRLJ, educator

Introduction

Katja VODOPIVEC

The experiment concerning the introduction of new educational methods in an experimental institution was carried out by the staff of the educational institution in Gorenji Logatec in co-operation with a research team from the Institute of Criminology of the Faculty of Law in Ljubljana and other professionals, as well as with the institution's inmates. The experiment lasted four and a half years, from the beginning of 1967 until the end of June 1971.

When we, the professional consultants, initiated the experiment in 1966, we had neither an institution, a staff nor an institutional director. We only knew that there existed a gap between theory and practice in the methods of educating personally and behaviourally disturbed youth in Yugoslavia, a gap that the theoreticians had not yet succeeded in bridging, despite considerable effort. But we had faith in each other's ability to work, and in the method of group counselling as a tool that could contribute to a reunion of theory and practice.

In retrospect we look on our decision at that time as adventurous, since we knew that all educational institutions have a lack of staff, and that people generally choose such work with reluctance, especially highly qualified workers. We were also aware that the experimental results could be negative. Although we pointed these things out to those who were willing to support and finance the experiment, we knew that their support was an expression of their favourable expectations.

Within four and a half years the experiment brought together, directly or indirectly, roughly 150 people (consultants, staff and inmates). In our interactions with each other, which often had a more than intellectual and professional colouring, we all experienced a wide range of fears, disappointments, pleasures, surprises, and both positive and negative emotional reactions. In illustration we might mention that the staff, who had no previous experience in work with behaviourally disturbed youth, experienced tensions before the first inmates arrived in the institution; that in the first week following the admission of inmates some of the consultants wanted to telephone the institution practically every day to find out if the inmates were still there and if anything untoward had happened during the night, but restrained themselves for fear of increasing the staff's tensions; that the consultants suffered personally in the face of the staff's resistance and carelessness; and that we experienced great personal satisfaction for any kindness shown us, and rejoiced over every postcard that we received from the teachers and inmates on their excursions together.

Throughout the experiment we were aware that the wealth of experience that grows out of the relationships between people could not be captured in any description of our experiment, and particularly not in a research report. Determination of facts and even their quantification is simply something other than the essence of interpersonal relationships. In this respect, as undoubtedly in many others, experiments in social science differ from experiments in natural science. The means at our disposal for presenting the results of experiments in the social sciences are extremely modest in comparison with the richness of the actual phenomenon. Therefore we feel that our presentation is only a pale shadow of the happenings we describe.

Six researchers worked on the experiment for four and a half years. The records gathered in the institute during this time are immense. They include the valuable diaries written by the institutional staff. Thus it is understandable that we faced a dilemma in trying to write a final report on the experiment, in particular because one of the financers of the work required that the report be short and concise. Since all of us involved in the research contributed to it, we all wanted to help write it. Therefore we decided first to prepare a more or less exhaustive report (of about 800 pages), which we would then summarise to produce the final report.

In this summary the various researchers are responsible for different parts of the text. The length of the different contributions in no way reflects a difference in the degree of involvement of the contributors. Therefore we wish to state explicitly that we were all maximally involved in the experiment (considering our respective responsibilities outside the experiment), and that we all participated equally in producing the results, such as they are.

Financial support for the research was provided by: the Secretariat for Education and Culture of the Socialist Republic of Slovenia (for renovation of the facilities); the Boris Kidrič Research Fund in Ljubljana; and the Department of Health, Education and Welfare in the USA, particularly its division for research and demonstration projects in the field of rehabilitation (the main source of financial support for the experiment, and a partial source of funds for the purchase of new equipment for the educational institution). Special thanks are due to all of our financial supporters for making the experiment possible, for having confidence in our work, and for the contribution they made to the results of the experiment with their understanding and consideration.

The researchers wish to express special thanks to the entire staff of the educational institution in Logatec; to Miss Marjorie M. Farley, international research specialist in the Office of Research and Demonstrations, Social and Rehabilitation Service USA, for all the consideration she devoted to the professional team, for her helpful criticism and suggestions, and for literature which she sent; to both experts: the psychiatrist, Dr Vojin Matič from Belgrade, who evaluated the composition and work of the professional team, and the psychologist Eugene S. Jones (director of the educational institution in Sacramento, California, in the United States), who offered organisational and technical help to the staff of the educational institution in Logatec; to Carl F. Jesness and R.H. Moos for sending psychological tests and directions for their use; to Stane Obranovič, psychologist at the Institute of Sociology, University of Ljubljana, who, together with the psychologist Skalar developed the methods of statistical analysis of the results and carried out most of the computations; to Dr Milan Lampret, counsellor at the Republican Statistical Office, who did the remaining calculations; to the administration of the Institute of Criminology of the Faculty of Law in Ljubljana and to Mila Kulnikova for their careful typing, duplicating and book-keeping work in connection with the experiment; and to both translators, Jana and Eric Hansen, for their conscientious efforts to remain true to the meaning of the original text. The institute also gives particular thanks to all the part-time professional consultants who contributed to the research and approached the experiment as their own personal responsibility.

Since the experiment has been financed mainly by the Department of Health, Education and Welfare of the USA and approved by it we want to draw attention to the specific conditions in which the experiment has been carried out. It might be that for these reasons the experiment is hardly comparable with the work in educational institutions in other countries. The particulars of the experimental scene were as described below.

The educational institution at Logatec is a so-called small institution (can provide boarding for forty to fifty inmates).

The management of the educational institution is based on the principle of self-government of the staff. The director of the institution is the executive of the self-government decisions of the staff. The management problems are therefore different from such problems in other countries.

The population of inmates reflects the particulars of the Slovene culture and subculture. Before admission to the institution, the majority of the inmates were exposed to heavy economic and emotional frustrations. There were no inmates who would live in spoiling family conditions. We do not have youth gangs in the way that the big cities in the USA or in Europe have them. There were no drug users among the inmates. Thus, one cannot ignore the fact that the results of work with a different population of inmates could be different from ours.

As a therapeutic method we have chosen primarily the method of permissiveness, counselling and guidance for inmates. Behaviour modifications as a method of treatment have been taken into account as far as proposed by the staff. We considered this method of treatment as a supplement of minor importance, compared to the first approach.

Our expectations regarding the results of the experiment were not oriented towards the greater efficiency of educational efforts. The aim of the experiment has been defined in another way. But, it has to be noted that the expectations regarding the issue of the experiment were not the same for all members of the research team. The differences in this respect are reflected also in the presentation of our findings (some authors tend to show better results obtained with inmates than others do). However, we were of the opinion that the expectations of research members could be different up to a certain point, provided they did not contradict each other. In this sense we wanted to preserve the principle of permissiveness also among the research members.

The experiment, as an empirical research, was demanding towards the staff of the institution. In our opinion the question of whether such experimentation is acceptable from the ethical point of view depends on the conceptual starting-point. Therefore, in presenting the results, we cannot and do not want to limit ourselves only to negative or positive findings. The conceptual problems, which entitle the researcher to conduct his experiments with people, are, in our opinion, of the same importance as the results themselves. That is why we have dedicated more space in our research to the conceptual problems than has been the case in many similar studies.

K.V.
Ljubljana, 17 January 1973

PART I

Concept of the Experiment

1 Historical Origins [1]

Bronislav SKABERNE

A proper understanding of the current situation in institutional education is not possible without knowledge of the historical origins and efforts which have led to the present state of affairs. In different periods and in various places individuals established the bases for institutional care, which were then adopted and developed by others and thus transmitted from generation to generation and from one country to another. Many principles of institutional care have been incorporated into the general spiritual culture of Europe, of which Slovenia is a part.

Ancient times

During the time of the tribal system the entire responsibility for the child and his education belonged to the chieftain of the tribe. The tribe offered the child security, and in turn the tribal chieftain had unlimited power over the children, including the power of life and death. The Hebrews recognised this right as being God's will. Similar provisions are found in Hellenic laws, the Spartan laws of Lycurgus, Solon's laws in Athens, and in Roman law (the law of the Twelve Tables).

With the development of civilisation came the first limitations on the father's right over the life and death of children. Already in the time of Roman emperors the father of the immediate family group was deprived of the right to kill his children, leaving him with only the right of punishment.

In these times institutions for poor children were founded primarily for political reasons. The benefactors wished honour during their lifetime and after their death. Mercy and charity were neither Hellenic nor Roman virtues. There was no basis for it in either the beliefs or the philosophy of those times.

The phenomenon of Christianity brought with it the first privately organised charity. Christianity developed the idea of the natural equality of all people and their mutual interdependence. A reflection of this is found in the Christian commandment to love one's neighbour. This commandment also resulted in charitable help to the needy.

In the early days of Christianity individuals cared primarily for those

3

children who had lost their parents, particularly those who were victims of the persecution of the Christians. Private Christian charity was organised according to congregational groupings and was first carried out in families.

The increase in poverty encouraged the church to begin caring for orphans, foundlings, abandoned and poor children, as well as for adults. These institutions were called hospitals. The hospitals originally served a number of purposes and carried out various activities, but were primarily asylums for all the needy homeless, both young and old. Thus this cultural period is characterised by institutionalisation.

The Middle Ages

At the time of the Carolingians every city with a bishop had a hospital led by priests. Charlemagne (742–814) accelerated the founding of hospitals, particularly by cathedrals and monasteries.

Following the Crusades (1096–1270) the feudal nobility and knights also began to build hospitals, and in the fourteenth and fifteenth centuries the nobility actually competed in the building of charitable institutions. Many hospitals were also founded in the cities. Although the cities administered the hospitals, the clergy was allowed a wide range of action in the work with the beneficiaries. Consequently hospitals at this time had a religious character, life within their walls being similar to that in a monastery.

In the Middle Ages children were not cared for because they needed special education, but rather, as was the case with adults, for social reasons. A very heterogeneous group of children were cared for in the hospitals: from foundlings to children who had been abandoned by their parents or whose parents had died. Children were cared for in the hospitals at least until they became capable of supporting themselves with begging. It is characteristic of thought in the Middle Ages that such children were to remain in the poor class.

Towards the end of the fifteenth century, but before the Reformation, the idea of professional education appeared.

From the Reformation to the middle of the eighteenth century

Christianity emphasised the significance of indulgences (which secured forgiveness of sins and salvation after death) by giving money to charity. The Reformation brought with it a different way of evaluating charity. It rejected the idea that salvation could be attained through good works,

4

independently of morality. For example, Luther demanded that the state assume responsibility for the care of the poor, which was to include only those who were truly in need of help. Under the influence of these thoughts, Europe experienced a reorganisation of care for the poor, with the state assuming increasing responsibility for this function. The influence of the Reformation and humanism began a transformation of views on the meaning and aim of life, as well as the meaning and aim of support of the poor. However, the people in political power at that time still considered poverty to be a moral problem, despite the fact that it was essentially a social problem.

In this period (the end of the fifteenth century) some German cities began to produce regulations governing beggars ('Bettelordnungen') which made special provision for children and required that they be given employment.

In countries that did not undergo the Reformation, care of the poor was reorganised under the influence of humanism. Efforts to care for the poor were systematically described in 1526 by the Spanish humanist Johan Ludvig Vives (1492–1540) in his work *De subventione pauperum sine humanis necessitatibus. Libro duo: primus de subventione privata, alter de subventione publica.* Vives represented the view that young people should be forced to work; that training for work should begin with childhood; if necessary, they must be removed from a menacing family environment and placed in institutions; that these institutions should be administered in the spirit of the humanistic ideas; that education in the institutions should not be limited to reading and writing; and that Christian piety should serve as their example.

Among those enthusiastic for Vives' ideas was the Hapsburg Emperor Charles V (reigned 1519–56). In October 1531 he made a decree concerning care of the poor, and in July 1548 he issued another one in which he stipulated that hospitals must accept widows, orphans and those of the poor who were unable to earn their daily bread. The decrees of Charles V, and some of the decrees of the Council of Trent (1545–63), provided the foundation on which the church and state built their care of the poor.

With time the care of poor children as well as care for the poor in general became a function of the mercantile economic politics of the countries of that period. In the sixteenth century institutions for forced work were established in England. These institutions accepted for instruction not only beggars and vagabonds, but also children and juveniles. In this way a new kind of institution arose. It was hoped that forced work for adults and children would stamp out beggary and reorganise care for the poor. The workhouses were originally an integral part of efforts to solve the problem of the poor while at the same time securing the work force necessary for the early development of manufacture. Business management was often taken over by production organisations which developed out of the old guilds. The government's function was the maintenance of discipline and the support of production. To these ends use was made of the most severe corporal punishments.

Similar institutions were also founded in France and in Amsterdam in the sixteenth and seventeenth centuries. In contrast to the English and French institutions, the Dutch institution was a penal institution. Here strict education and hard work (in fear of God) were intended morally to elevate the juvenile criminal, beggar or vagabond, and train him to be a useful member of society. Education through work awakened interest to the extent that Dutch parents began sending their disobedient and lazy children to the Amsterdam institution. In addition to the one for boys, beginning in 1597 there was a similar institution in Amsterdam for girls. These institutions represented something new in the history of care for the young. They signified the beginning of specialised institutional treatment of educationally deprived and delinquent youth for the purpose of their bettering themselves through work.

German Hanseatic cities in particular began to imitate the Dutch institution in the seventeenth century. The Thirty Years War slowed for some time the founding of more of these institutions in Germany, but after the war the founding of such institutions continued.

The first institution for forced work in Austria was founded by Emperor Leopold I in Vienna in 1671. Following the example of Vienna, similar institutions were founded in other Austrian cities.

In the seventeenth century a significant contribution to institutional education came from the efforts of August Hermann Francke (1663–1727), who founded a famous orphanage in Halle in 1694. Francke required that the teachers know the characteristics of the students. He required that the students be treated as individuals. The teachers had to enter their observations on special cards which were presented at the monthly tests of the students. He advised unqualified teachers to quit. In 1713 he prepared instructions for teachers in which he appealed to them to exercise self-control and display exemplary behaviour.

Francke's education led to a rationally regulated life of untiring activity. The emphasis of his education was on religious instruction, all other teaching being subordinate, though also lively and clear. The children had to be continually occupied with useful work, and each child could be trained for the work that suited his abilities. Francke arranged for gifted children to obtain higher education. Orphans were given training necessary to the 'generally useful man'. Francke's students did not do their work for personal gain, but only in order to receive training in the work. It was forbidden to force the children to work with physical punishment.

Other orphanages in Germany adopted Francke's principles, which were also supported by teachers who had been trained in his institution. This development was all the more significant since many of the orphanages at that time were workhouses established for economic and mercantile reasons. Many of the orphanages founded in Austria in the reign of Maria Theresa (1740—80) were of this kind.

Age of enlightenment

The ideas of enlightenment which appeared in the second half of the eighteenth century gave new initiative to care for the young. The philosophy of enlightenment was based on the belief that the cultivation of the intellect can abolish not only ignorance, but also all other social deficiencies.

Because of the economic crises which appeared in various parts of Europe towards the end of the eighteenth century, the question of poverty remained one of the main problems of the time. The idea of educating the poor for work thus found fresh impetus, and once again institutions that employed the poor were founded.

Many children were trained for work in the orphanages. The hygienic conditions were very bad, the food monotonous. Many children contracted scurvy; many slept together in a single bed; mange and ocular diseases spread, and parasites were endemic. Mortality for children in orphanages was high.

These conditions were the reason for the beginning in Germany of a battle directed against the institutional education of children, and referred to as the 'Waisenhausstreit' ('battle of the orphanages'). In this dispute emphasis was also given to the lack of preparation of institutional children for life in the outside world. It was advocated that the children be sent to the country for care, so that they could develop more soundly and grow accustomed to work. The village schools were considered adequate for the education of poor children. A debate developed concerning the theoretical and practical advantages of institutional and family education. The views that were then current of the importance of work for children were also supported by some German pedagogues, such as Basedow (1723—90) and Salzman (1744—1811), because of the value they placed on the influence of work in the strengthening of health in the young.

Thus towards the end of the eighteenth century many orphanages were closed in the German-speaking parts of Europe, and children sent to foster homes on the basis of written contracts. In the country the foster children were under the guidance of a special warden, usually a clergyman.

The idea of joining basic education with manual labour also appeared in this period. Thus industrial schools appeared at the end of the eighteenth century, beginning with the school of Ferdinand Kindermann (1740–1801) in Czechoslovakia.

Despite the general dissemination of the ideas of enlightenment and the raising of children in foster homes, for delinquent youth there was still no alternative to the institutions for forced work. The administrators of these institutions were satisfied with monotonous work and cruel punishment as well as other forms of coercion. The work was not adapted to youth. They worked as adults under strict supervision.

Representatives of the enlightenment attempted to replace *ius puniendi* with *ius corrigendi*. Special correctional sections were established in the workhouses, in which juveniles were placed in order to remove them from the negative influence of the adult institutional residents.

At the end of the eighteenth century and at the beginning of the nineteenth, certain restraints were placed on social care efforts by the theory of Thomas Malthus (1766–1834) and liberalism. Malthus opposed organised social care for the poor. The ideas of liberalism were also in conflict with personal and public charity. Thus at the beginning of the nineteenth century the ruling agencies became disinterested in the problems of juvenile care, even though the Napoleonic wars and the current economic conditions had caused great poverty and want in many areas of Europe. This period was characterised by renewed private initiatives to alleviate the harsh circumstances of particularly threatened and neglected children. A significant movement in institutional care was that of the 'rescue houses' ('Rettungshausbewegung'), which spread from southern Germany through much of Europe.

The rescue house movement

Historians relate the beginning of the rescue house movement to the work of Johann Heinrich Pestalozzi (1746–1827). In his writings he emphasised the importance of affectionate family education for the natural development of children. Pestalozzi developed his ideas on institutional education in Neuhof, Stans and Yverdon. The literature describes him as brilliant creator of plans for institutional education in which ideas of instruction, work and communal life interwine. These ideas were applied by the Protestants Jakob Johann Wehrli (1790–1855), Christian Heinrich Zeller (1779–1860), Johannes Daniel Falk (1768–1826), and in particular Johann Hinrich Wichern (1808–1891).

The rescue house, as an educational institution, emerged from Pestalozzi's ideas about the educational capacities of the family. Thus these institutions were built to operate as big families with a family spirit and air of domesticity. The directors of the rescue house were mother and father, the teachers older sons and daughters. Everything was tied into a common household in which it was attempted to develop relationships similar to those in true families. The rescue house rejected on principle the admission of a student against his will. In order to preserve the family atmosphere as much as possible, the institution accepted only a small number of children – i.e., forty to fifty.

Whereas Pestalozzi encouraged industrial as well as agricultural work, industrial work was later rejected on principle, primarily because industrialisation was considered a cause of poverty, destruction of the family, and educational neglect. Agriculture and supplementary cottage industries aided the management of these institutions.

Parallel with the development of rescue houses, this period also saw the development of foster homes. A notable contribution to this area was made by Falk. In 1813 he founded the society of 'friends in need', with the help of which he began to take in children from the streets and then to place them with families, particularly with tradesmen and farmers. He tried to get to know the children in his home before sending them to a suitable family. In addition, he retained in his own home the more difficult children, who would not be able to adapt to a foster home.

In 1833 Wichern established a rescue house, called the 'Rauhes Haus' in Horn near Hamburg. He advocated the family group and individualised education. In this regard he emphasised that the educational institution may be similar to the family, but could never replace it. He limited the number of inmates in one group to twelve. Wichern required that it be determined for each child whether education in the family or in the institution were more suitable. Wichern did not favour married couples as leaders of the individual groups of students. One reason for this was the difficulty in finding couples in which both partners were suited for work in an educational institution. He also rejected the division of authority that such an arrangement would require.

For the teachers he founded a special seminar-like institution through which the teachers ('brothers') gained practical and theoretical training for work in educational institutions.

Released students were a particular concern for Wichern. The institution's teachers either corresponded with them or visited them.

Rescue houses spread from Germany into Switzerland, Sweden and Russia. In the nineteenth century, rescue houses became institutions which dealt with children who were difficult to educate. These institutions were to prevent youth from going to the correctional departments of the workhouses or to reformatories. Wichern also considered as rescue houses the reformatories in England and the Nettray institutions in France.

In Italy in 1846, Don Giovanni Bosco (1815–80) founded an educational institution for young people in a suburb of Turin. Don Bosco developed the religious educational system,[2] the basic characteristic of which was preventive education. The teacher had to be continually with his students as instructor, supervisor and caring father, and could not leave them until they were well enough educated to make use of freedom and to control themselves. Strict discipline was not considered appropriate, because it induces fear in students and forces them into hypocrisy. None the less, discipline was to be exact, but never petty. The teacher was not to intervene only after the offence, but rather was to direct all of his educational skill and concern towards preventing it. A cordial and trusting relationship was to develop between teachers and students. The teachers were to join in the children's games, come to know their problems, empathise with them and take an interest in the things that interest children.

In 1851 Hugel, a physician, published a book about charitable institutions for children from the lower social classes (*Über die sozialen Humanitäts Anstalten für die Kinder der unteren Volksklassen*, Vienna, 1851). From this book it is clear that he knew of the children's institutions of that time in England, Austria, France, Italy, Germany, and Switzerland, and that these institutions were already considerably differentiated in the first half of the nineteenth century. Asylums accepted abandoned children in order to protect them from moral decay. One kind of correctional institution dealt with helping young beggars and those who had erred into 'milder' undesirable habits. Another kind of correctional institution concerned itself with the rehabilitation of convicted juveniles. Mixed institutions also existed which accepted young people without any kind of differentiation. Hügel further differentiates between institutions accepting only boys, those accepting only girls, and those accepting both sexes. Similarly, he notes institutions that educate children within their walls, others that educate them outside in families (especially families of tradesmen) and, finally, those that do both. The institutions of that time also differed according to religion. Thus there were Catholic, Protestant and Jewish institutions. Hügel also divided institutions according to whether they had schools or not. The educational institutions for the most part had only schools for elementary education, but there also existed institutions with other kinds of schools, in particular trade schools. Hügel was of the opinion that the private educational institutions, in both Europe and America, functioned better than the institutions run by the state.

The development of educational institutions in Slovenia

The development of institutional education in Europe was partly reflected in those regions of Yugoslavia that until 1918 were under the Austro-Hungarian monarchy. This is particularly true for Croatia, Vojvodina and Slovenia. A detailed description of historical data for all of these regions would be too extensive and not directly relevant to our study. For this reason we shall restrict ourselves here to some historical information about Slovenia.

In general, Austria imitated solutions to institutional education that had been accepted in Germany. We were not able to find in the literature concerning Austria before the nineteenth century or after that time any significant personalities (with the exception of Aichhorn) who had a strong influence on the development of educational institutions.

We in Slovenia also had no figures who had achieved prominence in the area of institutional education. Until the end of the Second World War it was primarily a matter of imitation of those institutional educational systems developed on the one hand by religious organisations, and, on the other, state penitentiary agencies.

If we disregard the fact that in the Middle Ages Slovene cities had hospitals, we may say that the development of educational institutions began here in the second half of the nineteenth century. However, we find that in the preceding century various people left money in their wills to orphanages. Efforts on behalf of the Ljubljana orphanage go back as far as 1758.

In 1876 the Society of Saint Vincent Paul was founded in Ljubljana. This was a clerical charitable organisation. The work of this society marked the beginning in Slovenia of organised charitable work. In the year of its founding the society established a 'young peoples' home, where poor children who were in danger of getting into trouble were placed. In 1878 a girls' orphanage, a so-called 'Lichtenturn' institution, was founded in Ljubljana; in 1882 another institution called 'Marjanišče' was founded.

In 1847 a workhouse was established in Ljubljana. In 1874 a special department was organised for correctional inmates; that is, for juvenile offenders eighteen years old or younger. This department gained a very bad reputation. It was in large part due to the efforts of Fran Milčinski (1867–1932), a Ljubljana juvenile judge and writer of books for young people, that conditions in this institution improved somewhat before the First World War. In 1911 the correctional department of the institution for forced work in Ljubljana was renamed an educational department.

In the new country of the Yugoslav nations from 1922 on, this educational department was in didactic matters under the jurisdiction of the Higher Educational Council. In 1931 the school was moved out of Ljubljana to a publicly owned farm estate in Ponoviči near Litija. Here the students were exploited as a cheap work force. Throughout this period the school barely functioned, with little being done educationally. In 1936 the school was again moved to Ljubljana, and in addition came under the control of the religious organisation. The entire education was adapted to the Don Bosco educational system. The institution operated until 1945.

Following liberation, the institution was initially intended for war orphans. However, it soon reverted to its original purpose of the care of behaviourally and personally disturbed youth. In 1949 the educational institution was moved to Gradec at Črnomelj. Here the conditions were very bad. For this reason the institution moved again in November 1953, to a castle dating from the first half of the seventeenth century in Gorenji Logatec. Because of bad conditions in the institution, it was discontinued in March 1966. But by June of the same year a new educational institution had been founded in the same place. It was in this institution that the Institute of Criminology in Ljubljana conducted the research study that is described here.

Besides this oldest educational institution, a second, preventive educational institution was opened in Ljubljana at Rakovnik in December 1901. Despite great resistance on the part of the religious organisation, pressure from the Ljubljana city councillors caused the institution to become, in 1906, an educational institution, a 'rescue house' as it was called by Milčinski. This educational institution was in operation until 1945.

Between the two wars the new Yugoslav penal code of 1929 provided for two institutions for the correction of younger juvenile delinquents in Slovenia. Both institutions were housed in prisons, the young male prison in Ljubljana and the women's prison in Begunje. Limited funds prevented realisation of the regulations governing institutions for the treatment of juvenile delinquents. Both institutions ceased to function during the war, the institution in Begunje immediately after the occupation in 1941, the Ljubljana institution after the capitulation of Italy in 1943.

12

In 1938 a girls' school was founded in Crneče at Dravograd. This school was housed in a renovated castle. The institution was run by a congregation of school sisters. This institution also ceased to function upon the German occupation of Slovenia in 1941.

Care for youth in the new Yugoslavia that emerged following the Second World War centred initially on the care of children without parents and on war orphans. A number of homes were founded for the care of these children. In the first years after liberation it was not possible to devote special attention to behaviourally and personally disturbed youth.

In keeping with modern knowledge, the new Yugoslavia adopted the view that the problem of behaviourally and personally disturbed youth could not be the responsibility of charitable efforts by individuals and societies. Helping these young people became the responsibility of society. Government and self-government agencies in Slovenia founded the following educational institutions for these young people following the Second World War:

1945   A girls' school in Maribor. In 1948 this institution was abandoned, and a school founded in Višnja gora for girls from fourteen to eighteen years of age.

1946   An educational institution in Smlednik for children of elementary school age. With time this institution restricted itself to the training of behaviourally disturbed and neurotic children.

1948   An educational institution in Podsmreka at Višnja gora, which was discontinued in 1953.

1949   An educational institution for elementary school children with social and pedagogic indications at Veržej at Ljutomer.

1951   An educational institution in Planina at Rakek for elementary school children. In recent years this institution has trained mildly mentally disturbed and behaviourally disturbed children.

1952   An educational correctional home in Radeče for delinquent youths of fourteen to eighteen years of age.

1954   A transitional young people's home in Ljubljana, which functions as an observation centre. This institution moved to entirely new quarters in Jarše in Ljubljana in 1964. This is the only institution for behaviourally and personally disturbed youth that is housed in a structure built for that purpose.

1954   The educational institution in Preddvor at Kranj for elementary school children with social and pedagogic indications.

1961   An educational institution in Slivnica at Maribor for students from fourteen to eighteen years of age. This is actually a boarding school for behaviourally and personally disturbed youth, since the students there are apprenticed and work solely in the businesses in Maribor and the surrounding area.

1966   The previously mentioned educational institutions in Gorenji Logatec.

There are at present nine institutions in Slovenia that deal with behaviourally and personally disturbed inmates. All of these institutions are under the jurisdiction of the Department of Education, except for the educational correctional home in Radeče, which comes under the Department of Justice, as do the penal institutions.

We should note here that the number of institutions in Slovenia increased after the Second World War.

After 1945 the people who then began to deal with behaviourally and personally disturbed youth had no experience in this work. They also lacked any special education. This problem was complicated by inadequate facilities and material support, far below the requirements for modern treatment of these children and young people. Under such conditions the groups of teachers themselves sought and developed work methods as best they could. It cannot be denied that some individuals showed considerable initiative. It was not until 1965 that the pedagogic academy in Ljubljana founded a department for the training of special teachers for work with behaviourally and personally disturbed youth.

Efforts in institutional education in the twentieth century, particularly since the Second World War, are directed toward finding suitable work methods for dealing with behaviourally and personally disturbed youths. Most of these methods are still being tested. In our research we have wished to join this modern movement in the area of institutional education and care.

Notes

[1]   This article is an excerpt from a study 188 pages long.
[2]   Called the Salesian congregation of St John Bosco.

References

Dolenc, Metod, 'Fate of the Ljubljana workhouses' *Kronika slovenskih mest* no. 2, 1937. (*Chronicle of Slovene Towns*)

Dra, Konrad, *Die Fürsorgeerziehung und ihre Entwicklung in Österreich*, Vienna 1938.

Jagodič, Vojko, 'Some History of the Institution for Education and Correction of Younger Juveniles', manuscript, probably from the year 1940; see also *Slovenski narod*, from 23 March 1940. (*Slovene Nation*)

Jagodič, Vojko, 'Our special schools' *Prosvetni delavec* nos 18 and 19, from 25 November 1953. (*Weekly Journal For Education*)

Jarc, Evgen, 'Fundamentals of modern protection of children in Slovenia' *Kronika slovenskih mest* no. 1, 1936. (*Chronicle of Slovene Towns*)

Handbuch der Heimerziehung, Verlag Moritz Dieslerweg, Frankfurt a. M., Berlin, Bonn, 1952.

Hippel, Robert, 'Beiträge zur Geschichte der Freiheitsstrafe' *Zeitschrift für gesamte Strafrechtswissenschaft* vol. 18, 1898.

Hügel, Franz Seraph, *Über die soziale Humanitäts Anstalten für die Kinder der unteren Volksklassen*, Prandel et Co., Vienna 1851.

Kos, Milko, 'Ljubljana in the Middle Ages' *Knjižnica 'Kronike'*, Ljubljana 1955. (Library of *Chronicle of Slovene Towns*)

Krebs, Albert, 'Wichtige Daten zum Jugendstrafvollzug' *Zeitschrift für Strafvollzug*, 1962.

Kržišnik, Anton, 'Social policies. History of social policies and social services in pre-socialist social systems', manuscript, Višja šola za socialne delavce. Ljubljana 1967. (College for Social Workers)

Lichtenturns Institution, An account for the institution from the beginning until the manuscript has been written.

Liese, Wilhelm, *Geschichte der Caritas*, Caritasverlag, Freiburg/Br., 1922.

Mihelčič, Fran, 'History of Rakovnik', manuscript, Ljubljana 1952.

Milčinski, Fran, *Our Neglected Youth and Kranjska, its Ruling Stepmother*, Ljubljana 1907.

Ratzinger, Georg, *Geschichte der kirchlichen Armenpflege*, Herder'sche Verlag, Freiburg/Br., 1884.

Rehm, Max, *Das Kind in der Gesellschaft*, Verlag Ernst Reinhard, Munich 1925.

Rohden, 'Rettungsanstalten' in *Enzyklopädisches Handbuch der Pädagogik* vol. 7, Hermann Beyer und Söhne, Langensalza 1908.

Rüger, Helmut, *Heimerziehungslehre*, Luther Verlag, Witten 1962.

Scherpner, Hans, *Geschichte der Fürsorge*, Vandenhoeck et Ruprecht, Göttingen 1966.

Schuber, 'Rauhes Haus' in *Enzyklopädisches Handbuch der Pädagogik* vol. 7, Hermann Beyer und Söhne, Langensalza 1908.

Skaberne, Bronislav, 'Problems of neglected children and youth in Slovenia', manuscript, Ljubljana 1953.

Skala, Anton, 'Institutions for education of children and young juveniles' *Izdanje doma maloletnika*, Belgrade 1934. (*The Home for Youth*)

Skala, Anton, 'On the education of developmentally effected children' *Državna založba Slovenije*, Ljubljana 1962. (The Slovene Publishing House)

Stritar, Albin, 'Some data from the chronicle, "Deško vzgajališče"', manuscript from the Slovene School Museum, Ljubljana 1952. (*The Home for Maladjusted Youth*)

Subotić, Dušan, *Six Basic Problems of Criminal Law 'Gece Kon'*, Belgrade 1933.

Uhlhorn, Gerhard, *Die christliche Liebestätigkeit*, Wissenschaftliche Buchgesellschaft, Darmstadt 1959.

Volčič, Fran, 'The historical development of the training school for boys at Selo by Ljubljana', manuscript, Ljubljana 1939.

Wichern, Johann Hinrich, 'Rettungsanstalten als Erziehungshäuser in Deutschland' in *Enzyklopädie des gesamten Erziehungs- und Unterrichtswesens* vol. 7, Verlag Rudolf Besser, Gotha 1869.

Zdešar, Anton, 'Clerical care for our poor' *Bogoslovni vestnik*, Ljubljana 1940. (*The Theological Herald*).

2 The Aim of the Experiment and Preliminary Hypotheses

Katja VODOPIVEC

As we have seen, care for socially and educationally deprived youth originated in the early Christian period. The historical elements of this care were charity, hospitalisation, forced accommodation to work and later to learning. These elements are still present in the institutional education of behaviourally and personally disturbed youth.

By the end of the eighteenth century, and even more in the nineteenth and early twentieth centuries, some practitioners were expressing doubt about the sufficiency of such educational methods. A still wider dissemination of doubt about the effectiveness of force and charity was to be found particularly after the Second World War, in public as well as professional circles. None the less, this conception in practice remains, having grown and persisted through the centuries, so that even now it is present in institutional education in most countries. It is not easily overcome even among professional workers, not to mention in public opinion. The prevalent opinion holds that socially disturbed youth deserves understanding, but requires a firm hand.

One of the basic questions facing us is: why are new theoretical ideas and practical experiences of enlightened individuals so slowly and with such difficulty incorporated into practice?

In recent years criticism of institutional education has become increasingly sharp. Many theoreticians feel that the institutions should be abolished and replaced with other forms of care for behaviourally and personally disturbed youth. This leads at least to the following questions:

— What is the modern conception of an institution? Is it a substitute family education for ten, twenty, or forty juveniles, or is it restricted to institutions with greater capacity? Does it include institutions of an open type which send inmates to work and to school in the community (so-called hostels), or is it restricted to institutions of the closed type?

— Why do we reject institutional education in principle? Is it because we have not succeeded in creating authentic human communication and a therapeutic atmosphere in institutions? Or is it because we are convinced that even with such conditions it is not possible to help these youths successfully?

– Have we found, or may we in the future hope to find, a form of extra-institutional treatment of youth which would entirely replace institutional therapy? May we for these reasons now entirely abandon concern for the development of institutional education?

Perhaps there will be fewer educational institutions in the future, and those that remain will be substantially different from the existing ones. However, we feel that an unrealistic leap beyond the time and place in which we live poses dangers equal to those posed by persistence of the status quo.

For these reasons we pursued an experiment in an educational institution at a time when there was much discussion and many contributions to the literature about extra-mural education of young people. None the less, we feel that the experiment's successes and failures will still be relevant for some time for our country and perhaps for others.

Situation

In Yugoslavia in 1966, educational work in institutions was carried out primarily by primary school teachers who functioned in the institutions as teachers, instructors and administrators. Most of the institutions also employed a psychologist and a social worker, who, to the best of our knowledge, were rarely able to take part in the educational work. These and other kinds of professional workers still represent intruders in our institutions and in the institutions of other countries.

The teacher's education prepares him primarily for the transmission of subject matter, and not for the role of an observer of personal problems and helper. In work with behaviourally and personally disturbed youth, the basic question is what and whether there is anything we can contribute before we have removed the source of the disturbance.

In Yugoslavia the special education of teachers for work with personally and behaviourally disturbed youth is a recent development (1963). So far there have been few such graduates, and even fewer have been employed in educational institutions.

In 1959 a special inquiry was conducted in Slovenia (population 1,700,000) among educational staff concerning their personal problems and interests, their relationships with inmates and other staff, and their

18

living conditions. The inquiry was supplemented with field interviews and with professional opinions from an extended group of experts. The researchers hypothesised that conditions in educational institutions caused the staff to experience continual psychic tension because of the negative relationship that the inmates have to authority. In keeping with varying personality structure, interests, and ability to tolerate frustration, individual staff members deal with this tension in different ways.

> Because of situations which necessarily (also) cause failures, the teacher's frustration tolerance decreases, and because the tolerance decreases, failures arise ... with increasing frequency. Teachers bring this basic attitude to the entire educational collective.... The teachers rationalise their mistakes.... Because there are usually a number of such teachers in any group, their justifications become intertwined and mutually reinforcing. As a result, rational restraints are reduced, causing an increase in the number of aggressive actions. Thus rationalisations of aggression are again strengthened until the conviction arises that aggressive interventions are a necessity in educational activity.[1]

Thus it appears that our administrators and teachers in educational institutions were forced into work which, without blame on their part, they were not able to carry out successfully. This kind of situation holds for all of Yugoslavia.

Experiment

The workers of the institute were convinced that it was not possible to conduct an experiment with a new conceptual plan in any of the existing institutions in Slovenia. These institutions had an ingrained system of work, with a staff that reacted to continual conflict relationships with the inmates by perpetuating an aggressive vicious circle. Neither occasional nor continuing courses for the staff could significantly influence relationships in the institutions, since institutional staffs were convinced that theoreticians were not familiar with the institutional situations and were unable to help them with their difficulties. To a certain extent this was true, since the hiring of staff was non-selective, without the requirement of appropriate education, and the staff was continually exposed to frustrating situations. The demands of the theoreticians for alternative modes of dealing with inmates in essence constituted a new burden for the staff. The theoreticians were not able to offer on-going gratifications for new experiments nor to provide occasionally more favourable responses on the

19

part of inmates, since the theoreticians were not sufficiently integrated into the everyday life and problems of the institution.

Thus the institute hit upon the idea of a special team of professionals working according to the principles of group counselling for a four-year period with a new, young staff that would be free of experience in institutional work, and thus more accessible to influence and personality changes than staff with habitual methods of behaving and fixed patterns of relationships with inmates.

The hypotheses of the experiment were as follows:

1   Educational work with behaviourally and personally disturbed youth is demanding, requiring teachers with appropriate higher education and appropriate personal orientations. Thus the hiring of staff for educational work in institutions must be selective.

2   Life in the institution and the institutional atmosphere should reflect as much as possible the variegated life on the outside. Thus, teachers with varying educations should work in the institution so that they can enrich each other with the variability of their opinions towards life situations; the heterogeneously educated professional collective should provide the inmates with a miniature reflection of the highly varied life on the outside.

3   Some exceptional personalities have already succeeded in becoming teacher-artists in the institutional situation. However, such personalities are much rarer than would be required to meet the needs for personnel in the institutions. The important question is whether it is possible, through intensive professional help, to enable staff of average ability and motivation to attain greater success and experience greater satisfaction in their work.

4   Permissive leading of inmates should be the work orientation of the entire institutional collective. The hypothesis is that permissive educational methods do not threaten society more than do repressive ones.

5   The method of group counselling which the professional team of the institute would use as its basic method of communication with the institutional staff can contribute to a lessening of antagonisms between theory and practice and to the strengthening of theoretical knowledge in practice.

6   It is not possible to treat all inmates, with their various behavioural and personal disturbances, in the same way, with identically structured staff and in identical institutional settings. Thus it is also necessary to

choose selectively the inmates who are to be accepted into the new institution. As few inmates as possible should be rejected from the new institution. Rejections of individual inmates should be individually justified.

7   During the experiment, three population groups will mutually influence each other: the consultants of the institute, the institutional staff, and the inmates. On theoretical grounds one might expect that some unfavourable dynamics would exist among the three groups at the beginning of the experiment, in particular mutual distrust, aggressiveness and partial servility. In the course of the experiment, these dynamics should change into greater understanding and more democratic co-operation. It can be anticipated that the groups of inmates, teachers and consultants will change from an original state of rigidity, authoritarianism and fixed positions to a state of greater adaptability and flexibility in the solution of problems.

Thus the goal of the experiment was to help the staff develop a permissive, understanding relationship with the inmates, with elements of enlightened leadership, the resolution of personal conflict situations, and thus an elevation of the level of tolerance. In this way the institution at Logatec was to achieve educational results at least comparable to those of similar institutions, without increasing the inmates' threat to society either during their stay in the institution or after their release. Thus it was not the goal of the experiment to obtain, during the time the inmates were in the institution, a better re-educational result in the sense that more inmates would become capable of actively and normally joining in life on the outside following release. Experiments have shown that similar educational results are obtained with different educational methods if the results are tested after a longer interval of life outside the institution.[2]

The time that the inmate spends in the institution − one and a half or two years − is no more than a modest oasis in the individual's journey through life, with its social disharmonies, its ups and downs of success and failure, its repeated confrontations stemming from the discrepancy between illusion and reality, and individual's premature burden of social discrimination and stigmatisation. If, as a result of our experiment, the new educational institution would not signify an additional obstacle to the personal development of the inmate, we should be satisfied.

On permissiveness

> If you cut off the tongues
> of those who lie, and cut off
> the hand of those who steal,
> one day you will be master of
> mute and one-handed freaks.

Fernand Deligny

Upon hearing of our experiment at Logatec, one of our guests commented that a bias towards permissive education can be as *a priori* as a bias towards repressive education. This is true. Faith in the value of permissive educational methods is more a matter of ideological conviction than the result of the conviction that it is possible to measure its positive effects empirically. In the final analysis, simple elimination (read: execution) of all socially undesirable people is the most effective and cheapest means of social defence (Törnudd).

Permissive educational attitudes are often equated in literature with uncritical acceptance of the idea of humanism which springs from the romantic utopian tenet that man is by his nature good. Paedocentrism is another expression of this conceptualisation of permissive educational efforts. Conversely, repressive educational attitudes are usually equated with aggressiveness and violation of the free expression of the individual.

Here it is not so much a question of which positive capabilities of young people can be released by permissive education, and which capabilities — positive and negative — can be suffocated by repressive education: the basic problem of our research is the institutional staff and their personal identity.

Various authors hold different opinions about the degree to which human aggressiveness is immanent and to what degree it is culturally acquired.[3] There is also a question of what we mean by aggressiveness. We know that man is an expansive[4] and creative being. These qualities necessarily affect the interests of others. Man is forced by the drive of self-preservation aggressively to defend against attack. Aggressiveness as an active process of social change is not always harmful.[5] If in our case we limit the concept of aggressiveness to physical and psychological repression of the developing man, then we are obviously speaking of destruction. Regardless of whether or not it is true that man has two primary instincts, the instincts of self-preservation and destruction (Freud), through the socialisation process it is possible to evoke man's destructive potential, and to cultivate and develop it.

From this viewpoint aggression seems more dangerous for those who use it in the educational process, or at least approve and allow it, than for those upon whom it is directed. For the more that aggressiveness penetrates social life, the more it moulds the psychic structure of people. The individual becomes at once more aggressive and more malleable (Marcuse).[6]

Aggression which is approved or required by public opinion, or by people in socially responsible positions from their employees, signifies the development of destructive forces as well as a weakening of personal responsibility for them, a weakening of conscience and a feeling of guilt. In this case, as well as in other examples, aggression is no longer the effect of decisions of the individual, but rather something external to him: the bureaucracy, administration, or public opinion. The individual becomes a tool, devoid of an ethical standpoint, a tool that can be neither guilty nor responsible.

Repression is at times a highly necessary reaction to the aggressiveness of others — a kind of defence and prevention. It is ethically acceptable so long as it accompanies man's immanent creativity. In the area of education, creativity means the evocation of the positive potentials of another person. Repression devoid of the essential component of human creativity becomes pure violation of the rights of others, an aggression and destruction.

The educational staff in the institution may well be either a collective of free, autonomously thinking and creating people or a group of hierarchically structured, obedient servants.

We conclude these considerations with the hypothesis: if the research team should succeed in demonstrating experimentally that a permissive educational method does not threaten society or the individual more than has been the case previously, then their efforts would have been justified. For repression by itself — because of the content inherent in this concept — is not and cannot be creative work.

Notes

[1] The research was prepared for the fifth congress of the International Association of Educators for Maladjusted Youth, Rome, 17—21 June 1960.

[2] Weeks; Jesness; Gibbens, p. 31; Bailey, p. 509; Hood-Sparks, p. 191, 192; Wilkins, p. 7. Jesness found significantly different results for the experimental and control group fifteen months after release, but not after thirty-six months after release.

³ See contributions to 'Réunion interdisciplinaire qui s'est tenue à l'UNESCO du 19–23 mai 1970: Comprendre l'aggressivité'.
⁴ Schultz-Hencke, pp. 28–32.
⁵ Tiger, p. 24.
⁶ Marcuse, p. 22.

References

Aichhorn, August, *Verwahrloste Jugend. Die Psychoanalyse in der Fürsorgeerziehung*, 4th ed., H. Huber, Bern and Stuttgart 1957.

Bailey, C. Walter, 'Correctional outcome: an evaluation of 100 reports' in A. Carl Bersani (ed.), *Crime and Delinquency*, Collier-Macmillan and The Macmillan Co., London and New York 1970, p. 505.

'Comprendre l'agressivité' *Revue internationale des sciences sociales* vol. XIII, no. 1, Paris 1971.

Deligny, Fernand, *Graine de crapule*, Ed. du Scarabée, Paris 1960.

Gibbens, T.C.N., 'L'identification des problèmes – clès dans la recherche criminologique' *Etudes relatives à la recherche criminologique* vol. VI, Conseil de l'Europe, Strasbourg 1970, pp. 13–37.

Holmes, Gerard, *The Idiot Teacher*, Faber and Faber, London 1952.

Hood, Roger, and Sparks, Richard, *Key Issues in Criminology*, World University Library, London 1970.

Jesness, Carl F., *Comparative Effectiveness of Two Institutional Treatment Programs for Delinquents*, California Youth Authority.

Jesness, Carl F., *The Fricot Ranch Study: outcomes with small versus large living groups in the rehabilitation of delinquents*, State of California Youth Authority, 1965.

Jones, Howard, *Reluctant Rebels. Re-education and group process in a residential community*, Tavistock, London 1960.

Makarenko, A.S., 'Pedagogičeskaja poema' *Mladinska knjiga*, Ljubljana 1950. (Youth Library)

Marcuse, Herbert, 'Agressivität in der gegenwärtigen Industriegesellschaft' in *Agression und Anpassung in der Industriegesellschaft*, Suhrkamp Verlag, Frankfurt a.M. 1968.

O'Neil, A.S., *Theorie und Praxis der Antiautoritären Erziehung*, RORORO, Hamburg 1969.

Redl, Fritz and Wineman, David, *The Aggressive Child*, The Free Press, New York and London 1966.

Schultz-Hencke, Dr Herald, *Der gehemmte Mensch*, 2nd ed., Georg Thieme Verlag, Stuttgart 1947.

Slavson, S.R., *Re-educating the Delinquent through Group and Community Participation*, Harper and Brothers, New York 1954.

Tiger, Lionel, 'Comprendre l'agressivité', Introduction, *Revue internationale des sciences sociales*, vol. XIII, no. 1, Paris 1971.

Törnudd, Patrik, 'Sixth International Congress on Criminology, Madrid (21—27 September 1970); National Report', manuscript.

Vodopivec, Katja, 'The fifteenth anniversary of the Institute of Criminology at the Faculty of Law in Ljubljana' *Revija za kriminalistiko in kriminologijo*, Ljubljana 1969, pp. 209—13. (*Review for Criminalistics and Criminology*)

'The educator of maladjusted youth and his mental hygiene' Bronislav Skaberne *Revija za kriminalistiko in kriminologijo*, Ljubljana 1960, pp. 265—68.

Weeks, Ashley, *Youthful Offenders at Highfields. An evaluation of the effects of the short-term treatment of delinquent boys,* University of Michigan Press, Ann Arbor 1958.

Wilkins, Leslie T., *Evaluation of Penal Measures*, Random House, New York 1970.

3 Permissiveness — A Method of Treatment of Asocial Personalities

Vinko SKALAR

Permissiveness is a method by which we wish to obtain positive results in the resocialisational and re-educational process of asocial personalities. This concept of permissiveness has direct and indirect implications. Thus, permissiveness can be characterised as follows:

Thesis 1: Acceptance of inmates

Explanation

The staff must have a humanly warm, friendly and understanding relationship with the inmates, and must attempt to empathise with their stresses and problems, and to understand their ways of reasoning and reacting. Only in this way can one expect that the inmate will gradually accept the educator, trust him, accept his help and perhaps even identify with him. This does not mean that the educator must approve of asocial or antisocial behaviour. Instead he can repeatedly offer understanding, explanation and help, but should also express his disapproval of behavioural excesses and deviations and explain his position.

In order that the teacher would be able to accept the inmate as he is, without moralising, he should fulfil especially the following conditions:

(a) he should have a broad knowledge of developmental psychology, psychodynamics and the aetiology of asocial personalities, in order to understand the phenomenology of deviant behaviour and to be able to decide on the most appropriate reaction from among various alternatives;
(b) he should have special training for work with asocial personalities which would include self-analysis of resentments and prejudices against delinquent population;
(c) in the institutional setting he should have the possibility of continual release of tensions generated by his interaction with behaviourally difficult inmates;

27

(d)   in the selection of staff for work with asocial personalities, priority should be given to individuals with specific personality characteristics, among which a high social intelligence, with developed empathetic ability, is of particular importance.

Thesis 2: Provision for living and psychological space wide enough to prevent basically frustrated personalities from having their maladaptive behaviour patterns reinforced

Explanation

In recent times the population in juvenile educational institutions has become more homogeneous, at least as regards certain characteristics. The institutions receive primarily severely disturbed juveniles who interfere with their environment, and whose manifest pathological traits prevent the use of milder treatment measures. In spite of possible differentiation within the population according to phenomenological and aetiological characteristics, it would be possible to find for the greater part of the institution's population several personality traits which would tend to be valid for the majority. These traits are as follows:

— disturbance in the motivation for initiating and development of emotional ties
— social and emotional immaturity
— asocial or anti-social symptoms
— weak ego and superego
— increased aggressiveness
— escape to substitute gratifications (compulsive film-going, masturbation, alcoholism, drug addition)
— general passivity
— uncritical relation to one's own abilities, potentials and future possibilities
— distrust of adults, exaggerated in some to the point of paranoia
— lowered tolerance of frustration
— hypersensitivity

The above characteristics are the result of frustrations which have hindered or deflected normal personality development.

Thus we have to deal with people who have failed in life, become frustrated, and become deviant in personality and behaviour; people who try to draw attention to themselves with maladaptive behaviour, and to assert themselves; people who constantly use various means to express their dissatisfaction with themselves and the environment, towards which they are distrustful and hostile. They lack perspective and escape to substitute gratifications. These people lack normal human contacts and emotional relationships, are hindered in recognition and self-assertion, and are constantly punished, disappointed and ostracised.

If such juveniles find themselves in narrowly confining living space (where they feel pressure and coercion, where opportunities are offered which they are usually unable to utilise, where they feel their environment to be more a punishment for past excesses than an opportunity for the future), we may expect that they will adapt to this environment, become temporarily integrated into it, but without hope of their changing their attitudes or identifying with their educators. The repressive environment will confirm their deviant traits and behaviour.

Is permissiveness a solution we can without reservation accept in place of repression, if our point of departure is solely 'to do no harm'? We know that it is not, for an immature, unstable charge may experience permissiveness as a more serious threat than repression. A repressive system, though on the one hand damaging, on the other hand offers a clarity and a consistency that generate a feeling of security. For the immature juvenile, a permissive atmosphere creates a feeling of insecurity and inner confusion. It assumes self-initiative and active participation of which the inmate is not capable; it assumes an ability to make decisions on the part of inmates who are not accustomed to doing so; and it assumes a self-restraint that is lacking.

Permissiveness by itself can lead to serious excesses, to a deterioration of discipline and a reinforcement of undesirable personality traits — in particular passivity, increased recourse to substitute gratifications, and an increase in asocial and anti-social activity. Thus the degree of permissiveness must be graded with reference to the level of maturity of the juveniles; permissiveness must not be allowed to deteriorate into anarchy or a *laissez faire* educational system.

We conceive of permissiveness as a dynamic expansion of the living space, with which it is necessary constantly to consider the given population and living conditions in the light of a continually perceived goal: acceleration of the juvenile's maturation, and removal of the hindrance of an either excessively strict or excessively permissive atmosphere.

Thesis 3: Dynamic resolution of inhibited motivational areas, conflicts and resentments

Explanation

The dynamics process that the juvenile experiences in a permissive atmosphere has been described in detail by Aichhorn,[1] Slavson[2] and Mailloux.[3]

To the extent that this entire process is coupled with intensive intervention on the part of the teacher, which must be directed towards analysis of the inmate's behaviour, a reduction of tensions, help towards the creation of maximally stimulating living conditions within the institution, and so on, we may expect that the inmate's behaviour will gradually become more balanced, his contact with his teachers more sincere, that he will become more accessible to positive influences and will begin a positive process of integration and social learning. Schematically we anticipate the following process to be triggered for asocial juveniles in a permissive atmosphere:

(a) malintegrated, rigid, hypersensitive, inhibited, inwardly cramped personality enters the institution;
(b) dissolution or weakening of incentives which continually give rise to maladaptive behaviour (this phase leads to insight by the inmate into his own problems on the one hand and the establishment of open human relations on the other);
(c) gradual reintegration and new social learning with the help of group and individual treatment methods.

This is only a rough outline, and could be elaborated in greater detail, especially if the whole system could be tested in various juvenile institutions.

Thesis 4: Facilitation of full expression and free communication on all levels

Explanation

It has great diagnostic value for the staff and great therapeutic value for the inmates if the juveniles have the opportunity to express themselves, their feelings and points of view, freely, without endangering their position in the institution. The educator will be able to adjust his actions, to control and evaluate critically his previous actions and, where necessary, correct them. For the inmate free communication will constitute a way of releasing tensions and a possible way of directly influencing life in the institution. With the teachers' help his expressions will manifest themselves in increasingly acceptable social forms. Encouragement of free communication has a special therapeutic value for asocial juveniles, for most of them are inhibited and tense about expressing themselves. This is an expression of their disturbance in the area of social relations; it inhibits a rapid and successful social maturation.

Free communication in the institution can take place in formal groups (therapy groups, group educational work, individual conversations), as well as in informal contacts on different levels. But in each case it is necessary to develop gradually the specific game rules within which communication must take place; otherwise it can deteriorate into mutual insults. The staff must approach free communication with considerable tolerance and always be prepared for surprises and provocations.

Thesis 5: Development of creativity, originality, authenticity, acceptance of responsibility and acquisition of positive social experiences

Explanation

Responsibility and creativity in asocial juveniles can be fully developed in the process of reintegration only if there are opportunities for participation in decisions affecting plans and activities, so that the juveniles can participate in creating their own living space and future. In this the juveniles need the help of the teacher in the role of adviser, and not in the role of guard or authority. Participation in specific activities, such as school, workshop or hobbies, should be the juveniles' right rather than duty. For example, the juvenile should himself decide whether to study or become apprenticed to a trade, whether to go to school, and the like. His free decision also implies responsibility and acceptance of the rules of the game for the various activities. Gross violation of work discipline or rules of an activity results in temporary loss of the right to participate, but does not call for the teacher to pressure the juvenile. Co-operation, participation and the opportunity for free decision-making all provide the juvenile with strong motivational factors which tend to increase his activity and to strengthen desirable behaviour.

Thesis 6: Facilitation of success, self-assertion and self-realisation

Explanation

Most asocial juveniles are disturbed in the area of self-assertion; this may be either basic frustration in the motivational area or a consequence of stigmatisation caused by commitment to an educational institution. Study of the aetiology of juvenile delinquency reveals that frustrated motives of self-assertion are often one of the significant aetiological factors behind anti-social behaviour.[4] Thus the entire organisation of the institution and the orientation of the staff must be stimulating, enabling the juveniles to succeed, assert themselves and find self-esteem within the limits of socially acceptable behaviour patterns. This is a particularly difficult task for the educational staff in cases of inmates who are deficient in both emotional and productive capacity. Their behaviour as well as their deficiencies literally cry for repressive modes of reaction. However, it is precisely here that the teacher must break the vicious circle of the inmate's permanent failure and defensive reaction on the one hand, and his own repressive reactions on the other.

This question concerns the entire stimulation system of the institution, as well as the basic orientation of the staff towards inmates as expressed in their expectations and belief in the success of their pedagogic work.

In connection with stimulation, it would be necessary to replace the present predominantly punitive system with a positive stimulation system. This would not mean that it would be possible to exclude punishment entirely from institutional education, particularly in cases of the emotional breakdown of teachers; however, punishment should be used only in certain circumstances,[5] in a way that would not lead to negative and undesirable educational effects, but that would hinder the juvenile's negative behaviour.

In general it would be desirable to transfer the penal function from the educational staff to the administration of the institution, to the police (to the extent that the inmates violate the law outside the institution), to courts and to the pressure of public opinion in the local community into which the institution is integrated. The teacher, as adviser and therapist, should distance himself as much as possible from the punitive function.

It was with these premises and conceptions of permissiveness as a method of work with delinquent and personally disturbed youth that we began experimental work at Logatec. We gradually transmitted various aspects of our views to the staff, and presented our concept in full at a seminar in

Portorož in December 1970 that was devoted entirely to the problem of permissiveness.

For the concept of permissiveness we relied primarily on psychodynamic findings and made use of the literature that is based on the psychodynamic and psychoanalytic therapeutic model (Schutz-Hencke, Annemarie Dührssen, Aichhorn, Mailloux, King, Redl, Slavson). We also accepted some of the principles of the neobehaviourist psychological system (Mowrer, Glasser), which incorporates, particularly recently, many elements of psychodynamically oriented theory (McCormick, Frazier).

We feel that the current level of development of psychological science makes it unjustifiable and also impossible to adopt any of the psychological systems in a pure and original form: unjustifiable in that each of the models contains insights that must not be neglected in practice; impossible in that the various systems of treatment make use of findings from all areas of psychologic science. Thus we find that systems and models which appear to have contradictory points of departure in fact have similarities in their application of theory to methods of treatment.

Thus we feel that our orientation does not show mere eclecticism, representing a simple compilation of views, but rather a reflection of the current state of psychological science and psychotherapy for the treatment of behaviourally and personally disturbed youth.

Notes

[1] Aichhorn, *Verwahrloste Jugend.*
[2] Slavson, *Re-educating the delinquent.*
[3] Mailloux, *Un symptôme de désocialisation.*
[4] Kobal, 'Reintegration of behaviour and the rigidity of disturbed personalities'.
[5] Skalar, *Experiences of an educator.*

References

Aichhorn, August, *Verwahrloste Jugend*, Int. Psychoanalitischer Verlag, Leipzig 1925.
Bedenić, Milan, *Mental hygiene*, 2nd ed., Medicinska knjiga, Belgrade, Zagreb 1964. (Medical Library)
Bergant, Milica, 'Permissive and repressive education' *Anthropos* nos. 1–2, Ljubljana 1971.

Bersani, Carl, A. (ed.), *Crime and Delinquency*, Collier-Macmillan and The Macmillan Co., London and New York 1970, pp. 542—52.

Dewey, John, *Democracy and Education*, The Macmillan Co., New York 1916.

Fenton, Norman, *Group Counseling, A preface to its use in correctional and welfare agencies* Lee Printing Company, Sacramento 1961.

Klüwer, Karl, 'Dissoziale Jugendliche in der Industriegesellschaft,' *Praxis der Kinderpsychologie und Kinderpsychiatrie*, 14, no. 4, 1965.

Kobal, Miloš, 'Reintegration of behaviour and the rigidity of disturbed personalities', Medicinska fakulteta, Ljubljana 1970. (Facùlty of Medicine. Duplicated)

Mailloux, R.P. Noël, 'Un symptôme de désocialisation: L'incapacité de communiquer avec autrui' *Annales internationales de criminologie* no. 5, 1966.

Popovic, Vidak, *System for carrying out the punishment of imprisonment in Yugoslavia*, Belgrade 1966, pp. 75—83.

Redel, Fritz, *The Aggressive Child*, The Free Press, New York and London 1966.

Slavson, S.R., *Re-educating the delinquent through group and community participation*, Harper Brothers, New York 1954.

Skaberne, Bronislav, 'Historical background, contribution to final report', Ljubljana 1972.

Skalar, Vinko, *Experiences of an educator. Aggressiveness in a behaviourally disturbed child*, Društvo defektologov Slovenije, Sekcija vzgojiteljev neprilagojene mladine, Ljubljana 1967. (Society of Slovene Educators, Section for Maladjusted Youth)

Skalar, Vinko, 'Staff problems with educational tasks in penal correction institutions and educational institutions' *Revija za kriminalistiko in kriminologijo* no. 3, 1968, pp. 121—4. (*Review for Criminalistics and Criminology*)

Ülo, Luuka, 'Treatment of aggression' *Unsere Jugend* no. 3, 1972, pp. 102—8.

PART II

Methodological Draft

4 The Institution at Logatec – Description

Bronislav SKABERNE

Following the closing of the previous home for maladjusted boys[1] in Gorenji Logatec, the Republic's Department for Education and Culture had professionals review a number of unoccupied buildings in Slovenia. On the basis of their opinions the conclusion was reached that educational and economic considerations indicated that it would be best to renovate and adapt the building of the closed institution at Logatec.

For this reason it was suggested to the municipal council of Logatec that a new educational institution be founded in the place previously occupied by the boys' educational institution in Gorenji Logatec. The municipal council of Logatec approved the founding of the institution on 10 June 1966.[2]

Gorenji Logatec lies in the western part of the Logatec plain at an elevation of 486 metres above sea level. It is on the main route between Ljubljana and Trieste, about thirty kilometres from Ljubljana. Round a church built in 1754 lie spacious two-storey homes belonging to craftsmen, merchants and shippers. The houses of farmers and workers lie behind this centre, crowded on to the hillside. The land is moderately fertile and is devoted mainly to livestock and forestry. Recently a number of people have found employment in industry located two kilometers away in Dolenji Logatec. Here is the centre of a combine consisting of a wood products industry (wooden articles, timber), a factory for aromatic oils, a farmers' co-operative and a recently constructed factory for corrugated cardboard. Gorenji Logatec has a number of pubs, and a cultural centre that contains a public library and rooms for various societies.[3]

According to the 1971 census, 7,552 people live in the 19,000 hectares of the municipality of Logatec. According to the previous census (1961) 31 per cent of the population was juvenile. About 35 per cent of the population is involved in agriculture and forestry, and 20 per cent employed in industry (the rest of the population is divided among various activities, none of which occupies as much as 10 per cent of the population).[4] 60.4 per cent of the population has completed elementary school, 4.8 per cent secondary school or college (data from 1969).[5]

The educational institution lies in the centre of Gorenji Logatec on the main road between Ljubljana and Trieste, and occupies a castle dating from the beginning of the seventeenth century. Originally the castle was the seat of the Logatec gentry; later it was owned by the Counts of Windischgrätz until 1848 when they relinquished it for office space. Until 1932 the castle housed the offices of the regional authorities. The castle has three storeys. Each corner has a small tower with its own floor plan.

Adaptation of the building began in June 1966. Central heating was installed, the living quarters of the students were renovated, as were the kitchen and bathrooms. In addition the most necessary equipment was purchased.

During the adaptation of the castle a new small workshop was constructed for metal-working and carpentry. On the ground floor of the previous living quarters there already existed an electrical workshop. The office space on the second floor was renovated.

The Department for Education and Culture provided 958,475 new dinars for renovation of the institution. With special financial help from the Department and the sale of resort facilities on the coast, the institution also purchased several apartments for staff.

In 1968 the institution demolished an outdated wooden barrack and in its place constructed a small building for a workshop and several classrooms. In the park behind the castle the staff and inmates prepared several playing fields for various sports.

In the course of four years the inmates have destroyed considerable property; it will be necessary to whitewash the buildings and purchase additional equipment. For these reasons, after four years of existence the institution cannot be considered to be in optimal condition.

In August 1966, during the renovations, the first staff positions were advertised. The first members of staff were employed on 1 December 1966. The staff were given theoretical training for the work and started to practise in similar educational institutions, and the shopmasters began work in industrial organisations. On 20 January 1967, the Institute of Criminology in Ljubljana started regular sessions with the existing staff.

The institution began to function on 20 September 1967, when the temporary head teacher and the social worker of the institution brought the first twelve inmates from the observation home in Ljubljana. With time all the available places in the institution (capacity fifty inmates) were filled.

The inmates are trained in the institution's workshops. The metal workshop has between seventeen and twenty-one working places, the carpentry shop twelve, the electric workshop six, and there are three for implement-sharpening. There is little opportunity for employment of inmates in the

Logatec industries, since these can fill their labour requirements from the local work force. From time to time an inmate succeeds in joining a commercial organisation in Ljubljana or finds employment with a private craftsman. Although the educational institution invested considerable effort in introducing inmates into regular commercial organisations, little success was achieved.

Most staff members live in Gorenji or Dolenji Logatec. Eight members of the professional council, including the principal, commute to work from Ljubljana or Vrhnika.

Notes

[1] Resolution for the discontinuation of the boys' training home in Gorenji Logatec from 18 March 1966, Uradni list SRS 9-49/66.

[2] Resolution of the municipal council of Logatec no. 022-11/66 from 24 June 1966.

[3] *Regional lexicon of Slovenia* vol. I, Državna založba Slovenije, Ljubljana 1968, pp. 180, 181. (The Slovene Publishing House)

[4] Data gathered at the municipal council of Logatec and at the Institute of Statistics (SRS) in Ljubljana.

[5] Plan for the development of schooling and education in SR Slovenia (1972).

5   Selection of Staff

Vinko SKALAR

In planning the experiment in the educational institution we also determined how the staff was to be selected. We established several formal criteria and special criteria which were to be applied by a professional subcommittee of the selection commission. This subcommittee consisted of a psychiatrist, a psychologist and a pedagogue.[1] The formal criteria for the educational staff were as follows:

1   Graduate or college education in pedagogic, psychological or social sciences. We were not able to require specific educational qualifications, since the orthopedagogical department of the pedagogic academy in Ljubljana was founded only in 1966, and had not yet produced enough graduates to fill our requirements.

2   Besides the educational criteria, we wanted to select young staff-members, without previous experience in other educational institutions. In other words, we wanted staff that would be more flexible and free from the habits of work with delinquents that are characteristic of staff in similar institutions. In addition, it seemed unlikely that we could interest well-established teachers in work in an experimental institution. We anticipated that younger people would be more likely to respond and would be easier to interest in modern work methods.

The formal criterion for instructors of practical subjects was completion of professional school in the area for which a position was being offered.

Both educators and instructors of practical subjects were required to include a doctor's report with their applications. The professional subcommittee that was to check the special criteria had the following responsibilities:

— to determine the personal stability and maturity of the candidate;
— to determine his intellectual level;
— to determine vocational preferences with particular attention to affinity and motivation towards the anticipated work.

The professional subcommittee applied special criteria to candidates for

41

positions as educators, shopmasters and for other professional positions in the institution (psychologist, social worker, nurse). Special criteria were also set up for selection of director and director's assistant. Special criteria were not anticipated for technical and other ancillary staff.

The members of the professional subcommittee used the following methods and techniques in their selection:

1 Psychiatrist: psychiatric interview, with which he attempted to determine the essential psychodynamic elements in the life history and present psychophysical status of the candidate.

2 Pedagogue: an interview by which he attempted to determine primarily the candidate's motives in connection with his future profession.

3 The psychologist used three psychological tests:

— Domino test (D_{48}), an intelligence test
— Rorschach psychodiagnostic cards
— 0—I (personal interest test).[2]

The professional subcommittee did not apply these criteria rigidly. It required that all the candidates that it recommended for work in the institution be mentally and physically healthy, emotionally stable and mature, and at least of average intelligence. In addition, the candidate had to be suitably motivated for work in the institution. The general criteria that the professional subcommittee selected were appropriate, since with them we were just able to select, from a relatively large number of applicants, the minimum number of staff that would allow the institution to function.

Before the beginning of the experiment and during the experiment the institution advertised positions five times. A total of ninety-one candidates applied. Sixty-six candidates came for interviews; of these, the subcommittee recommended twenty-nine and rejected thirty-seven. Of the twenty-nine candidates that were recommended, twenty were given positions in the institutions.

Let us examine some data which show the differences between the group of candidates which the subcommittee recommended and the group they rejected:

1 Psychiatric diagnosis

Candidates that the professional subcommittee recommended:

Diagnosis	No.
— mild immaturity	4
— mild neurotic disturbance	6
— neurotic disturbance	5
— mild personality disturbance	4
— without particular disturbance	10
Total	29

Candidates that the professional subcommittee rejected:

Diagnosis	No.
— alcoholism with secondary personality disturbances	10
— personality disturbance	9
— immaturity	1
— neurotic disturbance	7
— psychopatic personality traits	4
— epilepsy	1
— intellectual insufficiency	3
— without particular disturbance	2
Total	37

2 Intellectual level

Candidates that the professional subcommittee recommended:

D_{48} (raw scores)

M (arithmetic means) = 23·4 SD (standard deviation) = 6·02

Candidates that the subcommittee rejected:

D_{48} (raw scores)

M = 18·51 SD = 5·52

	Favourably evaluated group		Unfavourably evaluated group	
	No.[3]	%	No.	%
Group I (protocols with favourable constellation of test characteristics)	14	51·9	3	8·2
Group II (isolated deviations in the protocols)	9	33·3	24	64·8
Group III (protocols with pathological constellation of test characteristics)	4	14·8	10	27·0

The professional subcommittee were apparently not consistent in their selections, since they found deviations also in the group of favourably evaluated candidates – despite the fact that the candidates were, according to the established criteria, to be personally stable. We must note that our final decision was not based solely on the opinion of one member of the subcommittee.

Personality profile of the staff in the experimental institution

As mentioned before, of the twenty-nine candidates that the professional subcommittee recommended, twenty assumed positions in the institution. Their professional profile is as follows:

Teachers	8
Shopmasters	6
Other	5
Total	19

In the group described as 'other' we include the principal, the principal's assistant, the psychologist, the social worker and the nurse. During the first year of the experiment the position of psychologist was filled by a new worker. Therefore we are dealing with only nineteen, and not twenty, staff-members. Only the second psychologist is included in the group for which we prepared personality profiles, since he lived in the institution for a longer time than did the first psychologist.

We present the results of individual tests for the staff as a group. Breakdown of the data according to subgroups would have been interesting, but the small numbers would have made statistical analysis unjustified.

Table 5.1

Domino test

High school students	Experimental group	
	Test 1	Test 2
No. 273	19	19
M 26·05	24·63	26·68
SD 5·35	6·98	6·66
r = 0·01		
t = 0		
F = 0 (see pp. 179,180)		

Table 5.2

Rorschach psychodiagnostic cards

	Test 1		Test 2	
	No.	%	No.	%
Group I (protocols with favourable constellation of test characteristics)	11	57·8	9	47·4
Group II (isolated deviations in the protocols)	4	21·1	8	42·1
Group III (protocols with pathological constellation of test characteristics)	4	21·1	2	10·5

Note: For the Rorschach protocols we also analysed individual specific and general factors; for example, number of answers, order of answers, intermediate interpretations, colour interpretations, black—white interpretations, kind of experience, consent responses and so on.

The entire staff was tested again at the conclusion of the experiment; we have prepared tables (5.1, 5.2, 5.3) showing the data (parameters) of this second testing. For the Domino test (D_{48}) and the personal interest test we have included in the tables data of several groups from the general population on which these tests have been temporarily standardised in Yugoslavia. We tested the significance of the differences in the arithmetic means and standard deviations of the first and second testings.

Table 5.3

Personal interest test

Dimension		General population		Experimental population			
				Test 1		Test 2	
		M	SD	M	SD	M	SD
A +	Sincerity	9·09	3·48	8·58	3·31	10·00	2·43
A −	Insincerity	4·73	3·12	6·16	3·20	4·16	2·65
B +	Sociability	8·68	2·83	13·11	1·56	13·11	1·33
B −	Unsociability	5·15	2·77	1·63	1·38	1·42	1·12
C +	Extroversion	6·29	2·48	9·26	1·97	9·58	2·27
C −	Introversion	7·19	2·49	5·53	2·12	4·84	2·09
D +	Anti-neuroticism	12·16	3·18	15·63	2·65	15·42	2·48
D −	Neuroticism	6·61	3·03	3·74	2·35	3·05	1·54
E +	Anti-manic tendency	4·72	2·06	6·37	0·95	6·05	1·18
E −	Manic tendency	4·15	1·42	2·95	0·97	2·95	1·43
F +	Anti-depressive tendency	4·36	2·28	7·32	1·16	6·63	1·74
F −	Depressive tendency	3·95	2·15	1·89	0·88	2·26	1·69
G +	Anti-schizoid tendency	5·56	1·77	7·42	1·22	7·84	1·50
G −	Schizoid tendency	3·82	1·75	2·16	1·30	1·26	0·93
H +	Anti-paranoid tendency	4·90	2·17	7·00	2·19	8·16	1·38
H −	Paranoid tendency	3·73	1·90	2·21	1·81	0·88	0·92
I +	Vegetative stability	9·73	2·92	13·00	1·45	12·74	2·38
I −	Vegetative lability	4·40	2·47	1·84	1·46	1·26	1·33
O +	Rural life	3·65	2·77	5·05	2·15	4·84	2·81
O −	Urban life	5·78	2·90	4·37	2·41	4·47	3·04
P	Manual work	9·17	3·17	9·16	4·29	7·58	2·78
R	Science	10·91	4·04	12·32	2·97	11·00	3·09
S	Administration, bookkeeping	8·57	3·56	7·74	2·79	6·95	2·39
T	Work with people	9·44	3·65	9·16	3·44	9·42	3·15
U	Representative art	9·06	3·03	8·84	2·61	9·16	3·64
V	Literature, verbal activity	8·99	3·08	8·42	3·06	8·74	3·36
Z	Music	8·06	3·76	9·58	4·97	10·05	5·25
Ž	Social action	10·72	4·07	15·84	2·09	14·26	2·71

Sincerity	r = 0·01		t = 0·01		F = 0		
Insincerity	r = 0·01		t = 0·01		F = 0		
Schizoid tendency	r = 0·01		t = 0·01		F = 0		
Anti-paranoid tendency	r = 0·01		t = 0·01		F = 0·05		
Paranoid tendency	r = 0·01		t = 0·01		F = 0·01		
Vegetative stability	r = 0·05		t = 0		F = 0·05		
Manual work	r = 0·01		t = 0·05		F = 0·05		
Social action	r = 0		t = 0·05		F = 0		

We have shown the results of the statistical analysis only for those categories for which we found a statistically significant difference between the arithmetic means or standard deviations of the first and second testings. The correlations were high in most categories.

General conclusions

In our conclusions we also summarise those results that are presented in the original report.

1   We find significant differences between the group that the professional subcommittee recommended for work in the institution and the group that the subcommittee rejected. These differences favour the group that was favourably evaluated:

— The intellectual level of the rejected group is appreciably lower than that of the recommended group, which was near (but somewhat below) the intellectual level of the high school population on which the test was provisionally standardised.

— Personal stability, as measured by the personal interest test and with the Rorschach cards, was more favourably evaluated for the candidates that were recommended than for those that were rejected. The rejected group was characterised by a greater neuroticism, vegetative lability, manic tendency, depressive tendency, schizoid tendency, and paranoid tendency.

  The rejected group was characterised by a greater number of Rorschach protocols with unfavourable constellations of test characteristics expressing primarily neurotic personality structure.

— In the rejected group the psychiatric opinion was favourable for only two candidates; in all other cases, the diagnosis revealed clear personality deviation of one kind or another. In addition, the diagnosis for the remaining candidates was for the most part on a qualitatively different level, with less implication than for the candidates in the rejected group.

  Examination of the personal qualities of the candidates for positions in the experimental institution was justified, even though the commission did not check characteristics that were specifically relevant to institutional work. The role of the commission was primarily to eliminate those candidates unfitted for work in the institution because of

47

their personality structure; it did not attempt in its selection to guarantee maximally successful functioning of the selected staff.

2   We find the following relations between the group of staff and a group from the normal population, as shown in the tables:

— The intelligence of the group of teachers is at the same level as that of the group of high school students on which the test was provisionally standardised. This finding is favourable for the staff group, which was more heterogeneous in its previous education than the group of high school students — the staff group included six shopmasters who had only elementary and trade school education.

— The experimental staff group differed from the general population in the results of the personal interest test in all personality dimensions and also in some interest categories — the experimental group had more favourable results than those of the general population. In particular, the experimental group was more social, and showed less vegetative lability, and neurotic symptoms than the general population. In the interest categories, the experimental group showed greater interest in social action and in science than did the general population. The differences may be ascribed to the experimental group, which again confirms the soundness of the work of the professional subcommittee.

3   We find some differences in individual personality dimensions between the first and second testings of the staff. These differences are not so much an expression of changes in personality as of changes in opinion, more appropriate motivation, and a more creative relation with the test situation. The differences can be interpreted as expression of a freer atmosphere created between the institute team and the staff during the experimental period.

— In the second testing, the staff showed greater sincerity, less schizoid tendency, less paranoid tendency, and somewhat less interest for manual work and social action than was evident in the first testing, even though the results for the latter two categories are still above the level found in the normal population.

— The Rorschach protocols did not show significant differences between the first and second testings, either in individual elements or globally. Thus distribution of the protocols along the continuum of normality—abnormality does not reveal a significantly different picture between the first and second testings.

— The differences in the intellectual level between the first and second testing are not statistically significant, although the results of the second testing are higher — i.e., more favourable.

Notes

[1] Members of the professional subcommittee and the members of the institute team that led the experiment were not identical, except for the psychologist Skalar who was a member of both groups. By agreement the members of the institute team were not familiar with the results of the various tests of individual candidates, in order to eliminate any prejudice during the experimental period towards candidates that were selected.

[2] See chapter 7 pages 67 ff.

[3] In this case the favourably evaluated group numbers only twenty-seven, since the two psychologists were not tested with the Rorschach cards due to their familiarity with and even qualifications to administer it.

6   Group Work

Katja VODOPIVEC

Reasons for selection of the group counselling method

The main method by which we wished to change the attitudes of the institution's staff was group counselling. The individual counselling method was considered to be only a supplementary work method. There were various reasons for our orientation towards group counselling. Of particular importance were the following:

— Permissiveness can be achieved only by a group interaction.

— Group communication reduces the gap between the two conflicting cultures: the subculture of the inmates and the average social culture represented by the institution's staff.

— Group counselling has therapeutic significance in that it enlarges the opportunity for understanding and influencing the behaviour of the inmates without the use of force.

— The final phase of delinquent behaviour is subcultural grouping. Therefore the re-education process should also develop in the context of group interactions.

Conceptual problems

Group work may be defined in various ways. One definition which seems acceptable to us is that group work signifies mobilisation of all the forces present in the life of the group so that the personal and social potential of individuals and the group are maximally realised.[1] The advantage of group work is that it allows, with the help of verbal communication, the total involvement of the participants by binding them to each other also emotionally. The dialogue between 'I' and 'We' allows comparison of differing opinions;[2] consequently it allows recognition of and respect for differences between people. This fact is in itself significant for the development of social solidarity. In addition, the individual becomes aware of himself through interaction with others. Insight into the wide range of possible opinions widens the possibility for individual choice, and frees the individual from stereotypes and prejudices. This may make decision-making more difficult, but at the same time it becomes more sound and signifies an acceptance of responsibility for oneself and others.[3] Accumulation and exchange of opinions and information permits wider understanding of social life in the face of modern specialisation, group power greater than the power of individuals, and consciousness of the strength of social coherency.

The above are the positive aspects of group work. Objections against group work are described below.

Goals of group work

Some of the older authors (e.g. Klein, Fenton)[4] take social reality as a given quality to be taken into account and accommodated to by individuals and social groups. The objection to this concept of group work is that it means the manipulation of people in the service of goals external to the group, such as preservation of the status quo. A similar objection is that of functionalism (particularly in connection with group work in production), which serves the demands of the industrial society.[5]

More modern authors who deal with the problems of group counselling are aware that the objection is justified. Thus they advocate both a change in the social system, while recognising that it is not possible to change a part without changing the whole; and, at the same time also advocate group work (e.g. MacLennan and Felsenfeld).[6]

One of the basic premises of group work is acceptance of people for what they are at the beginning of the group-dynamic process and for what they become during the process. In the opinion of Marcuse, this approach can paralyse social conflicts and authentic opposition.[7]

These and similar objections are extremely important and deserving of consideration. They are justified to the extent that the goals of group work are those that are assumed by these writers. This implies that it is necessary to define the goals of group work in each separate case. Just as it is possible to use modern technical innovations to the benefit or the detriment of mankind, so it is possible to use knowledge about man and society to benefit or harm. The basic problem of contemporary society and science is to define the goals of each application of knowledge in the context of the whole, in so far as man can understand it.

Ethical problems

In 1951 the American Society of Social Workers formulated the following ethical principles for social work in general (and thus also for group work):

1   Unlimited faith in the integrity, worth and creative power of the individual.

2   Unlimited conviction of his right to have and express his own opinion and to act according to this opinion as long as his behaviour does not threaten the rights of others.

3   The uncontestable conviction of the immanent and inalienable rights of each person to realise his own fate in the context of a progressive but stable society.[8]

The ethical reservations against group work are that there is a tendency towards intrusion into the intimate sphere of the human personality following open discussion,[9] and that group work is a potential means of controlling people. A related problem is that of the confidentiality of intimate revelations, which restrains professionals in a way that it does not restrain other participants in a group.[10] An answer to these reservations would be that group work, like all other work, has specific limitations; and work with individuals is an indispensable supplement to group work.

Problems connected with principles of group work

Although it is true that the group process can meet some immanent human needs, it is also necessary to be aware that it cannot satisfy all human needs and thus that the scope of group work is limited.

Although it is necessary in the discussion of the individual and the group to consider psychodynamic, sociodynamic, economic and cultural factors, it is not possible to understand these influences in the cause and effect sense of natural science; rather, the individual should be respected as an active, creative being.[11]

In connection with acceptance of and respect for the differences between people, the reservation of Marcuse is of importance: that this position is a well-meaning neutrality which has nothing in common with the liberation of 'unrestrained, critical, radical thought and new intellectual and instinctual needs ...'.[12]

Two things should be said in connection with this reservation. First of all, group work in itself is a dynamic approach towards a specific goal which is not colourless and static. Among other things, this goal is also dependent on the average capability of the members of the group. Fur-

c

thermore, social change is not achieved only in the dimensions of radical dialectical conflict, but also with the help of organic growth and the overcoming of conflicts on a higher level. Thus we are of the opinion that groups exist which have specific goals and which may play a positive and progressive role in social development.

We may also include in the same category the danger of pragmatism if we consider democratic game rules as simply instrumental (Schiller, after Dewey). [13]

Acceleration of open communication between members of the group has negative and positive effects. The tendency towards assimilation into the group may hinder the member's individuality and his specific aspirations.

> ... the more closely an individual is aware of the group the more ardently he will strive for a good performance.... After all, what the individual wants is the appreciation of those he values: for this reason he will conform to their expectations. If they do not work hard, why should he? Since it is easier to conform to observed behaviour, than to infer from current practices what the ideal may be, the behaviour of the new member will be regulated by the average performance of the group, which may or may not be the ideal.... Group pressure, therefore, sometimes enables the individual to reach the correct solution, sometimes it confirms him in a wrong solution.... It may persuade a man to doubt the evidence of his own senses.... [14]

Thus, group work may lead to a reduction of deviations from the average (both negative as well as positive ones).

This is undoubtedly a problem that is immanent in group work. Group work is not in itself directed towards acceleration of exceptional creativity and of involvement, although in special cases it may also serve these ends. However, there are examples of special groups or special exceptional personalities who lead the group (in the area of our work, for example, Makarenko, Aichhorn, Redl, A.S. Neil, and so on). As a rule, the commitment of the members of a group toward a goal cannot exceed the commitment of the leader. If it does exceed the leader's commitment, it gradually leads such a group member out of the group process, makes him autonomous in his aspirations and growth, or leads him to form a new group. This is a normal, and desirable process of group dynamics. The problem here is that complete autonomy can signify isolation, which is not only a success but also a burden. In the final analysis 'potentiated individualism harbours the danger that the group may become a mass'. [15]

Problems of the techniques of group work

These problems are: unlimited confidence in a method of work which becomes a dogma and claims a total capability, [16] a fetish-like elevation of the method as an ideology, [17] a gradual transition into a routine, and a possibility of terrorising members, particularly when the group feels threatened. [18]

These are some of the problems that require the enlightenment of those who argue for group work and those who reject it in principle.

Conceptual problems of group work at Logatec

Goals

The goal of the experiment at Logatec was to determine whether it is possible, with intensive group counselling of the staff, to achieve a permissive institutional atmosphere which would not be less successful educationally than in other institutions, and which would be acceptable to the immediate and wider institutional environment and for the social atmosphere in Slovenia in general. The justification for such a goal came from the conviction that a repressive educational approach threatens authentic and creative development for both staff and inmates.

According to the basic concepts, the group work was to take place on three levels: in the professional team of consultants, between the consultants and the staff, and between the staff and the inmates. Thus within the context of the basic goal each of these groups had its own specific goal.

The goal of group work between the members of the professional team was mutual supplementary information on the various professional aspects of re-education and consultation work. From the very beginning the members of the professional team agreed on the one hand to have dealings in the institution only with the personnel, and not with the inmates, and on the other to serve purely in a consultative capacity, without exertion of any kind of control over the institution in the sense that anyone in the institution would be responsible to them for their actions. However, since the team conducted the experiment as a research project, it had to follow the development of the experiment with records and various tests. The staff knew that the experiment was to be described in a paper to be published in Slovenia and abroad. The staff were continually fearful that the results of the research might have unfavourable consequences either for individuals or for the institution as a whole.

In their group work with the staff, the team set as its goal the development of acceptance of the inmates and their behaviour, a permissive yet educational atmosphere in the institution, and scepticism toward prejudices. In general the team wished to accelerate the authentic development of each teacher as a unique individual, even at the price of variability in educational approaches. We anticipated that the staff would sooner or later form the inmates into groups appropriate to the personalities of the educators.

In their relationships with the inmates the staff were to use the method of group counselling primarily as a therapeutic tool, but also as an adaptive one. In this regard it is necessary to note that the inmates coming into the institution were almost exclusively ones who had committed offences against property or had behaved antisocially. Adaptation to institutional and social life signified in these cases a relative elevation of the cultural level of the inmates.

In addition, each institution has also to function within its internal organisation. This explains the tendency of the staff to adapt the inmates to the institutional and social environment, at least in the sense that the inmates should not threaten others or continually expose the staff to conflict situations. This reality must be faced also by the professional who has reservations against attempts to adapt people to reality.

From the beginning some members of the team were aware that there exist in every educational institution contradictions which are immanent in group work in such an environment, simply because it takes place in an artificial and forced situation. Specifically, inmates, therapist and institutional administration bring different expectations to group work. [19]

Ethical problems

At the beginning of the experiment all the staff were newly accepted; they were informed from the outset that this was an experimental institution. It was possible to observe that the staff felt uncomfortable about being the object of an experiment. We were frequently asked who was actually the object of the experiment – the staff or the inmates. Although we consistently explained that we were all the object of the experiment – the team, the staff and the inmates – our answer did not satisfy the staff. We accepted this as normal, since no one wishes to be the object of an experiment, even an experiment that could be of personal benefit.

The group counselling of the team and staff was in principle not psychoanalytically oriented. None the less, it was possible to anticipate situations that would require deeper analysis and individual contact between the consultants and members of the institution's staff. At the beginning of the experiment such contacts were more frequent than they become later, finally almost dying out. The institutional staff knew that individuals turned to consultants in conflict situations. Objections arose that staff-members were complaining about each other to members of the team.

It is probably true that at the beginning of the experiment members of the team were unsure of how to deal with such situations. However, we soon became aware that it was necessary to help the institutional member who found himself in a conflict situation to solve it himself. Thus in our individual discussions with staff-members we attempted to develop their own potentials and interests, at the same time avoiding discussion of the 'mistakes' of others. Despite these efforts, the fear of 'intrigues' remained, particularly for some staff-members.

The confidentiality of the discussions did not pose a great problem, since institutional life among the staff was so intense that no secrets could be kept except in unusual cases. But in some cases it happened that members of the professional team were not careful enough in defining what could and could not be taken from the team meetings and shared with the staff. However, there were few such situations, and those that arose were connected with other conflicts which had their sources elsewhere, and not in the poor keeping of secrets.

Principles

We knew from the beginning that the scope of group work is limited. Thus we required in the plan of our research a careful selection of staff; we sought a director for the institution for a whole year; we began the experiment with didactic seminars; and we wished to supplement group work with individual counselling.

At all levels group work signified a limiting and mitigating of conflict situations. None the less, such situations arose at all levels. We had variable success in our attempts to deal with these situations; the members of the team probably became fully aware only at the end of the experiment that solution of a conflict on a higher level can have a better effect than avoidance of the conflict.

Despite the fact that we wished to accelerate the authentic development of the individual, group work as a whole, on all levels, led to a reduction of deviations from the average. This average was not a compromise, but rather a developmentally dynamic totality which hindered those individuals who would undoubtedly have gone further and achieved greater successes if they had not been under the influence of the group.

Techniques

The techniques that we used can be named as follows: the meetings of the professional team were task oriented; the work of the team with the staff was growth and task oriented. We could say that the work of the team with the staff approximated therapeutic communities techniques.[20] We acted on the conviction that knowledge of group work methods was significant for the entire staff,[21] and was something they could apply in various situations, either systematically or occasionally, in work with the inmates. Thus we included the following workers in group meetings with the professional team: the director of the institution, the director's assistant, the psychologist, the social worker, educators and shopmasters. We repeatedly encouraged the staff to hold regular group meetings of leading members of the institution and ancillary staff members (cooks, janitors, seamstress, economist and drivers). Except for some isolated attempts, this kind of group work did not occur.

Notes

[1] Schiller, quoting from 'Bericht aus dem Nachbarschaftsheim' in *Nachrichten aus dem Pestalozzi-Fröbel-Haus*, p. 48.

[2] Lifton, p. 4.

[3] Lifton, p. 2.

[4] Klein, pp. 21, 123; Fenton, *Introduction* p. 9; Fenton, *Handbook*, pp. 2, 3, 18.

[5] Negt, p. 5.

[6] MacLennan and Felsenfeld, pp. v, 3, 45.

[7] Marcuse, *One-Dimensional Man*, pp. 35, 110.

[8] After Schiller, p. 58.

[9] Harrison, p. 32.

[10] Kleinsorge, p. 435.

[11] Schiller, p. 31.

[12] Marcuse, *Ideen zu einer kritischen Theorie der Gesellschaft*, p. 179.

[13] Schiller, p. 31.

[14] Klein, pp. 83–7. Štajnberger is of the opinion that the tendency to conformism is a relatively constant human characteristic which manifests itself in highly varied life situations (p. 177). See also Rakić, pp. 47–51; Rot; Fromm.

[15] Battegay I, pp. 9, 47.

[16] Schiller, p. 31.

[17] Negt, p. 13.

[18] Klein, pp. 69, 99.
[19] Kobal (1968).
[20] As described by Lifton, pp. 22, 23.
[21] Fenton, *Handbook*, p. 18.

References

Arn, L., and Perris, G., 'Mental-hygienic aspects of group therapy' in *Information and Rehabilitation in Group Psychotherapy* vol. I, Verlag der Wiener Medizinischen Akademie, Vienna 1968, p. 393 ff.

Battegay, Raymond, *Der Mensch in der Gruppe*, vols. I, II, Verlag Hans Huber, Bern and Stuttgart 1968.

Bion, W.R., *Experiences in Groups*, Tavistock Publications, London 1961.

Cartwright, Dorwin, and Zander, Alvin, *Group Dynamic*, 2nd ed., Row, Peterson and Co., Evanston, Ill., and Elmsford, NY 1962.

Fenton, Norman, *A Handbook on the Use of Group Counseling in Correctional Institutions*, Institute for the Study of Crime and Delinquency, Sacramento, Calif., 1965.

Fenton, Norman, *An Introduction to Group Counseling in State Correctional Service*, The American Correctional Association, New York 1958.

Fromm, Erich, *Flight from Freedom*, Nolit, Belgrade 1964.

Harrison, Roger, 'Some Criteria for choosing the Depth of Organizational Intervention Strategy' in *Information and Rehabilitation in Group Psychotherapy*, vol. I, Verlag der Wiener Medizinischen Akademie, Vienna 1968, p. 25 ff.

Hofstätter, R. Peter, *Gruppendynamik — Kritik der Massenpsychologie* RORORO, Munich 1957.

Klein, Josephine, *The Study of Groups*, 3rd ed., Routledge and Kegan Paul, London 1967.

Kleinsorge, Hellmuth, 'Medizinisch-Juristische Probleme bei der Gruppentherapie' in *Information and Rehabilitation in Group Psychotherapy*, vol. I, Verlag der Wiener Medizinischen Akademie, Vienna 1968, p. 435 ff.

Kobal, M., 'The contraversial role of the therapist in group work with dyssocial minors' in *Grupna psihoterapija*, II Jugoslovenski psihoterapijski seminar, Mokrice, 3. — May 5, 1968, ed. Sekcija za psihoterapiju Zbora liječnika Hrvatske and 'Lek', tvornica farmaceutskih i kemijskih priizvoda, Ljubljana, pp. 63–7.

Kolakovski, Lešek, *Philosophical Essays*, Nolit, Belgrade 1964.

Konopka, Gisela, *Soziale Gruppenarbeit ein helfender Prozess*, 2nd ed., Verlag Julius Beltz, Weinheim—Berlin—Basel 1969.

Lifton, M. Walter, *Working with Groups*, 2nd. ed., John Wiley and Sons, New York—London—Sydney 1966.

MacLennan, W. Beryce, and Felsenfeld, Naomi, *Group Counseling and Psychotherapy with Adolescents*, Columbia University Press, New York and London 1968.

Marcuse, Herbert, *One-Dimensional Man*, Veselin Masleša, Sarajevo 1968.

Marcuse, Herbert, *Ideen zu einer kritischen Theorie der Gesellschaft*, Suhrkamp, Frankfurt a.M. 1969.

Moreno, J.L., 'Introduction to the Fourth International Congress in Group Psychotherapy' in *Information and Rehabilitation in Group Psychotherapy*, Verlag der Wiener Medizinischen Akademie, vol. I, Vienna 1968, p. III ff.

Negt, Oskar, *Soziologische Phantasie und exemplarisches Lernen*, Europäische Verlaganstalt, Frankfurt a.M. 1968.

Rakić, B., *Educational Work in Small Groups*, Zavod za izdavanje udžbenika, Sarajevo 1967. (The Publishing House for School Text Books)

Rot, N., 'Influence of the opinions of the majority on the degree of conviction of persons of different psychological structure' *Sociologija* 1, Belgrade 1960. (*Sociology*)

Schiller, Heinrich, *Gruppenpädagogik als Methode der Sozialarbeit*, 3rd. ed. Haus Schwalbach, Wiesbaden—Dotsheim 1966.

Štajnberger, Ivan, 'Group leadership' in N. Rot et al., *Social Psychology*, Rad, Belgrade 1968, p. 161—209.

7 Test Instruments and Documentation

Vinko SKALAR

Instruments used in the selection of staff

A special subcommittee, consisting of a psychiatrist, psychologist and pedagogue, was responsible for selection of staff for the experimental institution. For diagnostic purposes the psychiatrist used the psychiatric interview, with which he investigated the personal stability and prevalent personality traits of the candidates. The pedagogue also used interviews, to determine the motivation of the candidates for work with behaviourally disturbed youth. The psychologist used three psychological techniques in the selection of staff:

— Domino test (D_{48}),[1] a test of intelligence. This test was introduced in Yugoslavia in 1961 with the permission of the Centre for Applied Psychology in Paris. In the same year the test was given preliminary standardisation on a group of 273 secondary school students in their senior year. The representative sample included students from eleven different high schools in Slovenia. The results of the comparison with the staff of the experimental institution are shown in Chapter 5.

— Personal interest test (0—I).[2] The 0—I is the Slovene adaptation of the Vienna version of the MMPI. The test was given preliminary standardisation in Slovenia in 1968 on a sample of 272 male and female high school students and on a sample of 208 male and female representatives of the general population. The test has been in use in Yugoslavia since 1959. It measures ten bipolar personality dimensions and eight interest categories. For purposes of comparison with the staff of the experimental institution, we show the results for the general population in Chapter 5.

— Rorschach's test[3], a definitely clinical test. In Yugoslavia this test is used in psychiatric and psychologic practice. Application of this test became particularly widespread after 1961, when the Institution for the Education of Staff and the Study of the Organisation of Work in Kranj held a one-year seminar on Rorschach psychodiagnostics which was attended by a large number of clinical psychologists.

The psychodiagnostic tests that were used in the selection of the staff were again given to the staff of the experimental institution at the end of the experiment in July and August 1971.

The entire documentation of the work of the special subcommittee of the selection commission, as well as the records of the final testing of the staff of the experimental institution, is available at the Institute of Criminology of the University of Ljubljana.

We must emphasise that selection of staff for educational institutions was not the custom here, but that this practice was retained in the experimental institution after the conclusion of the experiment.

Instruments used in evaluating the personalities of the inmates

The personality evaluation of the inmates was carried out by the psychologist of the observation centre in Jarše before their admission to the experimental institution. Until September 1968 no unified diagnostic instruments were used. After September 1968 the psychologist of the diagnostic centre agreed with the consulting team to use the following test instruments:

— Progressive matrices, a non-verbal intelligence test.[4] This test has been used in Yugoslavia since 1952, and in Slovenia since 1956. We applied it to groups of young people and adults, to groups of normals and deviants. The statistical results from a study of delinquent and non-delinquent youth from the year 1957,[5] as compared with the same parameters for the control and experimental groups of inmates, are given in Chapter 19.

— Bender test.[6] The Bender test has been used in Slovenia since 1961, when it was given preliminary standardisation on a population of 261 high school students from ten high schools and on a group of 314 young industrial workers of various kinds. The statistical parameters for these groups are compared with the parameters for the experimental and control groups in Chapter 19.

— MMQ[7] (questionnaire for determining the degree of neuroticism). This questionnaire has been used in Yugoslavia since 1954, but primarily in clinical practice. Therefore we do not have an appropriate control group from the normal population. Psychiatric and clinical psychologic practice has adopted the author's scale for the criteria for the determination of simulation.

— Mooney list for the survey of personal problems.[8] The Mooney list of personal problems contains seven sub-categories (health problems, school problems, family problems, financial and economic problems, problems of interpersonal relationships, problems in the area of assertion, problems of the intrapsychic realm) and a general category. This test has not yet been standardised in Yugoslavia, but has been given to numerous groups of normal and deviant juveniles. It is one of the tests used in the selection of candidates for the police cadet school of SR Slovenia. In Chapter 17 we present the statistical results for the candidates for the cadet school for 1970 in comparison with the experimental and control groups of inmates.

— Sentence completion test.[9] The sentence completion test has been used in Slovenia since 1960, particularly for groups of deviant juveniles and adults in clinical psychologic practice. This test was found to be a sensitive instrument for the determination of areas of frustration. It can also be used for people of below average intelligence, which is of importance since projective technics are for the most part applicable only to those of at least normal intelligence and with at least average verbal ability (e.g., Thematic Apperception Test).

The sentence completion test has not been standardised in Yugoslavia. We have not included the results of this test in our report, since we have not as yet been able to complete the quantitative analysis.

— Personal interest test $(O-I)^2$ (see previous section). We discontinued the use of this test after several months, since we found it to be inappropriate (too difficult) for the majority of the inmates in the experimental institution.

The psychologist of the observation centre thus made use of five instruments. He used the same instruments for repeat testing of the inmates upon their release from the institution.

In July and August 1971 we tested a selected group of inmates from the control institutions with the series of test instruments described above.

Instruments used in the measuring of attitudes of the staff

We used three attitude scales in the measurement of attitudes of the staff: the Schaefer-Bell scale, [10] F scale, [11] and semantic differential. [12] We chose these tests because they primarily measure, both globally and in sub-categories, the bipolar attitude dimension of authoritarianism: permissiveness.

— The Schaefer-Bell scale contains thirteen basic sub-categories (for authority, strictness, control, breaking the will, harshness, forcing independence, aggression, achievement, withholding affection, suppression of affect, equality, discussing problems and defensiveness) and six general categories (authoritarian control, 1 + 2 + 3; punitive discipline, 4 + 5; emotional distance, 6 + 7 + 8 + 9 + 10; egalitarian interaction, 11 + 12; custody orientation, 14 + 15 + 16; total custody orientation, 14 + 15 + 16 − 17).

In our Slovene translation of the Schaefer-Bell questionnaire we transformed the seven-level evaluation scale to a six-level scale. The reason for this change was:

The literal translation of the phrase 'strongly disagree' (or disagree very much) and the phrase 'strongly agree' (or agree very much) has a different meaning in Slovene from that in English. Therefore we changed the evaluative phrases as follows:

1   Not acceptable at all
2   Not acceptable
3   Hardly acceptable
4   Partially acceptable
5   Acceptable.
6   Fully Acceptable.

As the results of this change, our results cannot be directly compared with the results that Jesness presents in his study. The results differ to the extent of about 11·3 per cent. This is to say that our results are on average 11·3 per cent lower than Jesness' results.

— The F scale, which contains nine sub-categories (conventionalism, authoritarian submission, authoritarian aggression, anti-intraception, superstition and stereotypy, power and toughness, destructiveness and cynicism, projectivity and sex). We present only the general result.

— The semantic differential was constructed by Skalar, the psychologist of the consulting team, in the spring of 1967. As a basis three evocative words were selected: 'inmate', 'education' and 'educator'. We presented all three of these words to eight educators. Four were selected from the Observation Centre in Ljubljana, and four from the girls' approved school in Višnja gora. We asked the teachers to think freely about the given evocative words and the associations they had for them, and to record as many adjectives as possible for each word. These items were then arranged in order according to their frequency, and a contradictory item determined for each. Each item and its contradictory counterpart were then placed on a seven-level numerical bipolar scale. The evocative word 'inmate' had fifty-seven items, 'education' had 55, and 'educator' 52.

All three instruments were applied once every eight months to the staff in the experimental institution. The first test was given at a seminar before opening of the institution (or upon arrival of a new educator in the institution); the last test was given in February 1971, four months before the end of the experiment.

The attitude scales were also given to staff members from the control institutions. We gave four tests at the control institutions: the first was conducted in February 1970, and the last in April 1972. As was the case for the experimental institution, the interval between testings was eight months.

Instruments used in measuring the attitudes of inmates

We selected the Jesness inventory [13] for the measurement of the inmates' attitudes. This instrument measures attitudes related to several important aspects of the juvenile's socialisation or social adaptation. The questionnaire contains 155 questions, which correspond to ten basic sub-categories (social maladjustment, value orientation, immaturity, autism, alienation, manifest aggression, withdrawal, social anxiety, repression, denial) and the general category of asocialisation.

We gave the inventory to the inmates in the experimental institution at intervals of six months. The first test was carried out upon admission of the inmate into the institution, the last upon his release.

For the control institutions we conducted the first test for a group of inmates who were admitted between 1 September, and 31 December 1971. The first test was taken at the time of admission, and the last test on 1 June 1972.

Documentation of meetings with the staff of the experimental institution

During the experiment the consulting team had three different kinds of meetings with the staff: meetings with the entire staff (except for the auxiliary staff), meetings with the group of educators, and meetings with the group of shopmasters. We documented all three kinds of meetings according to the following scheme: presence (seating arrangement), participation (number of contributions), formal course and content of the discussion, and evaluation of the dynamics and contents.

Documentation of therapeutic communities

Therapeutic communities were introduced to the institution on 22 April 1970. They were scheduled to meet once a week and lasted one hour. They were regularly followed by a meeting with the staff which was devoted to analysis of the happenings in the therapy meetings. The therapeutic communities were formally led by the principle of the institution or his assistant, and were regularly attended by individual members of the consulting team. The psychiatrist, who gave the initiative for the introduction of therapeutic communities, often assumed a leadership role, both in the therapeutic communities and in the meetings with the staff.

We documented all the therapeutic communities, including the analytical meetings with the staff, according to the schema presented in the previous section. In the individual school years there were the following numbers of therapeutic community sessions:

1967/68	0	
1968/69	0	
1969/70	7	(introduced on 22 April 1970)
1970/71	34	(ending 23 June 1971)
Total	41	

In April 1971 the staff, on their own initiative, introduced an additional two therapeutic community sessions a week, these being intended primarily as a forum for discussion of the current affairs of the institution. The members of the consulting team did not take part in these additional sessions, which consequently were not documented. The experimental institution has continued with the therapeutic community sessions following the conclusion of the experiment.

Documentation of the educational process

The staff in educational institutions are obliged by the Republic's professional guidelines to document the educational process with daily records of the events in the educational work with the inmates. [14] This guideline is more or less followed in most educational institutions, but the institutions do not have a unified concept of the content and form of these diaries. In light of the generally accepted practice in other institutions, the professional team anticipated no difficulties in the documentation of the educational process in the experimental institution, but wished to improve gradually the quality of the diaries through the consultation process, and, together with the staff, to arrive at the most appropriate form for them. During the experiment the staff were given two schemas for the writing of diaries, with detailed directions for observation. The first one was prepared by the psychologist Skalar in November 1967, the second by the psychologist Mlinarič in November 1969.

We suggested to the staff that individual members of the consulting team might prepare comments on the daily entries in the diaries, and in this way give the staff an opportunity to compare their behaviour, actions and attitudes in the educational situation with the viewpoints of the consulting team, and thus gradually become more sensitive in their relationships with the inmates. We agreed that the diaries would be typed up at the Institute of Criminology on a weekly basis and then returned to the institutional staff and the files for each inmate.

Throughout the experiment the staff expressed extreme resistance to the writing of diaries. The main reason for this resistance is to be found in the general overburdening of the staff, and in their feelings of insecurity and fear that the consulting team would find out about their educational actions — about which they already felt unsure. In order to stimulate the

Table 7.1

Diaries: number of entries

	1967/68	1968/69	1969/70	1970/71	Total
Total number of entries	1,584	1,246	1,213	204	4,247
Number of entries by the teaching staff	1,034	1,161	1,083	124	3,402
Number of teaching staff	7	12	13	12	
Number of teaching staff who kept diaries	7	11	12	4	
Average number of entries for teaching staff who kept diaries	148	105	90	31	

Note: By teaching staff we mean teachers and instructors who were required to write diaries as part of their duties.

writing of diaries, the consulting team decided to give honorariums for these contributions. However, this stimulation was not effective either, since the staff neglected the writing of diaries more and more towards the end of the experiment. The number of reports from the staff for the individual school years can be seen in the Table 7.1.

The written comments on the diaries whre contributed by the leader of the experiment and the psychologist Skalar. Table 7.2 shows the number of written comments for the individual school years.

Table 7.2

Comments on the diaries

	1967/68	1968/69	1969/70	1970/71	Total
Total number of comments	299	173	43	12	527
Number of comments to the teaching staff	164	168	39	12	383
The percentage of comments relative to the number of entries by the teaching staff	15·8	14·5	4·0	10·0	

The number of comments on the diaries is small relative to the number of daily entries. The reason for the relatively modest response of the consulting team to the staff's diaries lies primarily in the fact that only two team members made it their duty to attend to this task. They responded primarily to diaries of teachers, specifically those who showed, at various phases of the experiment, a greater readiness for consultation and for co-operation with the consulting team in general. In 1969/70 the number of comments on the diaries falls drastically because of the absence of the psychologist Skalar and the increased work load of the leader of the experiment in this school year. Among other tasks she began to work systematically follow the functioning of the team.

The Bales evaluative scale [15] for the evaluation of group interactions could also be counted as part of the documentation of the educational process. This scale was given to the staff at an introductory seminar in September 1967. The staff were to fill out the evaluation scale once a week, each for the inmates in his own educational group. The staff rejected the filling out of the evaluation scale despite the repeated encouragement of the consulting team, and persisted in their refusal until the end of the experiment.

Documentation of the functioning of the consulting team

For the functioning of the consulting team we have three different sources of data, the psychiatric opinion, the observations of non-partisan observers at the meetings of the consulting team, and analysis of the self-evaluation conducted in June 1968.

— Psychiatric opinion. The consulting team asked the psychiatrist, Dr Matić from Belgrade, to conduct psychiatric interviews with the members of the consulting team and give his opinion of each, particularly in regards to the individual's intentions for the experiment. The first interviews were given by Dr Matić on 2 October 1967, and a second, control interview on 10–13 October 1971. Both times the psychiatrist gave his opinion for each individual, and after the second series of interviews also gave his opinion of the functioning of the whole team in the experiment.

— The consulting team had meetings once a week which were intended for analysis of the happenings in the experimental institution and synchronisation of viewpoints among the members of the team. These meetings were not specifically documented from the beginning of the experiment until May 1969. On 21 April 1969, on the suggestion of Miss Farley from the United States, the team decided to have a non-partisan observer taking part in future meetings, an observer who would systematically follow the functioning of the team.

We selected these observers from among our co-workers at the Institute of Criminology. They were Mrs Alenka Šelih, Mr Janez Pečar, and Mr Boris Uderman. An observer took part in a meeting for the first time on 12 May 1969, and we consistently followed this practice until the end of the experiment. We can divide the observations of the observers into two parts.

(a) Observations from 12 May 1969 until 12 July 1970. In this period the observers followed the dynamics and functioning of the consulting team according to the following schema: attendance, duration of meeting, content (subjects discussed), contributions of individuals in the group and of the group as a whole according to a special schema (sug-

gestions, search for information, giving of information, value judge-
ments, clarification, summarising), productivity of the group in ten-
minute intervals, emotional atmosphere, evaluation of the group as a
whole and conclusions. There were forty-two contributions according
to this scheme. Mrs Šelih contributed fifteen, Mr Pečar sixteen, and
Mr Uderman eleven.

(b)   Observations from 7 September 1970 to 31 May 1971. In this
period the observers used Bales's schema.[15] Uderman contributed
seventeen observations, Mrs Šelih twelve. The observers did not change
from meeting to meeting, but rather each of them was present at consecutive meetings for a determined period of time.

— Analysis of evaluations. In June 1968 the psychologist Skalar prepared
for the members of the consulting team a questionnaire, with which we
hoped to determine the motivation of individuals for work on the
experiment, attitudes in connection with the on-going experimental
work, and finally the perception of team members of their own role in
the consulting team. The questionnaire contributed towards members'
insight into their own roles in the team, to a greater integration and a
greater homogeneity of the team, and could give to the non-partisan
observer the possibility of insight into the functioning of the consulting
team.

Notes

[1]   Domino test (Anstey, Great Britain, 1943), French version (D_{48}).
[2]   Personal interest test (0—I), Šali Borut, Institution for the Productivity of Work of the SRS, Ljubljana 1959.
[3]   Bohm, Ewald, *Lehrbuch der Rorschach-Psychodiagnostik*, 2nd. ed.
Verlag Hans Huber, Bern and Stuttgart, 1957. *Rorschach psychodiagnostics* handbook, Borut Šali, Institution for the Education of Staff and the
Study of the Organisation of Work in Kranj, Kranj 1961.
[4]   Progressive matrices, L.S. Penrose and J.C. Raven, Great Britain 1938.
[5]   *Review for Criminalistics and Criminology*, no. 2, 1957, pp. 90—100.
Revija za kriminolistiko in kriminologico.
[6]   Bender Gestalt Test, L. Bender, USA 1938.
[7]   MMQ, Maudsley Hospital, Great Britain, 1948.
[8]   Mooney list for the survey of personal problems, Ross L. Mooney,
Office for educational research, Ohio 1950.
[9]   Sachs, J.M., and Levy, S., 'The sentence completion test' in L.E. Abt
and T. Bellak, *Projective Psychology*, A.A. Knopf, New York 1952,
pp. 370—97.

[10]   The Staff Opinion Survey, developed by Earl J. Schaefer and Richard E. Bell and adopted for institutional purposes by Jesness, (Jesness, F. Carl, *The Fricot Ranch Study*, State of California Youth Authority, October 1965, pp. 18–20, Appendix 1.)

[11]   The California F scale (shortened version): Miller, C. Delbert, *Handbook of Research Design and Social Measurement*, McKay Science Series, New York 1967, p. 301.

[12]   Semantic differential of our own construction (Skalar) with the evocative words: 'educator', 'education' and 'inmate'.

[13]   Jesness, F. Carl, 'The Jesness inventory' California Youth Authority, *Research Report* no. 35, 30 November 1963, pp. 67–78.

[14]   Statute of programming of educational work in training institutions, Uradni list SRS, no. 27, article 10, 1970.

[15]   R.G. Bales, *Interaction Process Analysis: A method for the study of small groups,* Addison-Wasley, Cambridge, Mass., 1950; summarised from Delbert Miller, *Handbook of Research Design and Social Measurement*, David McKay Company, Inc., New York 1964.

PART III

Implementation of the Experiment

8 Dynamics of Group Work and Group Counselling

Miloš KOBAL, Katja VODOPIVEC.

We planned group work on three levels: between the members of the professional team, between the members of the team as advisers to the institution's staff, and between the staff and the inmates.

We began with the first two forms of this work at the beginning of 1967; that is, in the preparatory phase. At this time — before the institution began functioning — the first institutional staff was assembled. The members of the team considered this necessary because the staff were not trained for educational work in institutions. The purpose of the staff's working in other institutions and work organisations, and of the weekly consultations, was to prepare them for work in the institution; the team meetings were designed to create greater homogeneity in the attitudes and the work methods of the team.

At the beginning the number of staff was small, and there were five team members. In the first two meetings with the staff we discovered that there were too many team members relative to the number of staff. Therefore we reduced the number of team members present to two, with different team members participating from meeting to meeting with the staff. We had no difficulties with this method of work in the preparatory phase. We attained a considerable group dynamic, and we felt that we had motivated the staff for their future work.

From January to September, when the first inmates were admitted, the members of the professional team had twenty-one meetings; the team-member consultants had fifteen meetings with the future educators.

Following the employment of additional teachers, the seminar with the staff, and the admission of the first inmates, we intended to base the group discussions on the daily educational problems that would confront the staff, and to intensify the consultations by reducing the number of participants.

We did not want to divide the educational staff into teachers and shop-masters (instructors), since we knew that in institutions there exist conflicts between these two groups of workers. We did not want the team's work to contribute to conflicts stemming from the nature of the work in the institution.

Therefore we intended to assign the educational staff randomly to two approximately equal groups, A and B. Each of these groups was to have at least one group meeting per week. Four members of the professional team were to lead these meetings, so that each of them would act as consultant one week per month — that is, for two meetings.

Although we were aware of the importance of continuity of communication for successful group counselling, in the context of this experiment we wanted to explore the possibility of using rotational consultants. We assumed that the consultants' attitudes and theoretical approaches were similar (we had previously worked together in research teams). We felt that it would be possible to discuss attitudes and methodology at weekly team meetings and in this way attain unity. We assumed that each member of the team was qualified to advise on all problems of treatment. We wanted to avoid excessive demands on individual team members — especially because some of them were only consulting co-workers of the institute.

In this way we began our counselling on 3 October 1967. After four group meetings the institutional staff rejected the method as it had been offered. They felt that they were getting too little practical help. In addition, a member of the other group had been criticised at one of the meetings. The staff feared criticism in the absence of the person criticised, and demanded meetings for the entire staff.

After heated discussion and with divergent opinions, the professional team of the institute decided to hold regular weekly conferences with the entire staff for the purpose of offering concrete educational help. These conferences were to be led by the team psychologist. (The experimental plan did not foresee conferences of this kind.) One of the team members (the team members participating changed from meeting to meeting) kept a detailed record of the contributions of the participants and also participated in the discussions. These records were the basis of weekly discussions among the members of the professional team (who received duplicated copies of them in advance), and in addition the rotation of the other members permitted all the team members to have contact with the staff.

From then on, — that is, from the end of October 1967 to the end of the experiment — these meetings took place regularly, although in time their content changed, and in the final phase, when the therapeutic communities were introduced, they acquired an entirely different significance. In addition, the members of the team were to give staff members who wished it individual help.

The members of the team were aware that the weekly conferences did not replace the intensive group counselling that had been originally planned.

We agreed that we would reintroduce group counselling in December 1967. But now we had a different conception of group counselling method: three members of the professional team were each to conduct ten consecutive group consultations. We agreed that each of the consultants was to adopt the work methods that suited him best: the leader of the experiment with emphasis on the determination of the roles of participants in the group and in the institution (social group work); the psychiatrist with non-directive methods of discussion of experiences in the group; and the pedagogue with study of selected literature. We agreed to explain the new methodological approach in greater detail to the staff.

There were twenty of these meetings: the first consultant had ten, the second eight, and the third two. The institutional staff were not satisfied with this method of work. They openly expressed their dissatisfaction on numerous occasions, and there was much passive resistance, particularly with absenteeism. By the end of the spring term, 1968, this kind of group work had also died out. In the winter term of 1968 the staff refused to participate in group consultations. The educators and instructors began to teach in the institutional school in their spare time. They excused themselves by saying that they did not have time for group work.

During this time there were group conferences once a week. The records of the contributions to these discussions reveal that the instructors made one-third fewer contributions than did the educators.

Once again the team decided on a number of modifications and interventions. It acquired some additional funds with which to stimulate the staff towards group work in their free time (with the understanding that it was a matter of obligatory training). The team offered to divide the staff into two groups: a group of educators and a group of instructors. The second psychologist was engaged for consultation with the instructors, and the psychiatrist decided to carry out consultations with the teachers. Every second week the sessions were to be held in Ljubljana (thirty kilometres from Logatec) in the afternoon, with the special purpose of permitting the staff who lived in Logatec to visit the city, perhaps the restaurants, and to attend the cinema or theatre. Travelling expenses and an honorarium were paid to the staff by the institute.

From then on the weekly group meetings with the staff, held separately with educators and with instructors, and taking place alternately in Logatec and Ljubljana, became a matter of course. The meetings with the teachers were permanently led by the psychiatrist, whereas the meetings with instructors were originally led by the psychologist Caserman. Later, when his other obligations kept him from doing this, the meetings were led by the psychologist Mlinarič.

We began the therapeutic community sessions in May 1970, and continued with them in the academic year 1970/71. Only then was the situation ripe for this kind of work for the team as well as for the institutional staff.

Table 8.1

Number of meetings by school year

School year	Meetings of the professional team	Team-staff group work	Team-staff conferences	Therapy groups	Seminars
1967 (preparations)	21	15	–	–	–
1967/68	28	24	41	–	1
1968/69	41	24 (12+12)	55	–	1
1969/70	40	38 (29+9)	35	7	–
1970/71	35	51 (20+31)	34	34	3
Total	165	152 (61+52)	165	41	5

Note: The first number in parentheses signifies the number of meetings of the psychiatrist with the educators, the second number in parentheses the number of meetings of the psychologist with the instructors.

The reasons for the rejection of group counselling must be sought in four directions: among the consultants, the administration of the institution, and the staff, and in the atmosphere of the entire institution.

First of all there was the erroneous assumption that the theoretical standpoints of the consultants and their attitudes towards institutional education were similar or even identical. In December 1967, we found that the expectations of the members of the professional team in connection with the experiment were also divergent. Rotation of the consultants was also unrealistic, in light of the differing possibilities for identification of the staff with individual consultants, a factor we had not considered in our plans.

We planned the experiment so that the professional team would advise the staff on problems of treatment and education, whereas the organisational problems of the institution were to be handled by the director (who was to be only one with experience in institutional work). However, we did not find an appropriate director for the school year 1967/68, and the institution functioned for one year without a director. The staff who worked in the institution had no experience in institutional work, not to mention organisational work. The institution obtained a director only at the beginning of the school year 1968/69. The new director took charge of an organisationally unstructured institution, with staff who had their own well-differentiated personalities, and were not prepared to submit to organisational schemes, which had been practically absent for a year. The director had no experience in democratic leadership of this kind of staff.

In this situation the director declined the additional burden of other forms of group work throughout the year 1968/69. At first he felt that there was not time for additional group work because of the need to organise more firmly the instruction of the inmates, and later, in the spring semester, he did not participate in group work.

The staff was young, without experience in work with personally and behaviourally disturbed youth, and unable to generate internal organisation and consolidate it. The staff expected the professional team to give help in the form of concrete proposals and willingness to take over parts of the work. In the second half of the year 1967/68 the staff requested of the professional team that one of its members assume the position of director, at least temporarily.

The group meetings brought to light the staff's aversion to the members of the team as theoreticians who did not understand the problems of practical work; in addition, they were dissatisfied that the educational staff were being observed.

Not the least problem was the fact that in Yugoslavia the role of the professional as an adviser is simply not known. The role of the adviser is usually accompanied by control over the work of the individual, control that has an influence on his evaluation, his promotion, and in the final analysis also in his further employment in the work organisation. For this reason, workers in all areas are accustomed for the most part to inspectors and supervisory commissions, and not to advisers who do not have such powers and also do not desire them. Thus it was inescapable that, for almost half the duration of the experiment, the professional team were identified with the inspectors and supervisory commissions.

For the above reasons the institution worked, at least until the beginning of September 1968, without a firm organisational framework. The staff certainly felt that such a framework was necessary, but themselves neither knew how nor wished to generate it, for this would have required greater individual discipline and work involvement. The institution was characterised by a *laissez faire* system, without systematic involvement of individuals, but rather with sporadic efforts and initiatives from individual educators, who acted to the extent that they were motivated to test their own specific abilities. The staff themselves continuously neutralised all such individual efforts with ridicule of those who wished to raise themselves above the average. This was a strong example of the reduction of individual efforts to the level of the average in the context of group work (Josephine Klein).

The staff accepted as a principle an extremely permissive atmosphere and considerable unplanned acquiescence to the inmates. This state, which may well be called anarchy, lasted until late in 1968/69. The inmates reacted to it in different ways, at times exploiting it, at other times not. However, it was particularly in the first school year that the institution had hardly any escapes of inmates. When an inmate did escape the institution for a day or so, he would return himself. In this year the institution never had to involve the police in a search for an inmate.

The years 1968/69 and 1969/70 saw the institution undergo organisational maturation and partial internal consolidation.

A problem is posed by the fact that in the literature there are no theoretical guidelines for the introduction of democratic organisational schemes and communication networks in institutions of this kind. The practical worker has no choice but to adapt experiences gained in industry to the organisation of educational institutions – of course, with many modifications. In addition, the directors of institutions are former teachers who have adopted the organisational experiences of their predecessors without ever considering in depth the questions of various kinds of leadership, decision-making and communication.

Since the question of the organisation appropriate to the institution that is not to be led autocratically remained more or less open until the end of the experiment, in 1970 we asked the Department of Health, Education and Welfare of the USA to send a special expert to help the institution function more effectively. The Department responded to our request and sent G. Eugene Salem Jones, superintendent of the Northern Reception Center Clinic, Sacramento, California. Unfortunately, Mr Jones did not come to the institution until 19 May 1971, and the last school year of the experiment ended in late June 1971.

In the planning phase of the experiment we anticipated staff resistance to professional consultants acting as 'theoreticians'. The overcoming of this resistance was also one of the goals of the experiment.

However, in the planning phase of the experiment we did not reckon with organisational difficulties of the magnitude that we encountered. We planned an experiment with emphasis on group counselling in the framework of a strong, or at least evolving, organisational scheme. In light of the fact that it was a new institution with new, inexperienced personnel, and due to the fact that in planning we did not even consider concretely who might be the director of an institution of this kind, we committed an error in the planning of the experiment. If we consider these difficulties, which neither the professional team nor the staff foresaw, we may evaluate the dynamics of the introduction of group counselling as adequate and sufficiently flexible.

Here it is also necessary to consider that group work during the experiment signified for the staff not only the possibility of easing tensions, but also a considerable additional burden of stressful situations. The team demanded of the staff understanding and acceptance of unpleasant inmates; the inhibition and mastery of normal aggressiveness in frustrating situations; the fulfilling and honouring of decisions that the staff had accepted; and individual education. During the entire experiment the developmental dynamics of the staff was the object of observation and testing.

It was in May 1969 that we first had the feeling that the staff had accepted the professional team of the institute.

The school year 1969/70 was, then, the most productive for the involvement of the personnel. On their own initiative the shopmasters, together with one teacher, developed a plan for the daily follow-up, with observation forms, of the work habits of inmates. The teachers became involved in seeking jobs for inmates and were able to find employment for nearly all released inmates (except for those who went into compulsory military service). One of the teachers began to work on an analysis of the behaviour and lives of released inmates. Another teacher developed an analysis of the success of education of inmates in the institution. The director's assistant and three instructors prepared a short report on the work problems of instructors in institutions of this type. The psychologist analysed the wishes and perceptions of free activity as expressed by the inmates and the staff. He also prepared a sociometric test for inmates and informed the teachers of individual educational groups of the results. He introduced for a selected group of inmates, an experimental psychotherapy which involved listening to music. The director prepared an article, concerning the methods of group work in the institution, for the congress of the Union of Associations of Workers in Rehabilitation of Yugoslavia. The institution as a whole received from the Republic a prize for successful work, and one teacher, a shopmaster and the psychologist received individual prizes.

In the school year 1970/71 several work methods had already become routine, and the search for new work methods diminished. The first teacher left the institution in 1970, the second at the end of the school year 1970/71.

9 Group Work with Educators

Miloš KOBAL

Introduction

The group of educators consisted of eleven male and three female participants (including the director, psychologist and social worker). Of these, seven men officially finished the programme of meetings from the end of February 1969 until 8 June 1971; two withdrew from the group by the end of its work; and two joined the group in 1971. Women were absent occasionally or for longer periods due to family circumstances. There were sixty-one of these group meetings, which were held once a week and lasted an average of one hour and a half.

The counsellor for these meetings — by profession a psychiatrist — based his role on the principles of non-directive group leadership (C.R. Rogers). He supplemented this with didactic clarifications of the principles of group work with inmates. When circumstances were favourable, he interpreted the dynamics of the group, and in exceptional cases also the dynamics of individual participants and of himself. The participants were to take note of their experience of themselves and of their readiness for therapeutic work with inmates. They were to re-experience these interactions in the relaxed atmosphere of non-directive communication with the therapist. By means of the didactic—interpretative work the teachers were to prepare themselves for therapeutic work with the inmates and their groups.

The material gathered from these meetings allows for quantitative and qualitative analysis.

Quantitative analysis

Our data show the seating arrangements for each of these meetings. From these we constructed a sociogram. The most characteristic shows that seven participants interacted primarily with one of the educators who had university education. The therapist was selected by three participants in particular.

We scored all the verbal contributions of the participants according to the following criteria:

1   Discussion of individual inmates or smaller groups of inmates
2   Ideological deliberations (including all contributions which were derived primarily from general convictions, past experiences and neurotic rationalisations)
3   Didactically informative contributions
4   Confessions of individual participants
5   Discussion of other participants
6   Discussion of other groups (i.e., the groups that were included in the experiment, the group of shopmasters, the professional team of the institute, and so on)
7   Contributions which were directed towards the group of participants itself
8   Catharsis.

Contributions scored in this way are presented in Table 9.1 according to the kind of problem and the individual periods of group work. The table presents separately those contributions that represent orientation towards the group or towards problems of individual participants. Orientation towards problems of the group increases until January 1971, and then again falls in favour of more intensive discussion of the inmates. Ideological deliberations increase to their highest point in the second period of 1969/70 and then again appear intensively during the entire year of 1970/71.

Qualitative analysis

Characteristics of individuals in the group and of the group as a whole

Only by functioning did the group become familiar with the important general and other characteristics of those who made up the group. We became acquainted with these characteristics in three areas in particular:

1   Each participant had to reveal how he regarded therapeutic treatment of inmates with the dyssocial syndrome. The therapist attempted to give weight to experiences showing that simple reward and punishment are not sufficient in the treatment of inmates, and to prove this with didactic and interpretative examples. He pointed out that it is necessary to understand the inmates also from the standpoint of their unconscious, objective personality mechanisms, and to give preference to a therapeutic approach. Other approaches were to be combined with the therapeutic approach or were significantly to supplement it. Analysis of the data does not support

84

Table 9.1

Verbal contributions of the participants

Kind of problem	School year and semester					Total
	1968/69	1969/70		1970/71		
	II	I	II	I	II	
Number of meetings	12	18	11	5	14	61
Number of contributions:						
1 Inmates	58	207	63	37	315	680
2 Ideological deliberations	15	160	139	120	224	658
3 Didactic	39	105	36	29	138	347
4 Confessions	10	96	60	79	52	297
5 Other participant	19	70	58	76	54	277
6 Other group	10	82	41	41	50	224
7 Own group	11	16	27	22	12	88
8 Catharsis	1	3	2	1	–	7
Total	163	739	426	405	845	2,578
Average number of contributions per meeting	13·6	41	39	68	60	
Structure of the contributions:						
1 Inmates	36	28	15	9	38	26
2 Ideological deliberations	9	22	33	30	27	26
3 Didactic	24	14	8	7	16	13
4 Confessions	6	13	14	20	6	12
5 Other participant	12	10	14	19	6	11
6 Other group	6	11	10	10	6	9
7 Own group	7	2	6	5	1	3
8 Catharsis	–	–	–	–	–	–
Total	100	100	100	100	100	100
Orientation towards the problems of the group or participants (4+5+7+8) in percentages	25	25	34	44	13	26

the conclusion that any of the participants attained satisfactory proficiency in the therapeutic approach to the inmates. All participants still considered as more important the evaluation of the inmates in the context of good, tolerable and bad behaviour. However, all participants were prepared for, and capable of using at least occasionally the principles that could be called the 'therapeutic approach'.

2   The personal characteristics of the participants revealed themselves in relation to group work with the inmates as a reference allowing a wide area for the inmates' behaviour, but at the same time setting natural limits to this behaviour. All the participants accepted group work with the inmates as a permanent or temporary form of their activities. However, the

majority of the participants expressed open or covert resistance, particularly against the permanence of this work. The participants resorted to group work with the inmates in an informal way, in connection with given situations, irregularly, and at various times of the day. At such meetings a dynamic developed to which the educators were receptive. The participants were able to report significant experiences within their groups, and, despite the irregularity of group work, the inmates also often increased their awareness of the group. Thus the participants acquired to a considerable degree the ability to use group work with the inmates for the resolution of daily situations and typically short-range goals. Continuous group work of the kind appropriate to its systematic principles was not attained at any time during the experiment.

3   Finally, the characteristics of the participants revealed themselves in the solution of individual neuroses and in the functioning of the group itself. With time, all participants were willing to admit the possibility that their behaviour, on occasions or continually, was also led by unconscious impulses. They allowed personal interaction, brought to the group or to individuals within the group some of their own tensions, and allowed – not without some resistance and rationalisation – interpretation of some forms of their behaviour and verbal expression. In time this spirit led to a decrease in the rigidity of all the participants. New and more personal experiences were expressed, and new experiences, more appropriate to their work, were accepted.

We feel that in this sense all participants attained a certain common level, particularly those who participated during the entire period.

Functioning of the group of educators as a whole

To a certain degree, the tension and rigidity that were expressed in the structure of the group remained for the entire duration of group work. In addition to the demanding nature of the problem itself, this state of affairs was probably also influenced by the experiment. The group was characterised by group-dynamic phenomena that are generally recognised in this kind of work: manifest resistance, silence, unwillingness of the group to begin with discussion, avoidance of critical subjects, mutual supporting and excusing, rationalisation, regression and humour. If we put particular emphasis on 'silences', we must note that they were relatively rare – in the entire time we documented them only fifteen times. The consultant began the group meetings forty-two times, whereas the participants did so only thirteen times.

In the entire period the group of teachers dealt only with itself in eighty-eight contributions out of a total of 2,578 that were recorded, although some of the other contributions (didactic, confessional, ideological, and cathartic) were also in some way connected with the group and its function. Even more numerous, however, were the non-verbal communications and emotional ties that we were not able to count, but which allowed the group to function also after the conclusion of the experiment.

Special problems in the group

Out of the total of 2,578 recorded contributions, 658 were of the kind that we designated as ideological; these could be most simply rated as positive or negative. However, we did not have appropriate criteria by which to decide what kind of ideological contributions were predominant. Although individuals in the group made progress toward self-awareness, frequently – probably too frequently – they relied on a rational system of past experiences and general deep-rooted convictions. In any case, the ideological deliberations gave the group considerable cohesiveness, permitted the development of ties between the participants, inmates and other groups, and counteracted a tendency towards disintegration.

Catharsis was least frequent in the group, as it was recorded only seven times. Confessions were considerably more frequent – we recorded them 297 times. For the most part they expressed actual experiences of individuals in connection with their work. The participants truly contributed a part of their personal essence, and such confessions often tied into important interactions in the group. Confessions were most frequently contributed by those participants who also made the most ideological contributions.

In several theoretical works, the hypothesis is expressed that it is in group interaction that the group turns to itself with the greatest intensity, freedom and awareness. Our data does not support this hypothesis. In terms of verbal communication, only eighty-eight contributions were explicitly directed to the group itself, although discussion of individual participants, and in particular the relatively extensive confessional material, also undoubtedly contributed to the group's more successful functioning. The group was concerned with ideological matters and the problems of the inmates. Ideology was the main subject at twenty meetings, whereas the problems of the inmates were primary at twenty-three. These two bodies of contributions set firm boundaries for the work of the group and permitted both its survival and its, at least relative, homogenisation. It was in this manner that the group also more clearly distinguished itself from the groups of inmates as well as from other groups that were working at the same time in the institution.

At times the group of educators was quite tense towards other groups, suspicious, and prepared for verbal aggression. These tendencies were often directed towards the professional team of the institute, and the institute often played the role of the black sheep, or acted as a lightning rod for these tensions. Only with time did the group become more tolerant towards the team. We resolved the numerous tensions by verbal means as they arose in the everyday contacts between educators and instructors; the group of instructors was practically never the object of particular discussion and resistance.

Reflections of work with the inmates and their problems

The most numerous contributions were those dealing with inmates — a total of 680. However, these contributions were of varying value for the dynamics of the group and the personal growth of the participants. A small number of contributions originated from the systematic group work with the inmates or some other activity of this kind. Even fewer contributions were connected with the evaluation of the development of inmates over longer time periods. Contributions about inmates were of various kinds, including complaints about behaviour, information about unsuccessful and successful actions in actual situations or with specific inmates, general information about inmates, and prognostic evaluations. Frequently they contained questions directed to the counsellor or to other participants about means of solving various problems with individual inmates and specific actions or situations in the group of inmates. The educators derived the overwhelming majority of their contributions from actual work with the inmates — this was always apparent. Only a small part — in our opinion too small — was derived from group work with the inmates.

Evaluation of results

In the group of educators we were able to find sufficient proof that they reduced their use of repressive approaches to individuals and groups in their work with the inmates, and that they used more permissive and lay therapeutic approaches.

The educators' relatively prolonged and systematic collaboration in the special therapeutically led and directed group was one of the positive factors in the above-mentioned endeavours. In addition to didactic-informative contributions, in the group the educators often discussed inmates, their own rational and emotional standpoints and experiences, and, at least to some degree, achieved awareness of themselves in the group and of the group as a whole.

Some goals were not attained and were probably unobtainable with this kind of work. None the less, the teachers profited greatly in the development of their own personalities and in their ability to undertake specific kinds of work with their groups of inmates and with individual inmates.

Non-directive leadership was, in all probability, insufficient support for change in the personalities of the participants. Single interpretations and emotional experiences in the group could not bring about to any appreciable degree the desired and theoretically expected transformations. Additional influence from the organisation of the institution and the disciplinary responsibilities of the participants as employees were as a whole too weak seriously to contribute to the transformation of the teachers' personalities.

None the less, the results of the group's work throughout the experiment, and its numerous practical consequences, which we may well call a therapeutic influence on the present and future activities of the participants, are demonstrably positive judging by both quantitative and qualitative criteria.

References

Bierer, J., 'Therapeutic methods and procedures in the rehabilitation of psychiatric patients' *Zbornik radova int. simpozijuma o rehabilitaciji u psihiatriji*, Belgrade 1972, pp. 479–87. (*Symposium on Rehabilitation in Psychiatry*)

Bion, W.R., *Experiences in groups*, Human Relations papers, Tavistock Publications, London 1961.

Fenton, N., *Group Counseling*, Institute for the Study of Crime and Delinquency, Sacramento 1961.

Fenton, N., *A Handbook on the use of Group Counseling in Correctional Institutions*, Institute for the Study of Crime and Delinquency, Sacramento 1965.

Klüwer, K., 'Stationäre Psychotherapie bei Jugendlichen Dissozialen' in *Handbuch der Kinderpsychotherapie*, vol. II, Reinhardt, Munich 1969, pp. 808–17.

Rapoport, R.N., Rapoport, R., Rosow, I., *Community as Doctor*, Social Science and Tavistock, London 1967.

Rogers, C.R., *Client centered therapy*, Houghton Mifflin, Boston 1951.

Rogers, C.R., *On becoming a person. A therapist's view of psychotherapy*, Constable, London 1963.

10 Group Work with the Instructors of Practical Subjects

Franc MLINARIČ

Introduction

From the end of February 1969, group work with the instructors was arranged once a week. The meetings were held every week, alternately in Logatec and Ljubljana, until December 1969, when they were discontinued for a period because of the consultant, the psychologist Caserman. He was replaced by Mlinarič who had become familiar with the problems of the group and its members by substituting for Skalar during his study leave in Scotland. The psychologist Mlinarič led the group until the end of the experiment.

The group of instructors consisted of eight members (six instructors, the director of the workshops, and the consultant). The group had a total of sixty-one meetings. Participation at the meetings was very good (see Table 10.1), and there were practically no unexcused absences. We kept records of the contents of the group meetings.

Table 10.1

Number of meetings and participation

Semesters by school year	No. of meetings	No. of recorded meetings	Percentage participation
1968/69 II	15	12	88
1969/70 I	12	7	87
1969/70 II	2	2	93
1970/71 I	15	15	89
1970/71 II	17	16	87
Total	61	52	

Functioning of the group: group-dynamic indicators

Even though the basic orientation of the group was not analytic, and despite the fact that the group did not have a special observer with the responsibility of recording the experiences of the group, the records available to us do offer some group-dynamic indicators.

We considered the average number of recorded contributions of each participant in individual observation periods, and expressed it by percentages and corresponding ranks (see Table 10.2).

Table 10.2

Percentages and ranks of contributions

Group member	1968/69 II 1		1969/70 I 2		1969/70 II 3		1970/71 I 4		1970/71 II 5	
Number of contributions:										
Total	324		162		52		130		122	
Percentages and ranks:										
	%	R	%	R	%	R	%	R	%	R
Consultant	20·1	1	14·3	4	23·1	2	24·9	2	20·4	2
A	19·8	2	17·7	2	15·4	3	11·6	3	19·1	3
B	16·1	3	15·5	3	38·4	1	31·7	1	23·4	1
C	11·7	4	11·2	5-6	1·9	6-7-8	3·7	7	6·8	7
D	10·1	5	19·8	1	5·8	5	10·6	4	10·5	4
E	9·6	6	11·2	5-6	11·5	4	10·0	5	7·3	6
F	7·1	7	7·2	7	1·9	6-7-8	4·1	6	8·1	5
G	5·5	8	3·1	8	1·9	6-7-8	3·3	8	4·4	8

Three of the participants were consistently very active (one of them was the consultant). In the first two semesters three participants accounted for more than 50 per cent of the group's participation, and in the third semester 76·9 per cent. In the fourth and fifth semesters their total contribution decreased. The three least active participants, who in the first two semesters accounted for approximately 20 per cent of the total participation, made only 5·7 per cent of the contributions to the group in the third semester. Later, in the last semester, their participation increased to the level of 18·5 per cent.

In both cases we observed a change between the second and third semesters — that is, at the time the consultants changed. This change coincided with a decrease in the participation of the least active members and an increase in the total participation of the most active members.

Undoubtedly the change in consultants constituted a certain turning point in the functioning of the group, but it would probably be unjustified to ascribe all the changes to this fact alone. We must note that five months separate the second and third observation periods, during which time the group did not meet formally, although its participants lived, worked, and took part in other forms of group work together in the institution (as well as in sensitivity training outside the institution). This group interaction probably had some consequences for the dynamics of the group.

A partial explanation for the changes in the relative participation of

Table 10.3

Contributions by content

Subject discussed	1968/69 II 1		1969/70 I 2		1969/70 II 3		1970/71 I 4		1970/71 II 5	
Number of contributions:										
Total*	386		188		64		173		145	
Percentages and ranks:										
Subject discussed	%	R	%	R	%	R	%	R	%	R
Conceptual problems of education and of the experiment	49·0	1	34·2	1	31·6	1	28·2	1	22·6	1
Economic, organisational and other problems of the institution	14·9	2	12·0	3	12·2	4-5	10·7	3	13·7	4
Inmates in their work and instruction	11·6	3	11·2	4	17·1	3	10·6	4	5·9	7
Functioning of the group of instructors	9·5	4	15·8	2	19·4	2	16·7	2	9·4	6
Relationships outside the group	4·2	6	10·8	5	2·9	7	9·3	6	15·9	3
Members of the group discussing themselves and other participants	3·8	7	7·5	6	12·5	4-5	10·5	5	10·3	5
Theoretic and didactic subjects	1·1	8	6·4	7	−	8	8·6	7	18·3	2
Other themes	5·9	5	2·1	8	4·6	6	5·3	8	3·9	8

* The number of contributions classified by the subject is bigger, as the number of interventions because one intervention can deal with different subjects.

individual members following the above-mentioned interval is also offered by analysis of the thematic indicators of the group meetings (Table 10.3). Whereas in the first two periods the group primarily discussed actual technical—organisational problems, in the third semester more abstract subjects were given greater attention, and this obviously offered still greater possibilities for participation to those more active members who had already shown a marked inclination for ideological deliberations during the discussion of practical problems.

Participation of the two consultants during individual observation periods is generally interesting in that it raises the theoretical question of the actual role of the consultants. A categorical answer to this question is not possible simply on the basis of quantitative data concerning their activities; none the less, even these data suggest the conclusion that both of them to a certain extent forced their leadership role in the group. It is questionable whether the group sufficiently accepted their strong participation.

Did the group offer sufficient opportunity for participation to the less expansive participants? As mentioned previously, the less active members made their greatest number of contributions in the first two semesters, when the group were discussing primarily technical—organisational problems, and made considerably fewer contributions later, when attention was directed to more abstract subjects. However, the final increase in the participation of these members supports the conclusion that the group in general did not hinder them, and that it is necessary to seek explanations for their smaller activity outside the group, in particular also in the habitual personality trait determined patterns of behaviour of these participants. The consultant was of the opinion that the least active members profited much more than one would conclude simply on the basis of their verbal participation. This conclusion is supported by the unrecorded nonverbal behaviour of these participants, including the considerable attentiveness and interest with which they followed the discussion of others, their expressions of emotionally positive experiences, and in their readiness to follow the intentions of the group.

Functioning of the group: thematic indicators

Conceptual problems of education and of the experiment

Analysis of the thematic indicators of the group meetings shows that the group were consistently most interested in conceptual problems of education and, parallel with this, conceptual problems of the experiment. Particularly in the first meetings, the participants frequently turned to the description of the behaviour of individual inmates, expressed their insufficiency in leadership, and attempted to decide about treatment on entirely empirical grounds. They thought that correction of the inmates' behaviour could be attained only by extremely consistent and strict educational approaches. The first definite change toward more permissive educational attitudes was not observed until the fourth semester. The instructors began to recognise that work in the educational institution is considerably more demanding than it appears to the beginner, and that consistency and strictness are not the only formula for success. Parallel with this, the group came gradually to accept the viewpoint that the educators as well as the instructors must be capable — in the first place — of understanding inmates' behaviour. They began to understand that it serves no purpose directly to prevent expression of the inmates' inner tensions by various strict measures, since such an approach does not remove the causes of tension. We must state that the majority of the participants gave at least intellectual acceptance to this viewpoint, whereas emotional acceptance was characterised — until the last meeting — by significant periodic fluctuations, from positive emotional reactions to apathy, rejection and manifest resistance.

Discussion of conceptual problems of education was consistently closely related to discussion of the significance and purpose of the entire experiment. The initial powerful resentment generated by recognition that the experiment was directed at the staff as well as the inmates became milder with time but never disappeared entirely. The group remained sceptical about a final positive result of the experiment, for the group considered simple improvement of interpersonal communication an insufficient guarantee of success.

Economic, organisational and other problems of the institution

Discussion of conceptual problems of education and of the experiment often brought the group to a discussion of economic, organisational and technical problems of the institution. The group most frequently discussed the problem of the relatively poorly equipped workshops with their outdated machines. Gradually the opinion emerged that institutions of the 'Logatec type' require — more than any other type — well-equipped workshops with modern machines, so that the instructor, with a group of at most six inmates, would have sufficient opportunity for effective pedagogic work, unimpeded by such a great divergence between the

95

demands of permissive education and the effectiveness of the workshop.

The group attempted to find a partial solution to the organisational, economic, and other problems of the institution in more consistent leadership of the institution and greater work discipline on the part of the staff. The discussions were laced with expressions of easy-going tendencies such as were considered the natural result of insufficiently firm organisational guidelines. The group did not resolve the dilemma between the principle of organisational coercion of workers for work discipline and the principle of reliance on the workers' consciousness of the necessity for discipline. Although individuals accepted in theory the assumption that authentic personal growth of each individual during the experiment would lead to development of his responsibility towards his work and his self-discipline, this did not shake the conviction that this process was too slow and that the institution in its given circumstances could not afford it.

Inmates in their work and instruction

Even though the group, at one of the first meetings, clearly expressed their expectation that the meetings would primarily give them concrete help in the solving of pedagogic problems in the workshop, this subject was not often raised again. Initial complaints that the instructors could not control the situation in the workshops were gradually transformed into a consideration of the possibilities of appropriate motivation of the inmates towards work and learning. Thus, for example, in the fourth and fifth semesters there was considerable discussion of the possibility of group programming of work in the workshops and group evaluation of success at work. However, the group did not take a final position on these questions, nor did it consistently carry out these plans in practice.

Functioning of the group of instructors

This subject appeared in different contexts throughout all the observation periods. In the beginning the group primarily discussed the significance and goals of the group meetings. The questions of the work orientation of the group and the question of 'What are we going to talk about?' arose. The question of the concept of group work became particularly acute in the second semester.

There was a continual increase in references to the crisis in group work and to the tenseness of the atmosphere at the meetings. The group stubbornly held on to its initial work orientation, but at the same time recognised that the course of events was taking the group in other directions.

At this point the question of the group's functioning became strongly intermixed with conceptual problems about the entire experiment.

The new, theoretical—didactic work orientation of the group somewhat inhibited discussion of the subject of the group's functioning, but only temporarily, for it reappeared later to a greater extent and on a qualitively higher level. Particularly in the fourth and fifth semesters the subject of the functioning of the group arose in the form of résumés and analysis of the group dynamics at specific meetings, in the form of analysis of the reactions of the group to the behaviour of individual participants, and in the form of a generally very favourable evaluation of the functioning of the group as a whole.

Relationships outside the group

The problem of the relationships between the group of instructors and the group of educators was continually present in one form or another. It usually arose in discussions of organisational problems in the institution and in discussion of conceptual problems of education. Contributions to this subject were laced with obvious rivalry towards the group of educators, which did not change in content throughout the experiment. Of particular importance in this context was evaluation of the functioning of the group of educators in comparison with the functioning of their own group. The group never gave a particularly favourable evaluation of interpersonal relationships in the rival group, whereas expressions of the good functioning of their own group were frequent. It is of interest that the problem of relations of the group with the professional team of the institute appeared relatively infrequently. It arose primarily in connection with discussion of conceptual problems of the experiment, and hardly ever in the form of evaluation of direct relationships of the professional team with the group of instructors. Discussions of conceptual problems were often accompanied by manifest resistance, and in the background we could sense strongly ambivalent feelings toward the professional team of the institute.

The group avoided on principle discussion of individuals outside the group. None the less, some participants occasionally gave descriptions of the behaviour of individuals from other groups and passed judgement on it. Contributions of this type expressed sublimated aggressive feelings toward individuals in other groups (members of the professional team not excluded), feelings which were with time less visible, but never eliminated entirely.

Members of the group discussing themselves and other participants

The quantitative data show that the group paid more attention to individuals in the group in the last semesters, and that contributions to this theme were less frequent in the first two periods. In these, we most frequently encountered descriptions of personal experiences in the educational situation, without any attempt at a deeper analysis of one's own behaviour, whereas in the fourth and fifth semesters we found an increase in surprisingly perceptive and critical explanations of personal reactions in the educational situation. We even found entirely personal — almost intimate — confessions which had only a formally logical connection with the situation in the institution. There were also analyses of interactions in the group which were connected with analyses of the effects produced by individual participants. Of particular significance were the explicit expressions of favourable feelings in the group which were particularly frequent in the last semesters, whereas we did not find explicit expressions of unfavourable feelings, although they may also have arisen periodically.

Theoretic and didactic subjects

By the end of the second semester the group were demanding that their meetings also have a theoretic—didactic character. The opinion was expressed that it was impossible to meet the demands of permissive and professional treatment without sufficient information about it. Soon after the change in consultants the resolution was adopted that a part of the meetings would be dedicated to theoretical subjects from the areas of personality psychology and the aetiology of disturbances in maladapted youth. The agenda for didactic and other subjects was not specified. Usually the group desired a predominantly educational meeting when there was a lack of the appropriate atmosphere for discussion of other subjects.

In the area of personality psychology particular attention was given to the chapters about personality dynamics, whereas we attempted to illustrate the aetiological problems of juvenile delinquency with the classification of Hewitt and Jenkins.

Other subjects

A number of recorded contributions of individual participants could not be included in any of the above categories and were therefore included in the category 'other subjects'. It is necessary to note that the actual num-

98

ber of contributions included under this heading was greater than we registered. Particularly in the last two semesters, the group began their meetings with a discussion of diverse subjects, which they called an 'informal introduction', and which often led without special transition into the 'formal discussion'.

Some final generalisations

In evaluating events in the group of instructors, and the function of this group in general, we must not neglect the fact that it comprised a special category of workers which differentiated itself from the group of educators both in its professional structure and its status in the institution. The special status of the group of instructors (lower professional education, lower income than the educators) had significant consequences for the experiences of its participants — for their experience of the institution as a whole, of the other groups, and of the entire experiment. Their role as instructors of practical subjects, joined with their responsibilities for production and their role as educators, potentiated these experiences and gave them the character of conflict.

After separating themselves from the group of educators, the group of instructors intensively attacked their own specific problems, 'educational problems in the workshops', though these problems were with increasing frequency discussed in the light of broader institutional problems and led to the area of relationships with other groups. The original work orientation of the group became increasingly weak, and the group even expressed manifest resistance towards discussion of organisational problems. But at the same time the group also declined a group-analytical orientation, even though the participants felt and also expressed that 'it is necessary to talk about ourselves'.

It was obvious that it was unwise in this situation to force a group-analytical orientation for the resistance of the group was too strong. The group found a way out of this situation by adopting a new theoretic–didactic orientation. It was in the nature of non-directive leadership that the consultant allowed this orientation, despite the fact that it appeared to signify a regression.

We expected that this new work orientation would hinder group dynamics at the meetings, but this happened only in part. It is true that the meetings that were primarily didactic were somewhat less dynamic, and that the less active participants were somewhat inhibited. But it is also true that the other meetings were that much livelier. Above all, the emotional atmosphere in the group strongly improved. There were increasing references to the favourable atmosphere in the group, its good function, and so on. A particularly favourable atmosphere in the group was noted in the fourth and fifth semesters. At this time the group functioned as a nearly homogeneous whole with well-established statuses for the individual participants. The favourable emotional atmosphere made possible the actualisation of the group-analytic problems on a higher, more enlightened, less provocative, and occasionally almost therapeutic level.

We certainly cannot ascribe all the positive changes in the group to group work at the institution. A large contribution to the group's development was added by group sensitivity training, which we organised outside the institution for instructors from various institutions.

Not least of all, the feeling of external threat from the rival group also contributed to the consolidation of the group of instructors. The aggressiveness of the group was redirected outwards in sublimated, more-or-less manifest forms, and did not appear in the form of interpersonal tension in the group itself. It is interesting that this redirection did not have visible unfavourable consequences for the dynamics of the group.

It is questionable whether the group were aware of this external element, the influence of which the consultant did not consider inconsiderable. It is also difficult to say to what extent the group adopted various positive approaches and opportunities for enlightened coexistence with other groups. It is obvious, however, that the group achieved 'for itself' much more success than it achieved in other areas towards which the group work had been directed.

References

Brocher, Tobias, *Gruppendynamik und Erwachsenenbildung*, Državna založba Slovenije, Ljubljana 1972 (translation). (The Slovene Publishing House)

Cividini, E., and Klein, E., 'Transference and counter-transference in group psychotherapy' published in *Group Psychotherapy, 2nd Yugoslav Seminar on Psychotherapy, Mokrice 3—5 June 1968*, Gorenjski tisk Kranj, Zagreb 1969, pp. 45—53. (The Printing House At Kranj-Govenjska)

Jezernik, Drago, 'Groups and group dynamic' in Nikola Rot (ed.), *Social Psychology*, Rad, Belgrade 1972.

Mailloux, R.P.Noël, 'Un symptome de désocialisation: L'incapacité de communiquer avec l'autrui' *Annales internationales de criminologie*, Paris 1966.

Stoić, Ljubomir, 'The individual in the group' in Nikola Rot (ed.), *Social Psychology*, Rad, Belgrade 1972.

Štajnberger, Ivan, and Gavrin, Bihali Ivan, 'Leading the group'; in the same edition.

11 Group Meetings of the Members of the Team with the Entire Institution Staff

Franc MLINARIČ and Miloš KOBAL

Meetings before the introduction of therapeutic communities

Group consultation of the members of the team with the entire institution staff was at the beginning of the experiment directed primarily towards the offering of help in the solving of current problems in the institution. The staff demanded this help and also were in need of it because of their inexperience. The group meetings were originally in the form of conferences. The staff brought up current problems in the institution, and then together with the consultants — the psychologist and team member whose turn it was under the rota system — sought the most suitable solution. The staff's first feelings of resentment were aroused by the fail-

Table 11.1

Number of meetings

Semesters by school year	Number of meetings recorded
1967/68 I	22
1967/68 II	19
1968/69 I	30
1968/69 II	25
1969/70 I	21
1969/70 II	14 (7 + 7)*
1970/71 I	15
1970/71 II	19

* The other seven meetings in this period, and all the later ones, followed the meetings of therapeutic communities.

ure of the professional team to provide the ready-made solutions for the problems discussed that the staff expected of them (rejection of directive counselling by the professional team). On the request of the staff we also introduced study at the group meetings, a practice that was continued intermittently.

Practical and educational problems also predominated at meetings in the following semester, but with the difference that the group meetings were already directed more towards 'goals and action'. This new goal-direction focused attention on the question of the carrying out of plans of action, work discipline and interpersonal relationships.

Problems of interpersonal relationships became particularly acute in the third and fourth semesters. The meetings in those two semesters were no longer clearly directed towards 'goals and action', nor did they have a markedly analytical character. The staff's unfulfilled expectation that by this time there would already be positive, concrete and highly visible results of the experiment potentiated already existing antagonisms between various groups and subgroups in the institution. Aggressiveness which the group initially directed outwards (into the institution's immediate environment, towards the courts and social agencies was in this period directed primarily as more-or-less hidden aggressiveness towards the professional team of the institute; but subsequently it was directed inwards, fluctuating from tension between the group of shopmasters and the group of teachers to tension between individuals, staff and the director. The group meetings became increasingly analytical. Actualisation of experience in the group and the problems of interpersonal relationships were also potentiated by observation of group dynamics at the meetings – a practice we introduced in the fifth semester. These observations were recorded by the employees of the institution themselves and were presented to the participants of the meetings. Despite the fact that the staff chose the subjects for discussion, there was constantly strong resistance against the analytical character of the meetings. There appeared a particular kind of 'approach–avoidance conflict', which the staff dealt with by temporarily retreating into practical–organisational problems and with repeated demands that the meetings should have a primarily educational character.

The intensification of consultation work in divided groups (the group of shopmasters and group of teachers) led once more to the group meetings of the entire staff being directed more clearly towards the solution of organisational problems. This was the case until introduction of the therapeutic communities, at which time we discontinued these meetings.

Regardless of the final results of the group meetings with the staff – whether considered in an organisational, educational or analytical sense –

we should note that the meetings, in the form described and in the actual conditions of the experiment, were indispensable. It was necessary to accommodate the needs and expectations of the staff, despite temporary deviations from the basic premises of the experiment. This was necessary in order to carry out the experiment at all. These discussions also in time became oriented more towards group dynamics.

Meetings following the introduction of therapeutic communities

Following the introduction of therapeutic communities on 22 April 1970, the staff and those members of the professional team who were present immediately gathered for a discussion. This was the practice after all the forty-one therapeutic community meetings and was always related to their content and process. Problems of organisation and interpersonal relationships were usually of secondary importance at these meetings. The members of the professional team wished to make use of the situations that arose in the social process of the therapeutic communities. For this reason they actively contributed on a 'second level'. According to the records of twenty-three meetings (out of a total of forty-one) Kobal made the most contributions with 12·5 per meeting. He was followed by Mlinarič, with 11·6, and Skalar, with 9·8 contributions per meeting. Vodopivec made 5·8 contributions, Bergant 3·9 and Skaberne 2·8 per meeting.

These meetings had varied content. Greatest resentment was aroused in the staff when the inmates, in the opinion of some, allowed themselves excessive freedom and criticism of the staff. In such conflict experiences the members of the professional team attempted to direct attention to the value as well as the direction of interpersonal co-operation between the staff and inmates. Of course this sometimes deepened the crisis of individuals. On 13 January 1971, after twenty-two therapeutic community meetings, individual members of the staff sharply criticised the therapeutic community method and rejected it as inappropriate in the educational process. In our opinion, this crisis was necessary and natural. We see its positive roll in the airing of positions and in the renewed acceptance of therapeutic community meetings by the majority of the staff. After two weeks the crisis was over. At this time the administration of the institution agreed to introduce an additional two therapeutic community meetings weekly and these were preceded by meetings of the groups of inmates.

12 Therapeutic Communities

Miloš KOBAL

We considered therapeutic communities as a synthesis of all previous social processes in the institution and as egalitarian discussion among all participants (Rapoport). We also postponed working with this technique for these reasons.

As we have emphasised, the social processes in the institution and in the team did not proceed according to expectations. These processes were also shallow and, in addition, too infrequent and superficial, particularly in organised group work with the inmates. None the less, we considered the situation ripe for the introduction of therapeutic community meetings. We anticipated that the new social experiences in such meetings would favourably influence the other less-developed forms of group work. Furthermore, the members of the professional team would acquire an opportunity to meet with the inmates and in various ways evaluate their opinions as the experiment proceeded. These expectations were to a large extent fulfilled.

We introduced therapeutic community meetings on 22 April 1970. Therapy groups met forty-one times during the experiment. In keeping with the well-known principles of M. Jones and Rapoport, we emphasised that each group is a social experience that opens numerous questions and imparts new experiences. But it is necessary to analyse the contents of the meetings and the experiences in them on a 'second level' — at a meeting of the staff which immediately follows the therapeutic community meetings. We adopted the principles of equal rights for all participants, freedom of expression and behaviour. However, at the very beginning we also decided to limit the freedom of the meetings to the framework of 'guided democracy' (Bierer). In this way we wanted to prevent outbursts, insults, noise and possible physical violence. The social maturity of the inmates, which had grown out of previous social processes, was such that it was not difficult to introduce a democratic spirit into the therapeutic community meetings and to lead the groups in a democratic way.

We analysed all forty-one meetings. Their contents can in general be divided into the following three groups of problems:

1   The inmates and staff (including members of the professional team) tested each other on the questions and opinions about what the experi-

ences in the therapeutic communities were supposed to mean. The inmates were most prominent in their testing of the situation, but individual staff members also tended to find out to what extent the group corresponded or went against their preconceptions. The staff expressed their satisfaction and dissatisfaction with these confrontations during the therapeutic communities and more frequently at the meetings that followed them.

2   As was to be expected, the therapeutic community meetings spent considerable time on 'unimportant matters of everyday life' (food, cleaning, clothing, rules, repairs, and so on). By 'unimportant' we mean merely that many matters of this kind could have been dealt with without the therapeutic community meetings and that most of these problems were taken care of through the routine organisation of the institution. However, the dynamics of these 'unimportant' matters were important for the masking of real problems in the institution and in the lives of individual participants, and permitted a varied, socially justified balance.

3   Despite the shortness of the period about which we can report, the therapeutic community meetings dealt with a considerable number of basic problems which were essential for the purpose and educational goals of the institution. Exploration of the situation and 'unimportant matters' did not completely mask the tensions of individuals and of the groups of participants; a discharge of tension brought basic problems to the fore. We registered twenty-four such problems, which can be grouped by content as shown in Table 12.1

Table 12.1

Basic problems of inmates discussed in therapeutic communities

Problems	Number
Relationships with teachers	5
Relation to work	5
Conflicts and relations with the environment	5
Value of therapeutic communities and discussions in the institution	5
Punishable acts in the institution and outside of it	4
Total	24

The group functioned for too short a time for discussion of basic problems to become the dominant subject of their work. The problems discussed are shown in the Table 12.2.

Table 12.2

Problems discussed in therapeutic community meetings

Period	No. of meetings	Problems discussed			
		Testing	Unimportant matters	Basic problems	Other
22 April	7	6	4	2	5
1970/71 I	15	8	18	10	5
1970/71 II	18	10	17	12	9
Total	40*	24	39	24	19

* The records of one therapeutic community meeting were lost

Due to the dissatisfaction of the participants with the solution of numerous institutional problems, the staff of the institution introduced an additional two therapeutic community meetings beginning on 17 February 1971. These additional meetings were originally dedicated to discussion of organisational and disciplinary matters. The educators coupled these meetings with meetings of small groups of the inmates. This expansion of initiatives for meeting in groups, including therapeutic communities, soon exceeded the narrow boundaries of institutional organisation and discipline. Gradually the true interests of the participants were revealed and also partially satisfied.

References

Bierer, J., 'Therapeutic methods and procedures in the rehabilitation of psychiatric patients', translation in *Zbornik radova int. simpozijuma o rehabilitaciji u psihijatriji*, Belgrade 1972, pp. 479–87. (*Symposium on Rehabilitation in Psychiatry*)

Jones, Maxwell, *Social Psychiatry in Practice*, 1968.

Jones, Maxwell, contribution to *The Encyclopedia of Mental Health* vol. 6, pp. 1992–9.

Rapoport, R.N., Rapoport, R., Rosow, I., *Community as Doctor*, Social Science and Tavistock, London 1967.

13 Education of the Staff

Vinko SKALAR

The staff selected for work in the experimental institution were young, without specific training for work with behaviourally disturbed youth, and without previous experience in educational institutions.[1] This fact obliged the consulting team to transmit specific knowledge to the staff (directly or indirectly), regardless of the initially accepted principle that we would use indirect means of influencing the staff, primarily counselling in group dynamic interactions.

The realisation of education, its content, and the degree of involvement of the consulting team in the educational effort were influenced by two factors:

1 Somewhat divergent views in the consulting team on the problem of education.
2 The attitude of the institutional staff towards education during the experimental period.

With regard to the first factor, it should be noted that during the experiment three somewhat different viewpoints towards the problems of education could be identified in the professional team. These were: that emphasis should be given to group counselling in which education should consist primarily of a generalisation of the findings made by the staff in daily communications and at group meetings with inmates; that, besides the group dynamic interaction between the institutional staff and the consulting team, the staff was also to educate itself, with guidance from the appropriate literature, although the main initiative for education was to be left to the staff; and that, in addition to the group counselling, the consulting team should also take the initiative in educating the staff, an activity that should be one of the forms of co-operation between the staff and the consulting team.

As regards the second factor, it must be said that during the experiment we observed a specific dynamic in the relation of the staff towards learning, a relation that changed from uncritical acceptance in the beginning to rejection of learning in the first year and a half, then to individual responses and, finally, in the last year of the experiment, a clearly expressed wish for further learning on the part of the staff.

The resistance of the staff to further learning in the first eighteen months of the experiment can be ascribed to a number of causes:

— The staff were faced with work without the benefit of prior knowledge and experience in dealing with educational situations. The advice of the consulting team was not applicable in this situation, and in addition the staff did not entirely trust advice with a permissive colouring (primary personal inclinations, defensiveness in frustrating situations, the influence of public opinion, and so on). In this conflict the staff sought practical solutions without the help of the team, and saw no value in theoretical considerations.

— The institutional situation did not support a more intellectual approach during the early period of the experiment. The institution was not fully established, and besides their regular work with the inmates the staff were involved with fundamental organisational questions and with instruction of the inmates. For the most part the work was an improvisation with insufficient materials and untested organisation. The staff were unwilling to accept any demands which were not directly related to dealing with the situation at hand.

— The staff's material incentives were too low to compensate for the unfavourable work conditions.

On the basis of the foregoing, we may question whether the reasons for this relation to further learning might not also be sought in the personality structures of members of the staff. This possibility comes to the fore because it was never possible to stimulate the staff to self-educational effort, and because the staff more or less rejected, throughout the experiment, activities which required office and administrative work (the writing of diaries, evaluation of inmates, co-operation in plans and programmes, and so on). We do not have sufficient evidence for this supposition in our test results, and in fact we find that our population has an above-average interest in scientific work[2] — which instead suggests a latent readiness for theoretical work as well, provided that the situational determinants of the work are more favourable and stimulating.

The year 1969 marked a turning point in the relation of the staff to further learning. The staff began to point out gaps in their knowledge and with increasing urgency express their need for further education.

Both factors — divergent viewpoints in the consulting team and the attitude of the staff of the institution towards further education — influenced the dynamics of the staff's education throughout the various phases of the experiment, as these dynamics developed in two directions:

1   Familiarisation of the staff with theoretical findings about the delinquent population and concerning treatment of this population, about pedagogic, psychologic, sociologic and psychiatric aspects of institutional treatment and the like.
2   Familiarisation of the staff with the method of group work and the principles of group dynamic functioning.

Both approaches became interwoven, since we increasingly transmitted the theoretical information with consideration of group dynamic principles, and the group counselling meetings occasionally were transformed into didactic sessions. Despite this interweaving of the two approaches we shall discuss each of them separately for the entire experimental period.

Familiarisation of the staff with theoretical findings

We shall divide the forms of education according to their content into the following categories: educational seminars, group meetings with didactic elements, and self-education.

Educational seminars

During the experiment the team held six seminars for the staff. Two were introductory. The first of these was organised in September 1967, before the institution was opened; a seminar with the same content was repeated for new staff members in July 1968. The psychologist Bergant, from the psychiatric dispensary of the Psychiatric Hospital in Ljubljana, was engaged to prepare and lead the third seminar, and three seminars were prepared and led by the psychologist in the consulting team, Skalar, during the school year of 1970/71.

The introductory seminar given before the institution opened (and again in July 1968) was intended to give the staff a basis for work with behaviourally and personally disturbed youth in an institutional setting, as well as to give the staff an initiative for individual study. The topics of the seminars can be divided into three categories: (i) theoretical (the psychology of the young person, juvenile delinquency, aetiology, problem of aggression, documentation of the educational process); (ii) applied educational (educational principles, content of educational work, educational plan, methodology of educational work, materials for the stimulation of interest, organisation of employment in the institution); and (iii) topics that concerned specific institutional problems (commitment to the educational institution, admission criteria, preparation of the inmate for life in the institution, educational groups, relationships of inmates with their families, erotic and sexual problems of inmates, the problem of punishable acts in the institution, escapes from the institution, physical isolation of inmates, and the problem of privacy of correspondence which the inmates send or receive).

The seminar lasted four days. It was partly organised didactically, and in part according to the principles of group dynamics, with active participation of all those present. All the members of the professional team contributed topics to the seminar, and between them prepared 285 pages of materials (translation of foreign articles and adaptions of Yugoslav publications) for the participants.

The repetition of the seminar for newly-arrived staff in July 1968 was only partially successful. Due to erratic attendance by the staff, we discontinued the seminar on the second day. The failure can be ascribed primarily to bad planning and organisation. Specifically, it was unfortunate that the seminar was scheduled for the month of July, when many people were on holiday, and was held in the institution itself, where the participants in the seminar were continually involved in dealing with problems in the educational groups.

In June 1970 the professional team requested the psychologist Bergant to prepare and lead a seminar that would give the staff some theoretical psychological bases for work with behaviourally disturbed youth. Eleven teachers and professional workers from the institution took part in the seminar; the shopmasters were not included. The selection of topics was allowed to develop spontaneously for the first day, during which time it emerged that the expectations of those participating were as follows: (i) to get an overview of the various theories of disturbed behaviour and personality and of methods of treatment; (ii) to get information about the rules of treatment that are considered tested and established in the literature; (iii) to get confirmation of the correctness of their own actions.

In response to the wishes of the participants, the leader of the seminar gave the group a series of lectures on individual disturbances and the principles of treatment, with allowance for wide-ranging discussion and exchanges of opinions between the participants. The seminar lasted five days. The participants evaluated it favourably in a questionnaire given at the end of the seminar, and expressed a wish for similar seminars in the future, through which they could deepen their knowledge.

A fourth seminar, 'Permissiveness as a method of work with behaviourally disturbed and delinquent youth', was organised in December 1970. The seminar was organised according to the methods of group work, and synthetically presented the entire staff of the experimental institution with the idea of permissiveness, with practical examples from work with behaviourally disturbed and delinquent youth.

A fifth seminar, 'Fundamentals of psychotherapeutic treatment in the educational institution', was organised in February 1971, and a sixth seminar on 'Individual and group approaches' was organised in April 1972. The final three seminars were all prepared and led by the psychologist Skalar. They presented a synthesis of the efforts and viewpoints of the consulting team during the experimental period, and to some extent satisfied the staff's wishes for further education.

Group meetings with didactic elements

After initial resistance on the part of the staff towards any kind of additional work, including education, the staff began, in the winter semester of 1968/69, to express the wish that theoretical topics would be included in the discussions at group meetings with the entire staff. In the summer semester of 1968/69 these meetings became in part educational, with occasional transmission of theoretical and technical information. The meetings lasted in this form until the end of the school year 1968/69, when the psychologist Skalar, who had been leading these meetings, went abroad. In the school year 1969/70 the psychologist Mlinarič took over the leadership of the weekly meetings with the entire staff; he gave less emphasis to the transmission of information and led the meetings in a less directive way. The meetings with the entire staff lasted in this form until the introduction of therapeutic communities on 22 April 1970.

During this time group work became fully developed, separately in the group of educators and the group of shopmasters. Despite the fact that these meetings were primarily intended to be non-directive, both of the leaders also conveyed considerable theoretical information, so that the meetings occasionally had an educational character.

Self-education

Self-education by the staff never developed as the consulting team had anticipated. The staff was obviously over-extended and continuously in stress situations. As a result motivation for self-education was low and occasionally present only in certain individuals. The only record of self-education (which is incomplete and unreliable) consists in the register of literature borrowed from the library of the Institute of Criminology of the University of Ljubljana. This was extremely limited. Except for the psychologist, the staff took out no literature at all. Regardless of the specific institutional circumstances, self-education is probably not a suitable solution in the face of the modern dynamics of life.

During the experiment the professional team made available to the educational staff seventeen professional texts (total of 284 pages). Thirteen texts were newly translated from the foreign professional literature (190 pages), and four texts (94 pages) had been translated previously but had not been available to the staff. We are not including with these texts the materials prepared for the introductory seminar. We have no direct way of knowing to what extent the staff studied these texts, but from the comments made about them at the meetings we conclude that at least some individuals were familiar with them.

In the winter semester of 1969/70 the institutional psychologist encouraged the founding of a debating club. The idea was that once a fortnight the staff would meet in the evening to discuss specific technical topics which would be prepared by the participants. Participation in these meetings was intended to be voluntary. The debating club was established, but the meetings were irregular and did not become an established activity. In the summer semester 1969/70 the meetings were somewhat more regular. Our records show a total of eight meetings of the debating club.

Familiarisation of the staff with the methods of group work and the principles of group dynamic functioning

Throughout the entire experiment the consulting team attempted to train the staff for various forms of group work with the inmates (for example, group work with small groups, and therapeutic community discussions). Therefore most of the meetings of the consulting team with the staff were organised according to group dynamic principles, so that the staff would become more aware and gradually get the information necessary for group work. For the same reason we included the staff in seminars for sensitivity training. The teachers and other professional workers took part in regular, consecutive seminars in 1968 and 1969. These seminars were not organised expressly for the experimental institution. A special seminar was organised for the shopmasters. The organiser filled out the number of participants with shopmasters from other educational institutions. In 1969 and 1970 all the staff took part in another continuation seminar in sensitivity training.

Following the sensitivity training of the educators, who took part in the seminars alternately and not as a group, there were no visible changes, whereas the shopmasters, who took part in sensitivity training as a group, showed a persistent increase in homogeneity and inner consolidation following the seminars. They themselves perceived this and often spoke of it.

As we evaluate the dynamics and process of education for the experimental staff, we must ask whether clearer and more solidly conceived education of the staff, as a constituent part of the plan of the experiment, could not have contributed to different, perhaps more visibly positive, results. We feel not, for the manoeuvring room of the professional team during the experiment was quite extensive, complex, and dependent on a multitude of dynamic factors in the institution and outside it. If the professional team had not been sufficiently flexible in this situation, and if it had not considered the staff's inclinations and the climate of the institution in its interventions, the team would not have been accepted and its interventions would have been less effective than they were.

Most probably the experimental period was also too short for the staff, without prior specific education and practice in educational institutions, to become fully reoriented from a practical to a scholarly, considered, and theoretically grounded relation to the problems they faced. However, in the four-year period we achieved significant progress in this direction.

Notes

[1] See Chapter 5.
[2] See Chapter 5 (results of the personal interest test).

14 Individual Tutoring

Vinko SKALAR

In the original plan the professional team did not foresee individual tutoring as a continuing form of co-operation with the institutional staff. None the less, tutoring was begun even before the opening of the institution, at first spontaneously and later by plan, though it never became a systematic and continuous form of co-operation between the staff and the consulting team.

Dynamics and scope of tutoring during the experiment

Before the institution opened individual members of the staff that had been selected began to seek contact outside the regular meetings with members of the consulting team, especially the psychologist Skalar, who was also a member of the special subcommittee of the selection commission. They wanted to know how they had done in the tests, details of the experiment, and more about their role in the experiment.

At an introductory seminar, before the opening of the institution, the consulting team pointed out the possibility of individual tutoring as one of the forms of co-operation between the staff of the institution and the consulting team.

During the academic year 1967/68 some more permanent tutoring relationships were established. The psychologist Skalar also took over introduction of the newly accepted staff to the experimental institution. Meanwhile the institutional staff became more consolidated. Most of the staff rejected tutoring, and those who retained contact with tutors were considered disloyal by the rest of the staff. The professional team repeatedly raised the subject of tutoring at meetings with the staff, but without appreciable response.

In the school year 1968/69 the situation in the first semester was even worse in comparison with the previous school year; some tutoring sessions that had been regular became occasional. In the second semester the professional team conducted a survey in the institution concerning forms of co-operation with the consulting team. Most of the staff felt that tutoring did not work because of bad organisation. They suggested that meetings with tutors should take place in the institution at specific times, and that each member of the staff should have his own tutor to whom he could turn. Two educators expressed the wish to have a mentor who was not a member of the professional team. A workshop leader suggested that shopmasters should have their own mentor.

After the survey was conducted the tutoring had a short revival and reached its greatest extent to date. Most of the educators took part, while the shopmasters remained in the background. However, the professional team organised group meetings for them with the psychologist Caserman (later with Mlinarič). At this time the tutoring meetings were accompanied by written and verbal comments on the diaries. This lasted only for several months, however, since the consulting team was not physically equal to the task; for the leader of the experiment and the psychologist Skalar had the most responsibilities, and the part-time members of the professional team did not want to become more involved.

In the school year 1969/70 the tutoring meetings were reduced to a minimum. The leader of the experiment had regular sessions with the principle of the institution. All other individual contacts were abandoned, in part because the psychologist Skalar left for a period of study outside the country.

In 1970/71 we wished to renew the tutoring. The part-time members of the professional team stated in advance that they could not help with tutoring. In spite of this a survey was taken of how the staff felt about the matter. Most of them expressed a wish to have meetings with a mentor, but because of the limited capacity of the professional team these wishes could only be met in part. Meetings with tutors remained restricted to some of the educators, and the psychologist. The meetings were only occasional and did not attain a more continuing form.

Reasons for the partial failure of individual tutoring

1   There is no tradition of tutoring in Yugoslavia. In consequence, people are not accustomed to this form of work and do not consider it as helpful for their professional growth, but rather as supervision and control over their work.

2   During the experiment the staff of the experimental institution experienced the consulting team as a threatening inspection commission (more so at the beginning than at the end of the experiment). For this reason they considered individual tutoring as a means by which the team was attempting to gain access to more detailed information about events in the institution. This was particularly the case in the initial phases of the

120

experiment. As a result, those individuals who retained regular or even occasional contacts with their mentors were often considered disloyal by the rest of the staff.

3   Besides their regular work, the staff was burdened with countless meetings and other duties. The staff therefore declined any new form of work that was not absolutely necessary and generally assumed a defensive posture towards all additional demands.

4   The capacity of the consulting team was limited, particularly because the part-time members were not prepared to accept greater additional responsibilities.

After the close of the experiment the experimental institution retained some of the kinds of work that had been established during the experiment, but individual tutoring died out entirely.

15 Evaluation of the Functioning of the Professional Team

Katja VODOPIVEC

It is only natural that the professional team was made up of people with a human variety of both good and bad qualities. Furthermore, the dynamics of our work and mutual relationships were permeated with both rational and irrational elements.

Structure of the team

In the initial phase the team comprised five members: a psychiatrist, a psychologist, a pedagogue, a criminologist who was a lawyer by training (she had lectured for five years at the school for social workers on the subject of social case work), and an expert in juvenile criminology (he was a lawyer by training). The team later brought in another psychologist (originally Mr Caserman; later, in his place, Mr Mlinarič). In the end the team consisted of four men and two women.

Of the six team members, three were permanently employed at the Institute of Criminology and three in other institutions. The permanent workers at the institute were: the juvenile criminologist Skaberne, the psychologist Skalar, and the leader of the experiment, Mrs Vodopivec (who was responsible for problems of social work). Those working on the experiment part-time were: the psychiatrist (Kobal), the pedagogue (Bergant) and the two psychologists (Caserman and Mlinarič) who joined the group subsequently.

The above structure of the research team resulted in the following differences in relation to the experiment:

- The workers at the institute were more interested in the results of the experiment than the part-time workers. Since we introduced into the experimental plan our wish to form a so-called exemplary educational institution, we were committed to reaching this goal. Because of this the involvement in the experiment of these two groups of workers differed considerably.

123

— The burden of work was incomparably greater for the part-time workers than for the workers at the institute. Whereas the primary responsibility of the part-time workers was directed towards the institutions in which they were employed, we who were employed at the institute could identify our success or failure in the experiment as our success or failure in our work. As we grew closer on a human level, we found that the part-time workers experienced during this time other psychological stresses at their places of work.

— It is difficult to evaluate the other conditions of living that the two groups of workers experienced in their home environments. In this respect there were individual differences, but these differences probably balance out in comparisons between the two groups.

— The group of permanent workers at the institute were always available to the educational institution's staff, and visited the institution whenever one of the part-time workers was detained. Thus the majority of the information was gathered through this group. In group dynamics, the nucleus with the greatest amount of information has an objectively determined advantage over the other members of the group.

The professional profile of the leader of the experiment also probably posed a special problem for the group as a whole. From the literature and practice it is known that the majority of team groupings of this kind are led by psychiatrists. If such a team is led by a person who has, in the opinion of the psychiatrists, insufficient knowledge of psychologic and psychopathologic dynamics then such leadership is accepted with difficulty, especially by psychiatrists. Even though all workers accepted the leader of the experiment in advance (the leader was the initiator of the experiment and the one who selected the first workers; later workers were selected in consultation with those previously selected), our team was not spared the difficulties that always appear in such groups. The fact that the leader of the experiment was a woman may have contributed to these problems.

Normal developmental processes and interpersonal relationships

In four and a half years of more or less intensive co-operation, the normal sympathies and antipathies appeared among individuals and subgroups. These relationships changed many times. As is the case for people generally, we were not exempt from competition and situations of rivalry. We wanted to test ourselves in interaction with the staff and we each experienced a personal success if the staff of the institution accepted us more than they did other members of the team. It was important to know which team member expressed his opinions most convincingly; whose opinions were most frequently accepted; what the status of individuals in the team was; and who was to be given credit for the initiation or originality of some idea.

Although these are matters of human weakness, they are a reality with which all group dynamics must reckon. For only within this reality, and perhaps precisely because of it, are members of the group offered the possibility of mutual help and improvement. This is particularly the case when the group temporarily isolates individual participants. There were many such situations during the time of our work together as a group. From time to time we were aggressively inclined towards each other, but we also attempted to ease the tensions with mutual help, with understanding of the dynamics which led to isolation and which followed it. And not least of all we remained a unified team to the end of the experiment, despite all the difficulties and misunderstandings. It is none the less true that we more frequently functioned successfully on an intellectual level than on a level of mutual emotional acceptance. The team members did not relate to each other as friends either more or less than previously. We learned to respect each other more since in our work together over a longer time it became clear that none of us was without failings, and none without significant human and professional qualities.

Content of conflict situations

Although we should really also analyse all the situations in which the members of the team were in harmony and mutual support, it is a shorter and more usual procedure to analyse the resolution of conflicts. Such cases are fewer, in the dynamics of group functioning, than are cases of mutual complementing; otherwise the group disintegrates. Conflict situations were also in the minority in our group.

The contents of the conflicts can be divided into two general problems. Since we did not succeed in solving these two problems when they first arose, they returned in various forms and gave rise to a number of conflict situations. Here, we must not of course, neglect all the accompanying emotional repelling and attracting mechanisms, and also neurotic mechanisms, that prevented resolution of the problems solely by rational means.

Problem 1: Concept of institutional education

During the phase of team formation we wished to bring together a group of workers representing all the necessary (and available) professional profiles; a group of people with similar concepts of institutional education, who could accept each other. All five of those who had worked on the experiment from the beginning had known each other previously, and all had worked on various projects and expressed their viewpoints in written articles. These were the reasons for our selecting and accepting each other. There were no difficulties in this respect during the preparatory phase of the experiment.

When the first practical problems appeared — how to work with the inmates, how to organise the institution as a whole, how to react to lack of discipline among staff and inmates and to various excesses — we found that we were less in agreement than we had thought. There were also differences in viewpoints about the content of permissiveness, the degree of leniency and restriction, and the matter of reward and punishment. To be sure, many of the apparent differences in any conflict situation can be traced to poor and incomplete verbalisation — in short, misunderstanding.

In order more easily to formulate and also understand the essence of our differences, particularly those between so-called clinical workers (among whom I include myself) on the one hand and the pedagogue and the juvenile criminologist on the other, we decided at the beginning of 1969 that each team member would develop in writing his concept of institutional education. The psychologist Skalar was the first to do so. The pedagogue was particularly opposed to his concept. After we had discussed the acceptability of Skalar's concept at a number of meetings, the pedagogue developed her concept of institutional education. She incorporated viewpoints that had already been modified on the basis of our discussions and mutual exchange of influences. Thus the differences that remained were a reduction from the initial misunderstandings and conceptual differences. An analytical summary can be made of the points of difference for both concepts:

Goal of institutional education

The socialisation of the inmate in the sense of an active, creative, independent but tolerant relation with the world.

Supplementation of deficits from the period of primary and secondary socialisation. The third level of socialisation (creative, autonomous, critical relation to the world) is in general obtainable for only a minority of young people.

Development of self-control

Emphasis on emotional experience.

Emphasis on understanding and participating in the norms of average social life.

Educational methods

Therapeutic treatment is appropriate (insight, catharsis, support); other educational goals can be achieved in steps.

A complex educational approach in which therapy is only one of the work methods. Educational influences and processes unfold parallel to each other and simultaneously in an intertwining fashion.

Educational context

Rigid educational guidelines hinder the self-initiating involvement of the staff. Therapy should be the point of departure for the organisation and functioning of the institution.

Educational guidelines are necessary to attain unity of education, without which anarchy can appear, disorienting the inmates and making them ill at ease.

Function of the institution

The institution is a refuge from the reality which has broken the inmate.

The institution is a miniature reflection of reality based on the social and cultural norms under which we live. The institution should help the inmate to participate in this lifestyle.

Theoretical basis

Clinical therapeutic leadership towards self-control.	Therapeutic leadership and various forms of education and instruction.

Although the pedagogue set the goals of institutional education lower and more realistically, she was more demanding as regards other aspects of the institution's functioning and the transformation of the inmates. Her approach is more global than that of the psychologist. It is a question (in connection with institutional education of disturbed youth in general, as usually conceptualised) of whether it is possible for a global approach to be effective in the course of an inmate's one- to two-year stay in the institution. The personally disturbed young people come to the institution because of the situation in which they have lived for approximately sixteen years.

The other members of the professional team did not prepare concepts of institutional education. We gave verbal acceptance to the pedagogue's concept because it was more universal. But in fact, in the resolution of practical problems, the clinically oriented members of the team were inclined towards realisation of the psychologist's concept (with lowered aspirations for the goals of institutional education).

Problem 2: The institution as a whole — permissive inclination of personnel

In the plan of the experiment we set two goals that were probably mutually exclusive: the transformation of attitudes of the members of the team and of the institutional staff from less to more permissive, from more rigid to more flexible, with the help of group work on the one hand, and the formation of an exemplary institution on the other. Because we feared ingrained and rigid educational frameworks as found in existing institutions, we opted for a new institution and new, young and inexperienced personnel. At that time we did not take into account that under these conditions the experiment would require a more complex approach than had originally been planned, and that it would not be possible to measure clearly the results of the experiment since it involved multiple variables.

As mentioned before, significant practical problems appeared immediately. In contradiction of the psychiatrist's viewpoint and the experimental plan, the members of the team reoriented themselves to the conference method of solving the various practical problems. Because of the differences in their viewpoints, that reorientation was not clear and definite, but rather marked by uncertainty. The weekly meetings with the staff became a compromise between the conference method of work (with clear responsibilities and subsequent controls) and group counselling. The staff's initial motivation for work decreased because of disorganised work conditions, excessive work, insufficient gratifications, and so on.

As the leader of the experiment I became impatient in the third year. I was disturbed by the bad organisation of the institution and the personnel's lack of motivation. I corresponded with the psychologist Skalar about these problems while he was in Scotland during the school year 1969/70. In one of his letters Skalar attempted, in fourteen pages, to examine critically the situation of the team and of the institution.

Although, as we have noted above, Skalar was less demanding than the pedagogue as regards all educational measures (except therapeutic ones), and less demanding in what he required of the inmates, in this letter he was clearly more demanding towards the professional team and the experiment. He requested an expansion of the efforts of the team to train the institutional staff, recommending a discussion of analyses of the work of the team and staff every three months, intensification of individual tutoring, and intensive help with organisational problems of the institution and problems of stimulating and rewarding the staff. He requested up to two teachers for each group of inmates and pointed out the excessive burdening of the staff with work, problems, and group meetings. (The teachers at this time were also instructors at the institutional school, and did not have time either for furthering their own education or for preparation for their teaching. They were supposed to participate in various kinds of group meetings, including professional conferences in connection with the development of inmates. There was no time provided for recreation.)

This analysis, which was particularly critical of the professional team's previous efforts, was accepted by most of the team members, but was completely rejected by the psychiatrist. In his opinion Skalar's demands required a fundamental reorientation of the conceptual bases of the experiment and the taking on of a task to which the team could not be equal.

The role of mediator in this situation was assumed by a new team member, the psychologist Caserman. Later a similar role was played by Caserman's successor, the psychologist Mlinarič. They were skilled analysts unhindered by the earlier conflicts that continued to affect the other team members. He proposed that in essence two experiments were taking place simultaneously in the institution at Logatec, experiments which he referred to as A (after the original plan) and B (organisational, motivational and educational problems). It appeared that the team would probably have to decide to accept experiment B as well, since it was a prerequisite for conducting experiment A. The psychiatrist agreed with this in principle, but said that he would not work on experiment B.

The tension between the psychiatrist and the other members of the team continued and increased throughout the spring semester of 1970. The other members of the team acknowledged the need for experiment B, but were not able to carry out all of the demanding tasks. Particularly during this time, the psychiatrist probably felt that the other team members undervalued his work with the teachers as one-sided, as losing its significance in a tangle of unresolved problems. He judged the situation in the institution more optimistically than the other team members. In June 1970 he threatened to leave the team. At this time the staff, who had indirectly been informed of the conflicts and upset by them, offered to help the team to resolve the conflict situation. Despite all the weaknesses that the team had manifested before this time of crises, the staff showed with this gesture that they accepted the team and wished to work with the team as a whole.

A confrontation of differing viewpoints took place at a stormy meeting with the institutional staff (the meeting was also attended by Skalar and both psychologists, Caserman and Mlinarič). The majority of the participants revealed their feelings and views with considerable candour. Perhaps the institutional staff understood at this meeting for the first time the differences and dilemmas of the efforts of the members of the team. The psychiatrist remained in the team.

In 1970/71 we attempted to solve the problems of the so-called experiments A and B as follows:

Experiment A: Group work with the teachers and shopmasters continued, and the weekly meetings became analytical explorations of the therapy groups and lost their conference-like character.

Experiment B: First of all we brought in the clinical therapist and psychologist Bergant as leader of one of the seminars (the staff demanded confrontation of the views of the team with professionals who did not work on the team). Later the psychologist Skalar organised three two-day didactic seminars for the staff. We requested that an expert come from the United States to help us solve our organisational problems. The institution itself lightened the work load of its teachers by bringing in several other teachers to help with instruction. Tri-monthly analytic meetings did not occur. Individual meetings with supervisors died out.

In 1970/71 there were no longer any special disagreements between members of the team.

The results of both kinds of efforts were as follows:

— during the experiment the staff progressed from less to more permissive attitudes;
— during the experiment the institution was left by three workers with university education, one worker with high school education, and one worker with elementary education;
— the organisational efforts of the professional team and also the expert from the USA had no particular effect on the institution.

Dynamics of the conflict situations

Conflicts can be expected in group dynamics. And not only this: they are necessary for the developmental dynamics of the group and the participants in general. The essential problem is thus not the conflicts, but rather the way in which they are resolved. If a conflict results in a solution at a higher level, then the contribution of the conflict to the group dynamics is a positive one.

In our case the conflicts and their solutions were as follows:

	CONFLICT	SOLUTION
I	September 1967: Psychiatrist—leader of the experiment. The leader of the experiment and the acting director are interviewed by a daily newspaper. Psychiatrist: we don't know what the results of the experiment will be, and there was no prior unanimity in the team.	Agreement: public popularisation of the experiment is dangerous. We will not make use of it without the consent of the whole team.
II	October 1967: Psychologist Skalar—psychiatrist. Psychologist: non-directive leading of the staff and the rotation of consultants is not appropriate. The institutional staff is under too much pressure. Suggestion: more directive and didactic help are necessary.	The psychologist Skalar assumes leadership of the meetings of all the institutional staff, with use made of the conference method. The other members of the team take part on a rotational basis.

CONFLICT	SOLUTION
III October—December 1968: Tension between members of the team because the staff declines group work and limits itself to weekly conferences.	The team decides to pursue special group counselling with the teachers, and with the shopmasters.
IV March 1969: The pedagogue—the psychologist Skalar. The psychologist prepares a concept of institutional education. The pedagogue does not accept it.	The pedagogue prepares an alternative conception of institutional education. The team accepts her ideas with modification.
V June 1969: The psychologist Skalar—the pedagogue. Differing opinions about the concept of permissiveness.	Only in his contribution to the final report, made after the end of the experiment, does the psychologist Skalar give an opinion on the concept and significance of permissiveness that is accepted by all team members.
VIa December 1969: Leader of the experiment and the psychologist Skalar—psychiatrist. Letter from the psychologist Skalar: the organisation of the institution is weak, the motivation of the staff for work with the inmates low. Much of the blame for this situation is to be ascribed to the team. Psychologist makes suggestions for improving the team's work. The psychiatrist does not accept the criticism or suggestions.	Insight that two experiments are taking place in the institution at the same time: A and B. Psychiatrist is disinterested in experiment B. Tensions among the team members remain unresolved.

VIb June 1970: Pedagogue and leader of the experiment—psychiatrist. Pedagogue and leader of the experiment consider the situation in the institution to be bad. Psychiatrist does not accept this evaluation, and transmits his disagreement to the institution.

The institutional staff offers to help the team resolve the misunderstanding. A group meeting is held: confrontation of the different viewpoints before the institutional staff. The psychiatrist makes a new contract with the institute.

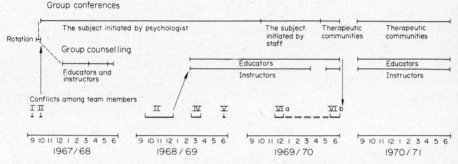

Fig. 15.1   Logatec: dynamics of the conflict situations and their solutions.

From Figure 15.1 one can see that the majority of the conflicts were followed also by restructuring of the group work.

Weaknesses and problems of the experiment

The conflict situations among members of the team also revealed some important weaknesses of the experiment, particularly in the planning phase, but also later.

1   The research problem was inappropriately defined in light of the goal of the experiment: an exemplary institution as the overall goal, and group counselling of the staff towards permissiveness as a partial goal.

2   We assumed similarities in the theoretical viewpoints of the participants without checking if this is in fact the case.

3   In the area of methodology we did not consider differences in group training and orientation in group counselling. The psychiatrist accepted and used the method of non-directive therapeutic group counselling ad-

vocated by Rogers; the pedagogue, organisational secretary, and leader of the experiment completed a number of short sensitivity training sessions, led by the psychologist Dr Otto Wilfert (an Austrian expert in group work) and having a social—pedagogic orientation; and the psychologist Skalar, who at the beginning of the experiment did not have group training, later received it after the method of Dr Wilfert.

4   From the standpoint of group functioning, it was unfortunate that we did not provide in advance for individual members of the team to have different roles. We erroneously assumed that we could all function in all problem areas. We also did not determine in advance the kind of professional roles that individuals wished to have in the team and the nature of their aspirations in connection with the experiment in general.[1]

In regard to the final goal of the experiment (an exemplary educational institution), those of us working in the institute were too demanding and critical towards the part-time workers (this applies particularly to the leader of the experiment). Thus all the team members got more criticism than praise and also gave more criticism than praise to the institutional staff. A situation was created in which the member of the team sought rewards from the institutional staff, and the staff rewards from the inmates.

In addition, we must also consider why more university educated workers than less well educated workers left the institution, and why neither the organisational efforts of the members of the team nor those of the expert from the United States succeeded. Hypotheses about these matters can only be speculative.

Most educational institutions have educators (or so-called parents of the educational groups) with elementary education, and special therapists with university education. There are constant conflicts between these two kinds of workers. Since we felt that the modification of personality is a task for highly qualified workers, we tried to entrust the entire educational process to highly qualified staff. In our situation, however, the university educated workers are not specifically trained for work with asocial and anti-social youth either. The psychologist Skalar assumed that it was also necessary to give supplemental training to these workers in order that they could work with such young people more easily. But it developed that those who were most qualified to also understand theoretically the behaviour of dyssocial juveniles (the psychologist and two pedagogues) were the first to leave the institution. At present in Yugoslavia we educate so-called 'special pedagogues' (having university and college education), who upon graduation generally do not take up employment in educational institutions. The work in educational institutions is hard, and professionals with university or college degrees can easily find employment elsewhere.

It is possible that we are dealing with work which in fact requires two kinds of workers. Possibly university educated workers could also work well in institutions, but for a shorter time limited in advance (perhaps a maximum of four years), or at least rotationally (for instance, four years in an institution and four years elsewhere). But above all it is very likely that a larger number of educators for each group of inmates could significantly change the educators' relation to and motivation for work with inmates.[2] The psychic strain on all workers, but particularly on university educated ones, from whom we require a permissive approach to the inmates, should in future be specially registered and analysed.

Organisational leadership — so-called management — has in modern times become a special discipline, particularly in the area of the management of business and administrative organisations. Business organisations that lack educated leadership can call on special service organisations for help in the development of organisational plans. In Yugoslavia, as far as is known to me, there are reservations about the success of such services and plans. Usually the leadership take these plans, which were prepared on request, and store them in the archives, while they continue to work as they had before the plans were developed.

Although one may accept the view that special or supplementary education in management is necessary, it is possible that the other forms of service help in this area are unsuccessful. Organisational schemes that disregard the characteristics of real people, their justified and unjustified aspirations, rivalries, and fears of loss or hope for gain in status — in short, the ever-present human factors in concrete work organisations — will probably establish lasting roots only with great difficulty. We suggest that the staff must themselves develop the organisational scheme and accept a suitable kind of leadership. In this, education in management can be a great help.

It is paradoxical that the greatest tensions among the members of the team because of the methods of working with the institutional staff and institutional problems were in the year 1969/70 — that is, the year that our retrospective evaluation shows to have been the most fruitful in terms of the involvement of the personnel. In this regard we should note that the psychologist Skalar left to study in Scotland in the autumn of 1969, and it is possible that his analysis relates mainly to 1968/69.

Although the staff prepared more analyses and proposals for improving work with the inmates in 1969/70 than in any other year of the experiment (for instance, it was proposed that there should be registration of the work habits of the inmates with observation protocols, and suggestions were made concerning the need for introduction of various forms of recreation), this did not result in any significant change in the methods of working with the inmates (the recording of work habits died out after several months, and no new recreational activities were introduced except for sports and music under the direction of a special teacher who had had success in introducing these activities previously). The arrival of the inmates at work, school, and the like remained a continuing problem.

However, in this year the staff in fact exerted great effort in the additional education of the inmates and in the search for jobs for those who had been released.

At least some of the team members anticipated that, in time, the staff would become motivated for self-initiated study, that they would begin regular observation of the personal development of inmates, that they would write diaries of their work with the inmates and, with the help of these records, analyse their work methods with the members of the team as mentors, and, finally, that they would arrive at an organisational form that they themselves would consider satisfactory.

These expectations were also not realised in this year; in fact, some team members evaluated a steady worsening of motivation for this kind of work and personal growth.

Thus a discrepancy developed between the expectations of some of the team members (including the leader of the experiment) and the efforts (and perhaps also the actual capabilities) of the staff. In this situation, some team members in particular probably made a mistake that often befalls people who find their expectations unfulfilled: they became impatient, and showed an inability to see positive efforts outside their specific expectations, and to give recognition for the progress that had been made or was in the making. Excessively oriented to the final goal of the experiment, an exemplary educational institution with enlightened and conscientious staff, we neglected the developmental process that was objectively possible. Not the least reason for our impatience was the fact that the third year of a four-year experiment was upon us.

Thus we feel that in the final analysis (as we shall see in the following chapters) the main success was the original plan for partial transformation of the staff and, as a consequence, transformation of the inmates. Although it cannot be documented quantitatively, we feel that the so-called experiment B was unsuccessful. It is possible that we lacked the necessary unity and training to carry out this experiment, and that it was simply not feasible in its intended form. This gives credence to the psychiatrist's insistence on the original, limited conception of the experiment. Unfortunately, he did not support his rejection of experiment B with substantive reasons, but rather on the basis of the consideration that the experiment, as a research project, must remain limited to the original conception because of the requirement of verification. He was not interested in the final goal of the experiment. The team members who were more committed to this goal could not accept his argument. But at the time we were not aware of all the pitfalls we were to encounter in broadening the experiment to include other areas of work.

Without reference to the final outcome of experiment B, we should note that some members of the team exerted particular efforts towards its success for the entire period of the experiment. Some team members suspect that if the team had not at the beginning offered to help the staff with organisational problems and education, albeit sporadically, some members of staff would have either rejected the team entirely or left the institution — i.e., the intolerable working situation. Thus we may consider that the efforts for experiment B were a prerequisite of the staff's remaining in the institution, gradually coming to accept advice, and in the end accepting the members of the team as partners in the pursuit of common goals.

Organisational dilemmas of educational institutions with permissive régimes

We have repeatedly noted that the staff were not able to solve the organisational problems in the institution during the experiment, either by themselves or with our help. We feel obliged to explain that it is not a simple process to reorient from a traditional method of running educational institutions to the democratic self-governing leadership of an educational institution with a permissive orientation. The dilemmas that arise in connection with a reorientation of this kind can be developed by a comparison between the viewpoints of the concept and significance of permissiveness cited by Skalar in Chapter 3, and the previous methods of leading educational institutions here in Yugoslavia. If some of the principles of permissiveness are valid for inmates, it seems unlikely that they would not also apply to staff, at least in a modified form. These principles, modified for the staff, imply:

1   mutual acceptance among the members of the working collective, without prejudice;

2   encouragement of active participation, self-determination, and the acceptance of personal responsibility;
3   the resolution of conflict situations and the relinquishing of resentments;
4   making possible free expression and open communication;
5   the development of creativeness, originality and authenticity.

The goal for the creation of this kind of atmosphere among the staff should be: the opportunity for maximal development of individual capacities and for promotion on this basis.

In contrast with these principles, the existing methods of leadership in educational institutions (those using methods of directive and self-governing leadership) are often based on the following assumptions:

1   mutual acceptance among the staff and possible prejudices are irrelevant;
2   the impulse towards active participation, self-determination and the taking of responsibility comes, for the most part, from the institutional administration, with few or no alternatives;
3   the approach to conflict situations consists primarily in the placing of blame — the easing of resentments is irrelevant;
4   because of the hierarchically structured organisational plan, free expression and authentic communication are not possible;
5   the development of creativity, originality and authenticity is hindered by fixed organisational schemes, daily schedules planned in advance, and the so-called need for unified education.

A successful transition from an old to a new organisational scheme is not possible with the help only of group communication; for we found that group communication also leads to a convergence of deviations from the average towards the average capacities of the participants.

By this we do not mean to say that it is impossible for educational institutions to have a successful democratic and truly self-governing leadership. On the contrary, we have practical examples of this (for instance, the social therapeutic clinic Van der Hoeven in Utrecht). However, theoretical systems for this kind of management are written primarily for manufacturing work organisations. In these organisations, however, significant stimulation for exceeding the average is provided by the finished product.

The results of educational efforts in institutions can be measured only at some future time after the inmate is released, if at all. Order and discipline in a group of inmates are not and must not be measures of the success of the teacher's work. The time that an inmate spends in an institution barely suffices to give him preliminary motivational encouragement to search for alternative life successes and goals in place of those accepted by him before his admission into the institution.

These are some of the dilemmas the solution of which probably requires more than a four-year experiment. According to the original plan our team did not even set itself such a goal, and, given its composition, was probably not adequately prepared for it.

Notes

[1] Analysis of the weaknesses of the research problem according to Ferracuti Franco, *Coordination of interdisciplinary research in criminology*, United Nations Social Defense Research Institute, Rome 1971, pp. 26, 27.

[2] The social therapeutic clinic of Van der Hoeven in Utrecht, intended for psychically disturbed delinquents from eighteen to fifty-five years of age, has, for example, three to four teachers for a group of between six and ten 'patients' ('Heilpedagogen' or social workers) who live in rotation with the group from 7.30 a.m. until 10.30 p.m. The entire clinic, which is of the open type, has sixty 'patients' and 140 personnel. This clinic is the prototype of institutions which function on the basis of self-government with the help of group work. (*Die Zeit*, Hamburg, September 1972.)

PART IV

Results

16 Dynamic Development of the Staff

Vinko SKALAR

Goal of the experiment

In the course of four years' work with the educational staff in the institution at Logatec (continuing group counselling and individual counselling with predominantly non-directive methods) we attempted to change their attitudes from what were assumed to be somewhat repressive, to more permissive, ones.

Measurement of attitudes and selection of instruments

We attempted to measure the results of continuing counselling over a period of time with three attitude scales: the Schaefer-Bell scale, the California F scale and the semantic differential.[1]

The experimental institution

The first measurements we made of the experimental group were conducted at the time the institution opened, in September 1967; the last were taken in February 1971 (the experiment was concluded in June 1971). In the intervening period measurements were made at approximately eight-monthly intervals. Not all the staff included in the measurement of attitudes were present in the institution for the entire time of the experiment. Some joined later, and were therefore included in the experiment later. Two educators left the institution prematurely, the nurse was absent on maternity leave twice, and an educator was absent for one year while he fulfilled his military obligations. For these reasons, the number of staff-members in the experimental group changed with time: the first testing included nineteen individuals (the entire group); the second, third and the fourth testings, seventeen; the fifth testing, twelve; the sixth and last testing, ten individuals.

The following table shows how long individuals were included in the experiment. (Note: the first number in parentheses indicates educators, the second instructors, and the third other staff members.)

4 years and more	8 (2 + 3 + 3)
3 to 4 years	6 (3 + 2 + 1)
2 to 3 years	4 (2 + 1 + 1)
1 to 2 years	1 (1 + 0 + 0)
Total	19

The staff who joined the institution later became incorporated into the experiment more quickly because of the infuence of the existing staff, who had in part already changed their attitudes.

Control institutions

The experiment did not originally provide for control groups. In the autumn of 1969 we decided to include them for the reasons cited below.

During the experiment one of the inmates at the institution at Logatec committed an offence and was transferred by the court to the institution at Radeče. The staff at the Logatec institution considered him to be unmanageable to such a degree that he had to be removed from there. We found out later that his degree of maladjustment, as measured by the Jesness inventory (asocial index and others), was not higher than that of other inmates. This caused us to reconsider the validity of the hypothesis that inmates sent to different institutions in Slovenia had different degrees of maladjustment. The team therefore decided somewhat belatedly also to start testing the staff and inmates in the institutions at Slivnica and Radeče. Within the Republic of Slovenia our choice of control groups was limited. Relative to the institution at Logatec, the roles of other institutions are somewhat more specific. The educational correctional Home in Radeče is more strict and accepts only delinquent youths referred by the courts. The institution provides schooling and training. In contrast, the educational institution in Slivnica is more open, with training being provided only outside the institution. It accepts youths both from the courts and social welfare agencies, youths who for the most part have completed their compulsory education prior to entrance into the institution. In the eyes of the courts and the social welfare services, the institution at Logatec should be somewhere between the two control institutions in the difficulties posed by its population and its strictness.[2] Despite the specific roles of the control institutions, both of them have points of similarity

144

with the experimental institution. Both deal with male delinquent young people of the same age as inmates of the Logatec institution. All three institutions (experimental and control institutions) have a similar environment, and all three were exposed to similar professional influences and influences of public opinion up to the beginning of the experiment in Logatec.

In both control institutions we selected from the staff the group that was most nearly like the group of staff-members in the experimental institution. The criteria for selection were: age, function in the institution, length of service in the institution and sex. After consideration of these criteria, which we were able to match only in part, we selected in both institutions two smaller groups. If other criteria had been added, selection would no longer have been possible.

From February 1970 to April 1972, we tested both control groups four times, at intervals of eight months.

Control group in the educational correctional home in Radeče

This group originally contained thirteen individuals. Since two educators left the institution during the experimental period (one of them after the first testing and the other after the second), we replaced them in the testing with the two educators who replaced them in the institution. In the statistical analysis, we considered the additional educators as additional members of the original group, and did not include them in place of the two who left the institution. Thus the group was increased to fifteen members for the first testing. The staff members who left the institution after the third testing (four) were not replaced. Thus the number of staff members tested in the educational correctional home in Radeče varied for the different testings.

Control group in the educational institution at Slivnica

This group originally included eleven individuals. The educators who replaced the educators (three) who left the institution after the first or second testing were replaced with others in a manner similar to that described for the educational correctional home in Radeče. Staff who left the institution after the third testing were not replaced. For reasons beyond our control, the number of staff-members became increasingly smaller with each testing.

We found significant differences between the experimental group and the control groups in the educational structure (the educational correctional home in Radeče had no staff-members with higher education, and most of the staff in the educational institution had only high school education), and in the structure of the functions of the staff in the institution (the educational institution in Slivnica had no shopmasters (instructors), and in the educational correctional home in Radeče the group of 'others' contained only one member). When both control groups are pooled as one group, the comparison is more favourable to the experimental group. Individual characteristics are shown in Tables 16.1 to 16.6.

Table 16.1

Numbers in the groups at different testings

Test	Experimental group	Control group
1	19	29
2	17	26
3	17	21
4	17	14
5	12	—
6	10	—

Table 16.2

Staff distribution by age

Age	Experimental group		Control group	
	No.	%	No.	%
20–25	6	31·6	4	13·8
26–30	10	52·6	17	58·6
31–37	3	15·8	8	27·6
Total	19	100	29	100

Note: At the time of the first testing, the average age of staff-members in the experimental institution was twenty-seven years. At the time of the first testing, the average age of staff-members in the control institutions was twenty-eight years.

Table 16.3

Staff distribution by education

Education	Experimental group		Control group	
	No.	%	No.	%
Vocational school	5	26·3	6	20·7
High school	3	15·8	13	44·9
Junior college	7	36·8	9	31·0
University	4	21·1	1	3·4
Total	19	100	29	100

Table 16.4

Staff distribution by sex

Sex	Experimental group		Control group	
	No.	%	No.	%
Male	16	84·2	22	75·9
Female	3	15·8	7	24·1
Total	19	100	29	100

Table 16.5

Staff distribution according to function in the institution

Function in the institution	Experimental group		Control group	
	No.	%	No.	%
Educator	8	42·1	20	69·0
Instructor	6	31·6	7	24·1
Other	5	26·3	2	6·9
Total	19	100	29	100

Table 16.6

Staff distribution by length of service in the institution

Years	Experimental group		Control group	
	No.	%	No.	%
0	19	100	0	0
1–5	–	–	20	69·0
6–10	–	–	7	24·1
11–15	–	–	2	6·9
	19	100	29	100

Note: At the time of the first testing, the average length of service for staff in the control group was four years.

Comparison between the experimental institution and the combined control institutions reveals differing characteristics, which are not, however, statistically significant (except for length of service in the institution). We explain the lack of statistical significance in these differences in terms of the small sample size for both populations. The differences between the populations are an expression of our efforts to select an appropriate staff for the experimental institution. Compared to the control institutions, this staff is younger, better educated, and at the time of the first testing had no experience in institutional work. Because of its relatively more complete staffing, the experimental institution had more workers in the group 'others'. Thus the starting points for the measurement of developmental dynamics were not equal, and this could not be helped.

Besides the reasons mentioned above which justify the combining of both control institutions as one group, we compared the two control groups on individual basic categories of attitudes in order to determine if there were significant differences between them. Because of the quadruple testing, the arithmetic means of the thirteen basic categories yields fifty-two possibilities. Among these we found only four statistically significant differences (two in the category 'irritability', one in the category 'defensiveness' and one in the category 'repression of feelings').

None of the other differences in the arithmetic means of the basic categories for the control institutions were statistically significant.

In our statistical analysis we included the first four testings for the experimental group, whereas for the control group the first three testings were included since the number of objects tested subsequently was too small for statistical analysis. Because of the small number of subjects, we also did not divide the groups into sub groups, even though it would have been interesting to compare the sub group of instructors and the sub-group of educators in both the experimental and control groups.

Selected statistical methods

We calculated statistical parameters for individual attitudinal categories: M (arithmetic means), SD (standard deviations) and in addition correlations (r) for individual relations.

For determination of the significance of the differences between the arithmetic means, a method was used in which the experimental group served as its own control for testings at different time periods. The method takes into account the correlation between the first and subsequent testings.[3] The significance of the differences was calculated by means of the method of differences and the T distribution.

The significance of the differences between the standard deviations (SD) within the groups on a temporally dynamic scale was calculated by means of the F distribution.[4]

Differences between arithmetic means for the experimental and control groups were calculated by means of the t distributions.[5] The differences between the standard deviation were evaluated for significance by means of the F distribution.[6]

For calculation of correlation coefficients we used the product—moment method.[7] The level of significance was derived from standard tables.

Method of presentation of results

Numerical results are presented only for the general categories.

In addition to the statistically significant differences on a temporally dynamic scale, we also show the trends numerically and graphically with consideration of all testings, including all those that were not considered on the statistical analysis.

Particular attention should be paid to the difference between the numbers (and consequently the arithmetic means and standard deviations) of the numerically and graphically presented trends and the numbers which were the basis of the statistical analysis. This difference is important only for the first testing (T_1) for the experimental and control groups. The total number for the experimental group for T_1 is nineteen, for the control group twenty-nine, while for our statistical analysis for T_1 we dealt with a number of seventeen for the experimental group and twenty-six for the control group. For both groups we equalised the number for T_1 with the number for T_2. The differences are a matter of hundredths, and the tendency of the trends in no case changes because of the differences in the sample sizes. Thus it is not necessary in the results to show separately the arithmetic means and standard deviations for T_1 which are derived from reduced numbers.

First of all we shall give the results of the Schaefer-Bell scale, and F scale, saving the results of the semantic differential for the following chapter.

Results and interpretation

1 *Authoritarian control (general average of category (1) authority + (2) strictness + (3) control).*

	Experimental institution			Control institution		
Test	No.	*M*	*SD*	No.	*M*	*SD*
1	19	3·22	0·498	29	3·15	0·537
2	17	3·15	0·428	26	3·30	0·514
3	17	3·09	0·513	21	3·34	0·502
4	17	2·92	0·534	14	3·31	
5	12	2·83				
6	10	2·87				

$r = T_1 : T_2, T_1 : T_3, T_1 : T_4 = 0·01$ $r = T_1 : T_2, T_1 : T_3 = 0·01$

$t = M_1 : M_4 = 0·01$ $t = 0$

$F = 0$ $F = 0$

The differences between the experimental and control groups are not statistically significant.

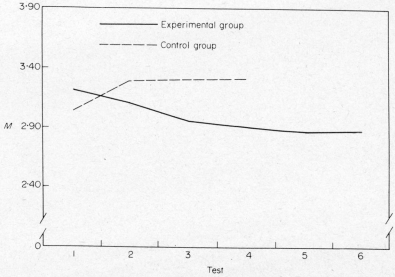

Note: The groups remain relatively homogeneous for all of the testings. The trend of attitudes in the experimental group is positive and continually decreases, whereas the trend is negative for the control group.

2 *Punitive discipline (general category of (4) breaking the will + (5) harshness)*

Test	Experimental group			Control group		
	No.	M	SD	No.	M	SD
1	19	2·59	0·377	29	2·67	0·489
2	17	2·77	0·455	26	2·89	0·511
3	17	2·75	0·549	21	2·94	0·562
4	17	2·65	0·553	14	3·04	
5	12	2·78				
6	10	2·86				

$r = T_1 : T_2, T_1 : T_3 = 0·01$ $\qquad$ $r = T_1 : T_2, T_1 : T_3 = 0·01$

$t = M_1 : M_2 = 0·05$ $\qquad$ $t = M_1 ; M_2, M_1 : M_3 = 0·01$

$F = 0$ $\qquad\qquad$ $F = 0$

The differences between the experimental and control groups are not statistically significant.

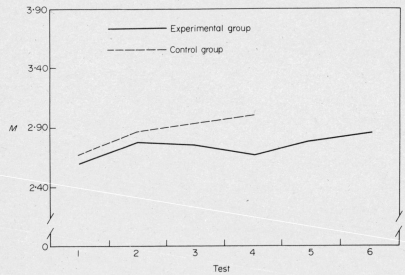

Note: The groups remain homogeneous for the different testings. The trend of attitudes fluctuates for the experimental group, but is generally negative; for the control group the trend is markedly negative.

Note: For punitive discipline a rising score signifies a negative trend.

3 *Emotional distances (general category of (6) forcing independence +
(7) aggression + (8) achievement + (9) withholding affection + (10) suppression of effect)*

Test	Experimental group			Control group		
	No.	M	SD	No.	M	SD
1	19	3·37	0·277	29	3·26	0·249
2	17	3·35	0·221	26	3·34	0·265
3	17	3·25	0·261	21	3·40	0·253
4	17	3·25	0·239			
				14	3·49	
5	12	3·20				
6	10	3·26				

$r = T_1 : T_2, T_1 : T_3 = 0·01;$ $\qquad$ $r = T_1 : T_2 = 0·05;$

$T_1 : T_4 = 0·05$ $\qquad$ $T_1 : T_3 = 0·01$

$t = M_1 : M_4 = 0·05$ $\qquad$ $t = M_1 : M_3 = 0·01$

$F = 0$ $\qquad$ $F = 0$

The differences between the experimental and control groups are not statistically significant.

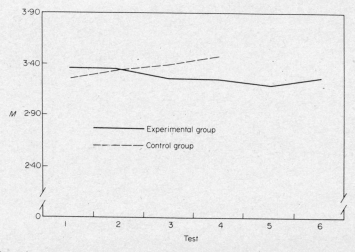

Note: For the experimental group the trend of attitudes falls moderately
in a positive direction, whereas for the control group it rises consistently
in a negative direction. The groups are homogeneous, with no statistically
significant differences between them.

4 Equalitarian interaction (general category of (11) equality + (12) discussing problems)

Test	Experimental group No.	M	SD	Control group No.	M	SD
1	19	4·67	0·430	29	4·67	0·354
2	17	4·67	0·315	26	4·45	0·431
3	17	4·64	0·379	21	4·49	0·455
4	17	4·69	0·349			
				14	4·33	
5	12	4·64				
6	10	4·62				

$r = T_1 : T_3 = 0·01; T_1 : T_4 = 0·05$ $r = T_1 : T_2, T_1 : T_3 = 0·05$
$t = 0$ $T = 0$
$F = 0$ $F = 0$

The differences between the experimental group and the control group are not statistically significant.

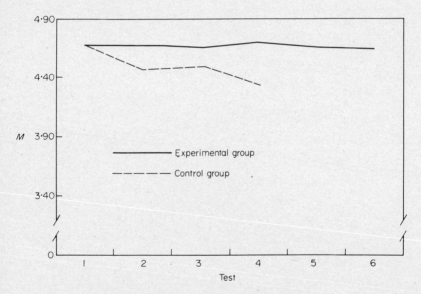

Note: The experimental groups remains on practically the same level, while the control group generally falls in a negativė direction. The groups are relatively homogeneous for all testings.

Note: A higher score in this case means a more positive attitude.

154

5 *Custody orientation (total category of (14) authoritarian control + (15) punitive discipline + (16) emotional distance)*

Test	Experimental group			Control group		
	No.	*M*	*SD*	No.	*M*	*SD*
1	19	3·16	0·330	29	3·11	0·341
2	17	3·16	0·279	26	3·23	0·354
3	17	3·09	0·365	21	3·29	0·369
4	17	3·00	0·351	14	3·33	
5	12	2·97				
6	10	3·02				

$r = T_1 : T_2, T_1 : T_3, T_1 : T_4 = 0·01$ $r = T_1 : T_2, T_1 : T_3 = 0·01$

$t = M_1 : M_3 = 0·05; M_1 : M_4 = 0·01$ $t = M_1 : M_3 = 0·01$

$F = 0$ $F = 0$

The differences between the experimental and control groups are not statistically significant.

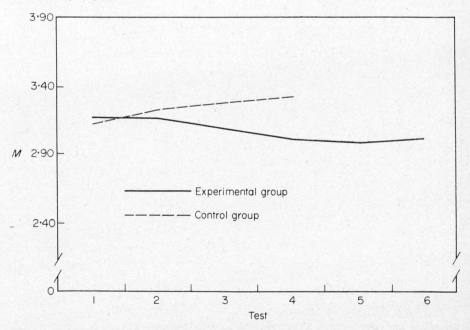

Note: In the experimental group the trend of attitudes generally falls in a positive direction, whereas it rises without exception in the control group. The groups remain homogeneous for the various testings.

6 Total custody orientation (= custody orientation–egalitarian interaction)

Test	Experimental group				Control group		
	No.	M	SD		No.	M	SD
1	19	2·72	0·522		29	2·64	0·509
2	17	2·72	0·417		26	2·85	0·548
3	17	2·65	0·562		21	2·95	0·574
4	17	2·51	0·533		14	3·04	
5	12	2·48					
6	10	2·57					

$r = T_1 : T_2, T_1 : T_3, T_1 : T_4 = 0.01$ $r = T_1 : T_2, T_1 : T_3 = 0.01$

$t = M_1 : M_3 = 0.05; M_1 : M_4 = 0.01$ $t = M_1 : M_2, M_1 : M_3 = 0.01$

$F = 0$ $F = 0$

The differences between the experimental and control groups are not statistically significant.

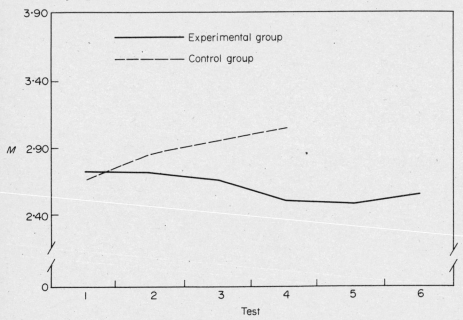

Note: The trend for the experimental group falls in a positive direction, whereas it rises continually in a negative direction for the control group. The groups are relatively homogeneous for the various testings.

7 *California* F *scale (general category)*

Test	Experimental group No.	M	SD	Control group No.	M	SD
1	19	3·22	0·444	29	3·20	0·485
2	17	3·10	0·584	26	3·30	0·596
3	17	3·08	0·560	21	3·36	0·672
4	17	2·94	0·657	14	3·39	
5	17	2·67				
6	10	2·88				

$r = T_1 : T_2, T_1 : T_3, T_1 : T_4 = 0·01$

$t = M_1 : M_2 = 0·05;$.

$M_1 : M_3, M_1 : M_4 = 0·01$

$F = 0$

$r = T_1 : T_2 = 0·01;$

$T_1 : T_3 = 0·05$

$t = 0$

$F = 0$

The differences between the experimental and control groups are not statistically significant.

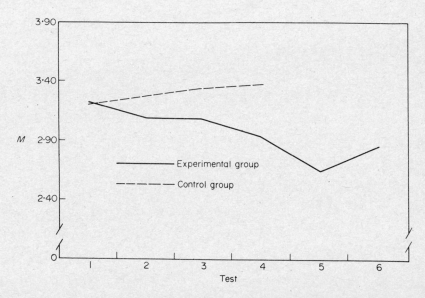

Note: The trend for the experimental group falls consistently on a dynamic time scale, whereas the control group shows a trend that rises in a negative direction. The starting point is nearly identical for both groups. The groups are relatively homogeneous throughout.

Summary

There are scarcely any statistically significant differences between the experimental and control groups. Out of seventy-eight calculations (of which thirty-nine (thirteen times three) were arithmetic means and thirty-nine (thirteen times three) were standard deviations) for thirteen basic categories, we found only six statistically significant differences. Four of these were for standard deviations and two were for arithmetic means.

In the general categories we found no statistically significant differences in either the arithmetic means or the standard deviations. We suspect that the numbers of both of the groups compared were too small and that the experiment lasted too short a time to allow us to find statistically significant differences between the groups.

Despite the fact that there were no statistically significant differences between the experimental and control groups, the characteristics of the experimental and control groups differ to such an extent that we may conclude that important differences do exist between the two groups. Let us examine some of these characteristics.

For the experimental group the correlations are statistically significant in all three relations for only eight categories (for three basic categories, four general categories, and for the F scale); for seven categories (for five basic and two general) the correlations are significant in two relations; in five categories (basic) the correlations are significant for only one relation. This means that the staff repeatedly changed some of their attitudes on repeated testings.

In contrast, we find that the control group has statistically significant correlations in all relations for sixteen categories (nine basic, six general and for the F scale), while we found no significant correlations in any relations for three categories. These differences between the groups allow the conclusion that the control group is more rigid in its attitudes than is the experimental group, which exhibited more fluctuations, searching and correction of attitudes.

For the experimental group the trend of attitudes is positive for eleven categories (six basic, four general and the F scale); a fluctuation in a negative and positive direction is found in six categories (four basic and two general); and a mildly negative trend (breaking of will, irritability, equalitarian tendency) is found in three categories (basic).

The control group shows no positive trend in any category; fluctuation is found twice (in basic categories); and a consistently negative trend is found in seventeen categories and the F scale.

The predominantly negative trends of attitudes for the control group and the predominantly positive trends for the experimental group point to important differences between the groups, despite the fact that we did not find statistically significant differences.

We would expect to find significant differences between the experimental and control groups since the experimental group was specially selected and employed for the first time in an institutional situation. Hypothetically, these differences should have been most obvious at the first testing, at a time when the staff in the experimental group had not yet been influenced by staff from other institutions, had not yet experienced frustrations in institutional practice and not yet accepted the philosophy that is on average characteristic of staff in educational institutions. In contrast, the staff in the control institutions were already working when they were first tested. If differences had been found between the two groups, the comparison of trends would still have been possible, although the results would have been on different levels.

Despite this hypothesis, we find (see graphs) that the differences between the experimental and control groups are smallest at the first testing — for some categories the results for the two groups are nearly identical. We assume that this is due to two conflicting factors:

1   The experimental group, as a representative of the general population, exhibited at the first testing an authentic, nearly repressive attitude towards the delinquent population (recent investigation of public opinion in Slovenia shows that the public is strongly repressively oriented towards the delinquent population). The predominantly positive trend toward greater permissiveness evidenced at the testings is presumably an expression of the influence of counselling.

2   The control group, as representative of staff in institutions, showed at the first testing a partially conformist attitude approximating to the theoretical principles to which they had been repeatedly exposed at seminars in recent years. On repeated testing, the self-control and conformity of the staff was reduced in intensity. They then expressed increasingly authentic and repressive attitudes.

We may conclude that the results for the experimental group are an expression of the influence of continuing counselling, in contrast to those for the control group, who did not have the benefit of this influence.

Semantic differential

Data analysis

In light of the fact that we gave emphasis in our research to changes in the attitudes of the staff reflecting the conflict between their repressive and permissive inclinations, we attempted in the semantic differential to isolate those items which were relevant to this category of attitudes.

We selected six competent and independent evaluators. All of them were educated as psychologists and currently or formerly employed in educational institutions. The seventh evaluator was the author of the test instrument (Skalar). We asked the evaluators to mark all the items in the categories of 'education' and 'teacher' which were, in their opinion, directly relevant to the conceptual continuum of repressiveness—permissiveness. In this way, we isolated from the total number of items seven for each category; these were items for which we found a high level of agreement among the evaluators, as is shown below.

'Educator': item	Degree of agreement
1 Democratic—autocratic	7
2 Mild—aggressive	7
3 Emotionally warm—emotionally cold	6
4 Friendly—official	6
5 Non-directive—directive	6
6 Sensitive—insensitive	5
7 Accommodating—strict	5

'Education': item	Degree of agreement
1 Democratic—autocratic	7
2 Non-directive—directive	6
3 Non-authoritarian—authoritarian	6
4 Relaxed—strict	6
5 Patient—impatient	6
6 Mild—strict	5
7 Yielding—unyielding	5

For both groups of items that were, in the opinion of the independent evaluators, indicative of permissive inclination versus repressive inclination, we decided to deal only with the total result, which theoretically could vary between seven (extreme permissiveness) and forty-nine (extreme authoritarianism). The total score reflect seven items scored on a seven-point scale.

We analysed the results with the same statistical methods as were used for the Schaefer-Bell scale and the F scale. We are aware that this in no way exhausts all the possibilities offered to us by the results of the semantic differential. A more exact statistical analysis would be possible, but we approached the data only from the standpoint that was appropriate to the goals of the experiment.

Test	Experimental group			Control group		
	No.	M	SD	No.	M	SD
1	19	24·50	6·587	29	23·14	5·519
2	17	22·94	4·904	26	22·19	4·519
3	17	22·22	4·685	21	24·34	4·685
4	17	22·41	3·679	14	23·79	
5	12	22·50				
6	10	21·43				

$r = T_1 : T_2 = 0.01$ $r = T_1 : T_2, T_1 : T_3 = 0.01$

$t = M_1 : M_4 = 0.05$ $t = 0$

$F = SD_1 : SD_4 = 0.05$ $F = 0$

There are no statistically significant differences between the experimental and control groups.

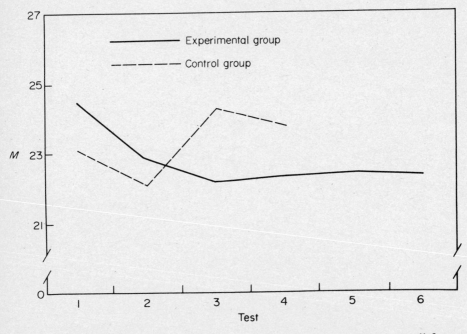

Note: For the experimental group, the trend of attitudes falls overall from a less to greater permissive tendency; the control group fluctuates but overall shows a negative trend towards greater authoritarianism.

Results and interpretation: item 'educator'

Test	Experimental group			Control group		
	No.	*M*	*SD*	No.	*M*	*SD*
1	19	18·95	4·992	29	17·05	4·560
2	17	18·50	3·974	26	18·82	4·738
3	17	19·17	5·159	21	19·48	5·075
4	17	17·12	4·635	14	19·00	
5	12	19·11				
6	10	19·43				

$r = T_1 : T_2 = 0·01; T_1 : T_3 = 0·05$ $r = T_1 : T_2 = 0·01$

$t = M_1 : M_4 = 0·05$ $t = 0$

$F = 0$ $F = 0$

There are no statistically significant differences.

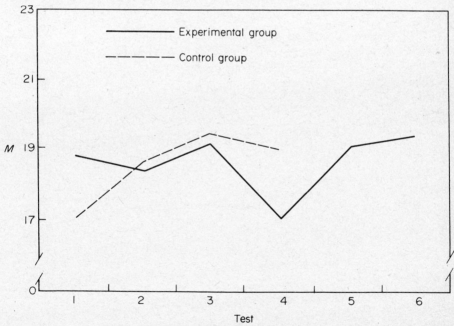

Note: The experimental group begins with attitudes that are less favourable than those of the control group. With further testing both groups become nearly equal, with the exception of the turn towards greater permissiveness at T_4 for the experimental group. Both groups are relatively homogeneous throughout.

Summary

The results of the semantic differential give a picture similar to that given by the results of the Schaefer-Bell scale and the F scale, both for the inner dynamics on a temporal scale for the experimental and control groups, and for the relation between the groups. The category 'education' yields clearer results than the category 'educator', perhaps because of the greater personal reference which the latter category probably evoked for the people tested.

Notes

[1] See Chapter 7. pp. 63–5
[2] The institution in Logatec accepts inmates on the basis of orders of the court and social welfare agencies. Except in one instance, all the inmates committed punishable acts before they were accepted into the institution, especially punishable acts against property.
[3] Boris Petz, *Basic statistical methods*, Zagreb 1964.
[4] Marjan Blejec, *Statistical methods for psychologist*, Ljubljana 1959, pp. 206–9.
[5] Ibid., pp. 154–5, 204.
[6] Ibid., pp. 156 and 206–9.
[7] Boris Petz, op. cit., pp. 82. 197.

17   Inmates (I)

Milica BERGANT

SUBCULTURAL MODELS OF SOCIALISATION AND SOCIAL CIRCUMSTANCES OF INMATES AT THE TIME OF ADMISSION INTO THE INSTITUTION

Although the work of the members of the professional team was primarily directed towards the educators and the other staff of the institution, and towards the changing of their attitudes, the inmates at Logatec and their re-education were also an object of the experiment. It was for them that the new methods of permissive education were intended. When new methods and processes for the treatment of material are tested in the area of technology, we are well aware that it is insufficient to know only the new technological process, and that it is just as important to know the raw materials on which the new process is to be used. If we pursue this simplified analogy, the succes or failure of our experiment depended to a large extent on the 'quality and resistance' of our material – the inmates; and in particular on the degree and kind of their disturbance and their ability to be receptive to resocialisation and therapeutic influences.

Modern dynamic psychology combines testing with analysis of anamnestic data gathered from the important periods and circumstances of the maturation, and in particular socialisation process. In this way an attempt is made to generate a more complete picture of the problems that are encountered. This is also the purpose of the analyses that we noted – subcultural models of socialisation and living circumstances of the inmates at Logatec with whom we worked. In the final analysis these circumstances (in addition to inherited dispositions) influence the emergence of dyssocial disturbances and give us the opportunity of evaluating the level and kind of the inmate's disturbance.

The sample for this study consisted of sixty-three inmates who were released from the institution at Logatec between 1968 and 1971. The data were gathered from extensive dossiers which contained the reports of social workers, psychologists, educators, the professional team at the observation centre, and so on, with sometimes a psychiatrist's report.

In this analysis we took as our point of departure the theory of socialisation which holds that biological dispositions emerge and become established only when given form and content by life and by educational models that influence the personality for an extended time and in developmentally important periods.

The inmates at Logatec were primarily from the city (80 per cent), with only a small number coming from farms or smaller villages. Most frequently their parents had migrated from country to city, drawn there by the intensive industrialisation of the post-war period. Their fathers were most frequently skilled workers (40·4 per cent), followed by unskilled workers (34·6 per cent), who comprise the group with the lowest incomes. Among the latter we also included fathers who were small farmers. In third place were administrative officers (16·0 per cent) and a small group made up of workers in public security and the Services (9·0 per cent).

Their mothers were for the most part employed (80 per cent). We should note here that one of our previous research projects[1] has shown that there is no connection between the employment of the mother and social disturbance in the children. The employment structure of these mothers was somewhat less favourable than that of the fathers. For the most part they were employed as unskilled workers.

On the whole the employment structure of the fathers of our inmates cannot be considered as being the lowest possible, since only a third of them are unskilled workmen. However, for 40 per cent of our inmates we found bad material conditions in the home: for 40 per cent the conditions were considered moderately good; and 20 per cent of the families of the inmates lived in very good material circumstances.

The data on housing conditions corresponds to the material circumstances. A question arises as to what extent the housing conditions influenced the social workers' estimate of the families' material circumstances. Because of the housing shortage in our cities, it is more difficult to better one's housing conditions than it is to increase the income of the members of the family. Because the families of inmates for the most part came to the city in the post-war period, their lack of adequate housing is even more pronounced, and because of their low incomes difficult to overcome — for the purchase of a dwelling requires considerable money and sacrifice.

It is also to be questioned whether the high percentage of materially disadvantaged families, in which both parents are employed, is not also the result of secondary causes, such as alcoholism or irregular employment of the parents, in particular the father.

A more disturbing datum than material circumstances and grade of employment is that concerning the level of education of the parents of our inmates. It is in fact considerably lower than one would infer from their employment structure. 53 per cent of the fathers and 35 per cent of the mothers did not complete elementary school. Also there were many fathers whose sole education was elementary school. Both of these categories are so inclusive that the average education of these parents falls well below the average for Slovenia. The proportion of the inmates' fathers who did not complete elementary school, and of those who completed only elementary school, is twice the average for the whole republic. An even worse picture of the cultural level of these families emerges if we compare the education of the parents of our inmates with the average for Slovene cities. In the cities the proportion of fathers without completed elementary school education is one-ninth of the comparable figure for the inmates' fathers; while the proportion of fathers with high school diplomas is three and a half times more than for the fathers of inmates.[2]

These data show that our inmates for the most part grew up in families that were below the cultural average for their environment — that is, in a subculture of poverty. It is known that life soon brings people in lower cultural strata into collision with higher cultural strata, to conflicts of the 'inferior' individual with his environment, to failure of his children in school and their premature choice of jobs. In an environment of higher civilisation and culture, success in life depends on the quality of the personality, as revealed in education, culture and personal stability. These factors also in large measure determine self-assertion, profession, income and possibly personal happiness as well. Our inmates, because of the pronounced sub-cultural status of their families, were deprived in youth of many of the requirements for success and self-assertion.

Disintegration of the family and dyssocial phenomena

Some of the signs of broken families are easily seen and documented in the families of the inmates at Logatec. In half of the cases our inmates lived in incomplete families (56 per cent) and only 44 per cent lived in families that were organisationally stable. Among the incomplete families reconstructed families were most frequent (19 per cent with the mother married for a second time), followed by children from divorced parents (15·8 per cent), children abandoned by both parents (8 per cent), illegitimate children (6 per cent) and foster children (3 per cent). However, we should not let the outward form of the family, be it complete or incomplete, impress us too much.

According to our criteria, the family is most incomplete, regardless of its form, when it does not fulfil its essential functions — the raising and education of its children. In this connection one must be impressed by a phenomenon which is on the increase in Yugoslavia — that is, the abandonment of an unwanted child by both parents. This category of completely disintegrated families makes up 11 per cent, an increase over the incidence found in previous studies. Most frequently mothers who have been deserted by a child's father give the child to their own mothers or to foster parents, and then move and have no further contact with the child.

Although previous Slovene studies of the aetiology of juvenile delinquency have shown a very unfavourable and disturbed picture of the father — reflecting, for instance, absence, unsatisfactory role in the family, alcoholism, lack of concern for the family, and desertion of the mother during pregnancy[3] — our analysis also revealed a considerably more negative picture of the mothers than had been indicated by previous studies. In the past children were more often abandoned by their fathers, but now, in increasing numbers, children are being abandoned by their mothers as well. Children react to this situation very sorrowfully, even if they have good foster parents. For example, in the institution we repeatedly observed a truly agonised 'sorrowful search for the mother' when inmates felt abandoned by the mother as well and thus shut out from their last family haven. Since mothers were such important family factors for half of those inmates in our group who lived in broken families, we devoted considerable attention to the description and study of them, with less attention to the fathers, who have been studied many times before.

Description of the fathers and mothers and family relationships

Many authors frequently present an oversimplified schema to the effect that the fathers of juvenile delinquents are very aggressive, whereas their mothers are warm and protective. After we had assembled from the dossiers of the inmates all of the available data concerning their parents, a descriptive scale emerged which included the pronounced characteristics of the mothers and fathers. We found that the characteristics of the fathers could be divided into four typical groups, while the inmates' mothers' fell into six groups and were thus more differentiated. (The mothers also possessed some characteristics that were more difficult to define into groups.)

In our description of the fathers our category of 'continual absence of a true father' also included substitute father figures, grandfathers, stepfathers or foster-fathers, who carried a father's educational role.

Description of fathers

1. The most frequent characteristic of the fathers of the Logatec inmates was marked aggressiveness (47·4 per cent), which was at times related to alcoholism. Their position in the family was usually that of a tyrant, or characterised by additional eccentric traits such as asociability. Many of the fathers were chronic alcoholics with aggressive traits. There were also fathers in whom brutal and aggressive traits became more pronounced under the influence of alcohol, with resultant physical abuse of wife and children. In these cases the wife and children feared the father and quietly rejected him.

The aggressive and fear-inducing father has been repeatedly found in studies of the aetiology of juvenile delinquents. The results of our research is thus another confirmation of the findings of Yugoslav and foreign research in this area.

2. A second group of fathers, numerically smaller and including about one-fourth of the cases, showed fewer negative aggressive—tyrannical traits, yet had other traits that are not suitable for someone involved in the raising of children. These are fathers who are not interested in their children, do not concern themselves with their children's education, and are probably also emotionally indifferent to them. Among them we also included older, sick fathers who were egocentrically occupied with health problems and showed no great inclination to concern themselves with the education of their children. It is of interest that the kind of father that shows no particular interest for a child and withdraws from the educational sphere is also frequently encountered at the child guidance clinics. These are fathers who no longer have a central patriarchal—authoritative role in the family. The wife is also employed, and the style of the family's life is more egalitarian and modern. However, the father does not find his role in the more egalitarian and less authoritarian atmosphere. Since the family life no longer rests on his shoulders, he feels fewer obligations and responsibilities. All the family obligations are transferred to the wife, for whom employment outside the home results in overwork and fatigue. In question is not only their relation to educational responsibilities, but also their emotional ties to the child, for often apparent emotional indifference is encountered.

3. The third group of fathers, which is not so numerous (17 per cent), is also frequently mentioned in discussions of the aetiology of youthful crime. These are fathers who show no responsibility towards their families. They show some asocial traits (like laziness), are quiet, good-natured

drinkers, or carousers, or continually erode their family life with infidelity. Among them we also included delinquent and mentally ill fathers, a numerically small group.

4.   The numerically smallest group (10 per cent) is made up of men who could be described as patriarchal, albeit somewhat modernised fathers. These are fathers who take great care for the material standard of the family, but are therefore preoccupied and have little day-to-day contact with their children. They serve as the main disciplinary force in the family, but are too clumsy, strict and demanding in their function as teachers, and tend to preach at their children. They are emotionally withdrawn from the children, though they are probably not emotionally indifferent.

Description of mothers

We were interested in the question of why the mothers of the inmates at Logatec were not able to compensate for the negative influence of the fathers, or why they were not better able to replace educationally passive fathers. Even if these mothers do remain self-supporting, this is not a reason, as many of our studies have shown, for neglect of their children. The fact that a mother becomes self-supporting is not in itself of fateful significance for her child. Some other unfavourable conditions must also be present: the mother must not be overburdened with care for the existence and education of a large number of children; her professional qualifications are important; and certain positive personality traits can be decisive – for instance, vitality and resistance, active relation with life, educational ability, and ability to assume some educational functions that are typically done by a father. Under typical functions of the father could be mentioned disciplining of the children, setting of limits for children's behaviour, and acting as a role model of someone who requires something from life, is experienced in life, and is well rounded. The mothers of our inmates obviously did not have these qualities, and their relation to life was primarily passive and yielding. In their relationship with their children there was also no evidence of particular activity or responsibility for the task of education. For the most part they also came from unstable, poorly educated, primitive families, and were 'used to hardship', expecting little in the way of stability of family and marital life. In the following descriptive scale we included in the category of absent mothers also substitute mothers, foster-mothers, and grandmothers who cared for the child.

1.   The largest group of mothers (44 per cent) show the following cha-

racteristics: for the most part primitive, apathetic women who gave birth to unwanted children. They neglect the child's education, and are emotionally indifferent to the child. Frequently they shun educational obligations or are even unaware of the significance of family education. In school records one such woman is reported as saying that she was not so stupid as to concern herself with the education of such a difficult child, on top of everything else. Others demand that the school cure the child's troubles. Such mothers consider their job done if they provide for the basic material needs of the child. They tend to have their children put in foster homes.

2.   The second largest group of mothers (20 per cent) is made up of women who are overworked, overtired and weak. Thus they are unable to change and redirect the unfavourable course of their family. These characteristics can be understood as the mirror image corresponding to the aggressive and tyrannical father. Some of them have a martyr-like quality. One mother of an inmate, born into a poor farm family, was partially deaf from birth and married off at a defenceless young age to an older small-tradesman. He was an alcoholic and was brutal towards both mother and children. The mother tried twice to hang herself, but was saved both times. All that such mothers succeed in doing for their children is to secure their basic material needs by means of thrift and careful housekeeping. They intervene on behalf of their children, and pity and defend them.

3.   The third group (12 per cent of the total) are mothers who are themselves socially deviant, practise prostitution, fast living and drinking. It is unnecessary to enlarge on their educational failings and meagre concern for the education of their children.

4.   A fourth group of mothers, about equal in size to the third group, is made up of women who spoil their children and attempt to defend and hide them from the more demanding or aggressive father. This kind of mother is often described by criminologists as typical, but was not frequently seen with our inmates. These mothers quietly reject the father, but are at the same time very unsure in their own educational efforts. If these mothers have a more dominant personality, then they spoil the child excessively or create disunity in the educational efforts. They defend the child and hide his mistakes from the father and the public.

5.   Less frequently we found mothers (9 per cent) who are socially stable and vital, but themselves create an aggressive atmosphere in the family. There have been numerous descriptions of the aggressive father in connection with dyssocial young people, but research to date has neglected the

171

unfavourable education and unpleasant family atmosphere which is caused by a verbally aggressive and often quarrelsome and hysterical mother. Such mothers must be added to the number of cases of aggressive fathers. In addition to aggressive fathers, these women contribute to a predominantly aggressive and unpleasant atmosphere of family life.

6. A numerically small (3 per cent) but yet recognisable group of mothers are those who live in reconstructed families (second marriages). It appears that this kind of family is on the increase in Yugoslavia, to such an extent that it appears more frequently in our sample than broken homes. These mothers are emotionally divided between the new marriage-partner and the jealous and difficult child who makes trouble and creates tension in the family. They gradually become estranged from the child.

From the description of the fathers, to which we have added a description of the mothers, we can deduce the prevailing atmosphere and the circumstances of family education of the inmates at Logatec. Among the fathers the predominant type is the aggressive, oppressive father, with whom we may group the verbally aggressive mother, who occurs somewhat less frequently. Thus our findings replicate those of earlier research: there is a predominance of unstable, aggressive families (39 per cent) near social disintegration. These families raise their children with sporadic and often excessive physical punishment and threats, and neglect all the positive aspects of education. We found inconsistent education in 25 per cent, which means that one of the parents was very repressive to the child while the other was permissive and usually attempted to shield the child from coercion.

From the most prevalent type of mother and those fathers in the second largest group, we may deduce a high percentage of the families in which the parents are emotionally indifferent to the child and emotionally deprive it. This deprivation may be expressed verbally, or may be masked by a superficial concern for the child's immediate material needs. In such circumstances the child comes to view himself as a stranger in the family, as an unpleasant burden on the parents, and as an unpleasant hindrance to their way of life. As was the case with physical aggression, the children also react to this with hate and the need for revenge, once they have failed in their legitimate demand for warmth and love from their parents. Emotional deprivation of the child (as well as aggressiveness in the family) has been frequently pointed out, in European and also in older American studies,[4] as an aetiological factor in delinquency.

Considering all our material, we may conclude that there is a pre-

ponderance of families that are aggressive or emotionally cold and rejecting to the child. It is likely too that aggressiveness and emotional deprivation are often joined together in one family.

Our method of gathering data did not allow us to determine the incidence of neurotic families. On rare occasions we also found permissive,
child-spoiling families, which distort the child's moral sense by insufficient
discipline.

As a result of such family relationships, we found markedly reduced
possibilities for the children to identify with their parents, or anticipated
reduced identification possibilities. It is also known that aggressive families
give rise to so-called identification with the aggressor, which is in fact a
psychological defence mechanism which fixates the child's development at
a lower level. Only 19 per cent of the inmates were able to identify strongly
with their fathers, while 38 per cent identified with their mothers. Supplementary identification with brothers or sisters appeared infrequently,
for generally speaking the sibling relationships were jealous or neutral.
Grandparents were more important as replacement role models. The poor
possibilities of identification with parents undoubtedly caused disturbances in the inmates' personalities; they also produced a tendency to seek
role models elsewhere, primarily in peer groups. We observed an intensive
attraction towards and readiness to identify with these peer groups
(96 per cent).

Accumulation of unfavourable educational and social circumstances and life traumas

The life stories of our inmates are characterised by a long series of unfavourable life experiences which occasionally accumulate to form a definite trauma. Such traumas are built into their lives, not as occasional or
chance events, but as concomitants of their lives over the years, including
during developmentally critical periods. From the inmates' dossiers we
could gather only the most visible and palpably unfavourable circumstances
of their lives and socialisation. But there was very little data about the
preschool period, though it is known that this period is the one in which
the child is most sensitive and liable to psychological scarring.

Social deviancy of other members of the family

The first socially disastrous circumstance we noted in the lives of the
inmates was the fact that 52 per cent of them came from families in which

173

other family members were socially deviant (most often parents). Social deviancy of the fathers and mothers was present in 44 per cent of cases, whereas brothers and sisters were deviant in 23 per cent of cases. If we look more closely at the social deviation of parents, we find that in most cases this consisted of alcoholism in the father. Out of sixty-three inmates at Logatec we had twenty-five cases where the father was alcoholic and three cases in which both parents were alcoholics. If we consider the destructive influence of alcohol on the entire family life and how much continual trauma is related to this social disease, then we may well say that in our group of inmates alcoholism was one of the strongest aetiological factors for dyssocial behaviour. It is typical of the educational atmosphere of the alcoholic family that physical punishment and revenge is out of proportion to the child's offences and mistakes; thus punishment loses its primary educational significance and becomes an end in itself in that it serves as the parents' easiest and most available means of discharging their own aggressive impulses. In such circumstances the child experiences on his own skin the unfavourable role of the weakest and least powerful, completely at the mercy of the whim and tyranny of the more powerful. Unfairness and cruelty surround him, and he develops hatred and the wish for revenge. We may also conclude that in many cases alcoholism is also the cause of poverty in the family, and the source of social stigma for the children, a stigma that by itself presses the child towards the edge of society.

Displacement of inmates

This is a second negative factor, with many far-reaching consequences. By displacement we mean that during childhood the inmate was sent away from the home for a period of one year or more, and in this way completely changed his socialising environment. Clinical psychology (Bowlby)[5] describes such displacement as a true life trauma or mental shock for the child. Displacement forcibly tears up the roots with which the child had emotionally and socially attached himself to his environment, and at the same time destroys the environment in which the child had built some sort of psychological stability based on a feeling of security. Displacement also implies the disruption of the identification process with 'significant others'. Repeated displacement makes identification and the forming of emotional ties with the changing environment impossible. Bowlby, who refers to the research of other authors, calls attention to the fateful consequences, in the form of emotional traumas, which result from displacement in the preschool period. He also finds unfavourable consequences during the school years up to the time of puberty, at which time the child begins to establish independence and is no longer so unconditionally dependent on his immediate environment.

The results of our survey reveal a very unfavourable picture of displacement. Only 38 per cent of the inmates spent their entire childhood with their parents – that is, were never displaced in childhood. All the other inmates, in other words the majority, were displaced at least once (21 per cent) or even several times (41 per cent) during childhood. In 10 per cent of cases the parents put their children in foster homes at an early age, 30 per cent were displaced during the school years, and repeated displacement in both developmental periods was found in 22 per cent of cases. Many of the children who were sent away from home in early childhood became educationally neglected and were already being sent by the foster parents or social welfare offices to institutions during the school years. Some of them were sent from one institution to the other before coming to Logatec, and showed fairly typical and unfavourable signs of hospitalisation. It is not surprising that these inmates included the most difficult cases, who were most often refractory to any kind of help in the institution.

The displacement of our inmates often took place in very poor social and educational circumstances. They were often sent from one unsuitable educational environment to one even less suitable, with resultant increases in educational neglect. They became uncaring, distrustful travellers from one environment to the next, unable to form emotional ties even with those who truly wished to help.

Physical defects of the inmates

We did not have any inmates with severe physical handicaps, since we did not accept into the institution invalids that would have required special help and rehabilitation. However, in our survey we found minor physical defects or psychosomatic disturbances such as stuttering, bed-wetting, hyperactivity, mild spinal deformities as evidenced by poor posture, and defects in appearance such as stunting of growth, protruding ears, poorly developed secondary sexual characteristics, and so on. We made note of these minor physical defects because they can make young people feel ill at ease and inferior, and make contact with other people, particularly the opposite sex, more difficult. Finally, they are often the cause for ridicule from others.

We found these kinds of physical defects in 46 per cent of our inmates. The number of inmates affected in this way is so great that physical defects should be included with the other disturbances and difficulties in life mentioned above. In cases in which the defect in appearance or other physical defect could be medically corrected, the institution at Logatec sent the inmate to a hospital.

Educational neglect

Educational neglect is the next serious life and socialisation circumstance which plays an obvious role in the aetiology of dyssocial behaviour in our inmates. By educational neglect we mean that the child gets too few suitable educational influences in the family. The child does not communicate with the culture of his environment on a proper level, and therefore is unable to develop those kinds of abilities which are important for life in society. Defects in the psychological sphere arise if spiritual and personal growth does not receive the necessary social and educational inputs and cultural experiences, which are the stimuli for growth of the mind. These are serious disturbances which are difficult, if not impossible, to correct in later developmental periods.

Among our inmates we frequently found that no one had seriously concerned themselves with the young persons' education, that they were 'homeless' children of the streets to whom no one showed real care, or for whose future no one felt any responsibility. In our inmates we observed an even more severe form of educational neglect, which did not affect only the moral dimension, but also intellectual capability: these inmates frequently had IQs that had been secondarily lowered to the lower limit of 'normal' due to lack of cultural and other educational influences. We also found poorly developed verbal abilities, and stunted emotional and social development and work capabilities. These most severe cases of educational neglect were typically seen in inmates from families of alcoholics, where in addition to the alcoholic father there was also a cold, neglectful mother.

In practice a case of this kind of educational neglect appears as follows. The mother and father take no interest in the child or his education, and the child is for the most part left to the streets, does whatever it wants and becomes wild and self-willed. No one raises the child or cares for the development of its abilities and necessary social qualities. From time to time the child is cruelly punished and roughly handled without regard to whether he actually did something bad or not, but simply because he is the most suitable and available object for the parent's aggression. We met with similar cases that involved very primitive self-supporting mothers who sent their child to one unsuitable foster home after another, became totally estranged from the child, but upon hearing of some problem with the child would beat the child with abandon.

Milder forms of educational neglect were also caused by the subcultural family environment in which no one knows how to raise the child and give him the higher level of culture that characterises the city. The parents of children in this situation were farmers who had moved to the city and had little education — less than their job skills. Their lack of education, together with their personal instability, resulted in their inability to adapt to the new city life, not to mention their inability to educate their children to live in the modern city environment.

We found the phenomenon of educational neglect relatively frequently in our inmates: 82 per cent of the inmates showed signs of severe or mild educational neglect. It was so frequent that we may include it among the typical aetiological factors of dyssocial phenomena in our population. The other characteristic finding related to educational neglect was that in our inmates it was most often accompanied by repressive, coercive education.

The high incidence of educational neglect is understandable in that it is a concomitant and result of the many other unfavourable circumstances of socialisation discussed above.

Lack of a true home

One of the traumas that we frequently found in the lives of our inmates was that they had been deprived of any true home. Such inmates had special problems in the institution, for at weekends, when other inmates went home, they had nowhere to go. For the most part they were not orphans, but rather children who had been abandoned, emotionally rejected and forgotten by their parents. They often grew up in foster homes, but when problems appeared they were also abandoned by their foster parents. Some of them grew up with grandparents, but when these people became infirm, the inmates had to go to other relatives, on whom they continued to be dependent. There were also cases in which the home environment disintegrated so much that all trace of human relationship was lost.

Inmates of this kind made up only 20 per cent of the total, but the loss of their hearth and home caused them great suffering. The high percentages related to the various unfavourable socialisation factors, such as family subculture, educational neglect, alcoholism and other forms of social decay, displacement of children in their early years, mild physical defects, and so on, indicate that they cumulate, interwine and condition each other.

177

The question inevitably arises of the severity of personality damage caused to inmates by all these unfavourable life and socialisation factors. This is particularly important because our educational institutions are increasingly being filled with difficult and seriously personally disturbed inmates. In 1963 Dr Kobal conducted a study in which he compared two groups of delinquents, one from London and the other from Slovenia.[6] The two groups were matched for punishable acts and other external characteristics. It was found that the Slovene group of young delinquents was more severely disturbed, more personally distorted, and characterised by more dangerous asocial traits than the London group. This can be partly explained by the more civilised and educationally demanding London environment, which by demanding more of the individual, leads to an earlier intervention by mental hygiene institutions for milder disturbances. But Dr Kobal also found that the Slovene group lived in considerably more difficult living and socialisation conditions than did the London group. Most notable was the greater prevalence of alcoholic fathers and strongly negative father figures in the Slovene group; the Slovene group also had more neglectful, emotionally rejecting mothers. In our research we compared the group of Logatec inmates with the Slovene and London delinquents studied by Dr Kobal in 1963. The comparison showed a worsening of the socialisation conditions for the Logatec group: the employment structure of the fathers was slightly worse; there were more alcoholic fathers and partially broken families, and somewhat more emotionally rejecting mothers. From these comparisons we may conclude that the young people coming to our institutions, including the institution at Logatec, are becoming more difficult to deal with and are characterised by greater asocial disturbances. This fact undoubtedly makes successful education more difficult.

Conclusion

In contrast to the wider environment in which they live, most inmates come to the institution from a so-called subcultural environment.

All the inmates included in our analysis were deprived in the primary and secondary socialisation process. In the primary phase of socialisation the inmates suffered their main deprivation in the emotional sphere, whereas in the secondary socialisation phase the main deprivation was in the area of school and other life successes.

Prior to their entrance into the institution most of the inmates did not have the opportunity of identifying with a positive adult figure. In their development the adult person signified either coercion or impotence, both coupled with emotional indifference. Positive role models from among adults were almost totally lacking.

In light of this history we could expect that the inmates would also transfer this relationship to adults to their relationships with the educational staff.

Notes

[1] Bergant, M., *Themes from pedagogical sociology — The incomplete family*, Cankarjeva založba, Ljubljana 1970; *The living conditions of delinquent youth,* collective authorship, Publication 4 of the Institute of Criminology of the Faculty of Law, Ljubljana 1960. (Publishing House Cankar)

[2] Statistical Year-Book of Yugoslavia 1971, Savezni zavod za statistiku, Belgrade 1971, p. 352. (Federal Statistical Office)

[3] Kobal, M., Biological and developmental aspects of juvenile delinquents, *Bilten republiškega sekretariata za pravosodno upravo* 2, Ljubljana 1964, pp. 1—9. (*Bulletin of Republican Department of Justice*)

[4] Cattel, Raymond B., *Personality*, McGraw-Hill Book Co., New York 1950, p. 239.

[5] Bowlby, John, *Attachment and Loss,* Hogarth Press, London 1969.

[6] Kobal, M., 'Juvenile delinquents from two different cultures' *Revija za kriminalistiko in kriminologijo,* Ljubljana 1965, pp. 101—34. (*Review for Criminalistics and Criminology*)

References

Bergant, Dr Milica, *Themes from Pedagogical Sociology — The Incomplete Family*, Cankarjeva založba, Ljubljana 1970 (Publishing House Cankar)

Bloom, Benjamin, *Stability and Change in Human Characteristics*, John Wiley and Sons, New York 1960.

Bowlby, John, *Attachment and Loss*, Hogarth Press, London 1969.

Brombock, *Social Foundation of Education*, John Wiley and Sons, New York 1969.

Cattel, Raymond B., *Personality*, McGraw-Hill Book Co., New York 1950, p. 239.

Glonar, Ivan, *School Success and the Guardians. Environment and Development of Slovene Children*, Državna založba Slovenije, Ljubljana 1962, pp. 82, 83. (The Slovene Publishing House)

Kneller, Georg, *Educational Anthropology*, John Wiley and Sons, New York 1965.

Kobal, Dr Miloš, 'Biological and developmental aspects of juvenile delinquents' *Bilten republiškega sekretariata za pravosodno upravo* 2, Ljubljana 1964, pp. 1—9. (*Bulletin of Republican Department of Justice*)

Kobal, Dr Miloš, 'Juvenile delinquents from two different cultures' *Revija za kriminalistiko in kriminologijo*, Ljubljana 1965, pp. 101—34. (*Review For Criminalistics and Criminology*)

Luria, A. R., *The Role of the Speech in the Regulation of Normal and Abnormal Behavior*, Pergamon Press, New York 1961.

Ottaway, A. K. C., *Education and Society*, Routledge and Kegan Paul, London 1964, pp. 33—4.

Riesman, F., *The Culturally Deprived Child: Mental Health and Achievement*, John Wiley and Sons, New York 1965.

'Social Conflicts and the socialist development of Yugoslavia' *Zbornik Jugoslovanskega društva za sociologijo*, Part I, Ljubljana 1972, pp. 350—1.

Statistical Year Book of Yugoslavia 1971, Savezni zavod za statistiku, Belgrade 1971, p. 352. (Federal Statistical Office)

Streib-Shanar, *Social Structure and the Family*, Prentice Hall, London and Toronto 1960.

Strodbock, Fred L. *Family Integration Value and Achievement, Education-Economy and Society*, The Free Press of Glencoe, New York 1961, p. 315.

The Living Conditions of Delinquent Youth, collective authorship, Publication 4 of the Institute of Criminology of the Faculty of Law, Ljubljana 1960.

18   Inmates (II)

Vinko SKALAR

DYNAMIC DEVELOPMENT OF THE INMATES

The purpose of measurement of the attitudes of the inmates

We decided to measure attitudes in the experimental institution at regular intervals of six months, so as to determine the changing effect of the permissive institutional atmosphere and the educational process to which the inmates were exposed. We used the Jesness' inventory (see Chapter 7)

Experimental group

Size of the experimental group

All inmates who were accepted into the institution during the experimental period (from September 1967 to 21 July 1971 – 105 inmates were accepted in this time) were included in our measurements of attitudes. Each inmate was to complete his first testing at the time of his admission into the institution. The average length of stay of the inmates in the institution during the experimental period was 18·9 months. Theoretically, an inmate could complete four testings in this time, though of course this did not hold for inmates who were admitted into the institution towards the end of the experimental period. Various objective problems also arose in the organisation of the testing, with the result that it did not take place entirely according to plan. For a number of inmates the first testing was not carried out immediately upon their admission to the institution, or delays occured on subsequent testings (because of holidays, escapes by the inmates, their employment outside of the institution, sickness, and so on). Some inmates refused to take the tests entirely; some refused to co-operate for individual tests. For these reasons the number of inmates became continually smaller on a serial temporal scale (L curve).

We could only include the first five testings in our statistical analysis, since the sample size for the sixth of testing three inmates did not permit statistical analysis.

Characteristics of the experimental group

The experimental institution accepted adolescents, behaviourally disturbed and delinquent male youths of fifteen to eighteen years of age, in compliance with the orders of the court or the social service bodies. The institution used selective certain acceptance criteria, a new practice for our institutions. The following categories of inmates were rejected: those who were mentally ill, youths with a marked psycho-organic syndrome, the mentally defective, the physically invalid, gypsies, and, in the first year of the operation of the institution, leaders of gangs. Thus during the time of the experiment the experimental institution, in contrast with other institutions in Slovenia, had a somewhat selective population, although the category of inmates that the institution rejected constituted a minority of the entire population of juveniles in institutions (about 15 per cent). We assume that the percentage of the rejected inmates was even smaller, since the criteria for rejection could only be applied in very clear cases. The criteria of rejection were also violated several times because of external pressures. Thus the selectiveness of the population in the experimental institution was more theoretical than factual. We shall show the other characteristics of the group in tables.

Control group

Originally we did not plan to have a control group, since the question of the social adaptability of the inmates was not the basic purpose of the experiment, and since there were no institutions in Slovenia that were comparable in all characteristics to the experimental institution. We did not decide to have a control group until the autumn of 1969, for reasons presented in Chapter 16, page 144. We were also interested in changes in the dynamics of the attitudes of the inmates in other institutions, because at that time we found positive developmental trends in the experimental institution. We selected a control group in the educational correctional home (ECH) in Radeče and in the educational institution (EI) in Slivnica — institutions that accept male, adolescent, delinquent youths, as does the experimental institution. In both control institutions we considered those inmates who had been accepted between the 1 September and 31 December 1970. We anticipated that inmates selected in this way could be tested at least four times by the spring of 1972.

Characteristics of the control group in the ECH in Radeče

In the ECH in Radeče we succeeded, between 1 September and 31 December 1970, in selecting a group of twenty-three inmates. During the experimental period some of them were sent to juvenile prisons because of new offences, and some escaped repeatedly or were prematurely released. Thus the group became smaller from one testing to another, and successive testings involved a continually decreasing number of inmates.

Characteristics of the conrol group in the EI in Slivnica

In the same time period as for the ECH in Radeče we were able to select twenty-three inmates in the EI in Slivnica. Also in this case the group became smaller from testing to testing, for similar reasons.

The selected groups from the control institution as one control group

The characteristics of the control groups from ECH in Radeče and EI in Slivnica (age, education, and reason for commitment to the institution) are very similar. Somewhat greater differences are found for the educational structure, but these are not statistically significant. Thus we decided to join both groups from the control institutions into one control group. In order to further evaluate the justification for this combining of groups, we also tested the differences between the two institutions for individual categories of attitudes in the Jesness inventory. We found statistically significant differences only for the categories 'withdrawal' and 'social anxiety'. For both categories, most of the statistically significant differences are in the standard deviation — the population of inmates in the ECH in Radeče is more heterogeneous than the population of inmates in the EI in Slivnica. We found only one statistically significant difference in arithmetic means — for the category 'social anxiety'. We found no other statistically significant differences between the two groups for any of the other categories.

Characteristics of the experimental and control groups

Table 18.1

Group size for individual testings

Test	Experimental group	Control group	ECH Radeče	EI Slivnica
1	98	46	23	23
2	93	38	20	18
3	61	30	18	12
4	42	17	7	10
5	20	–	–	–
6	3	–	–	–

Note: In the statistical calculations we considered five testings for the experimental group, and only the first three consecutive tests for the control group.

Table 18.2

Age (upon admission to the institution)

Age	Experimental group No.	%	Control group No.	%	ECH Radeče No.	%	EI Slivnica No.	%
14	3	2·9	–	–	–	–	–	–
15	22	20·9	5	10·9	2	8·7	3	13·0
16	29	27·6	16	34·7	7	30·5	9	39·1
17	35	33·3	16	34·7	9	39·1	7	30·5
18	14	13·4	7	15·3	4	17·4	3	13·0
19	2	1·9	2	4·4	1	4·3	1	4·4
Total	105	100	46	100	23	100	23	100

Note: The average age for the experimental and control groups at the time of admission was sixteen years.

Table 18.3
Education (at the time of release from the institution)

Grades	Experimental group		Control group		ECH Radeče		EI Slivnica	
	No.	%	No.	%	No.	%	No.	%
4	–	–	3	6·5	3	13·0	–	–
5	6	5·7	5	10·9	5	21·8	–	–
6	13	12·4	9	19·5	4	17·4	5	21·7
7	15	14·3	5	10·9	3	13·0	2	8·7
8	71	67·6	24	52·2	8	34·8	16	69·6
	105	100	46	100	23	100	23	100

Table 18.4
Punishable act (at the time of admission)

	Experimental group		Control group		ECH Radeče		EI Slivnica	
	No.	%	No.	%	No.	%	No.	%
Yes	104	99·8	41	90·0	23	100	18	78·3
No	1	0·2	5	10·0	–	–	5	21·7
	105	100	46	100	23	100	23	100

Selected statistical methods and the manner of presentation of results

For the testing of differences between the experimental and control groups, as well as for the testing of differences on a dynamic time scale for the experimental and control groups, we used the same statistical methods as for the statistical analysis of results from the staff (r, M, SD, and the significance of differences in the parameters M and SD), except in this case we used methods for large samples, with the exception of T_5 for the experimental group, for which the number was twenty. In this case we again used methods for small samples.

In comparing $T_1 : T_2 \dots T_1 : T_5$ we equalised the numbers of the groups. numbers were as follows for comparison of the various relations between the experimental and the control groups:

Experimental group		Control group	
$T_1 : T_2$ . . . . No. = 90		$T_1 : T_2$ . . . . No. = 37	
$T_1 : T_3$ . . . . No. = 59		$T_1 : T_3$ . . . . No. = 30	
$T_1 : T_4$ . . . . No. = 41			
$T_1 : T_5$ . . . . No. = 19			

We shall know the results for only some categories of attitudes; the results for the other categories are contained in the original material. We selected categories which, according to psychological criteria, globally and most typically characterise the degree of social maturity and adaptation. The selected categories were as follows: social maladjustment (1), value orientation (2), immaturity (3), manifest aggression (6), and the general category — asocialization (11).

Results and interpretation

1 Social maladjustment

Test	Experimental group			Control group		
	No.	*M*	*SD*	No.	*M*	*SD*
1	98	67·65	8·89	46	68·51	12·19
2	93	67·1'1	10·41	38	65·67	12·01
3	61	63·41	8·02	30	66·68	13·27
4	42	60·45	6·59	17	65·12	
5	20	60·94	7·99			
6	3	58·67				

$$r = T_1 : T_2, T_1 : T_3 = 0·01 \qquad r = T_1 : T_2, T_1 : T_3 = 0·01$$
$$t = M_1 : M_3, M_1 : M_4, M_1 : M_5 = 0·01 \qquad t = 0$$
$$F = 0 \qquad F = 0$$

There are statistically significant differences between the experimental and control groups for T_1 and T_3 in the standard deviations ($F_1 = 2·108$, significant at a level of 0·05; $F_3 = 2·813$, significant at a level of 0·01)

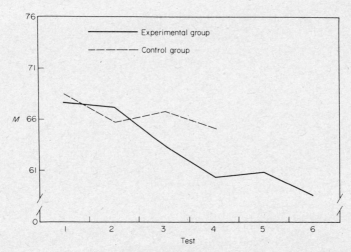

Note: The trend of attitudes generally falls in a positive direction towards smaller social maladjustment for both groups, but more markedly for the experimental group. There are statistically significant differences between the groups in standard deviations, which indicates that the experimental group is more homogeneous than the control group.

2 Value orientation

| Test | Experimental group | | | Control group | | |
	No.	M	SD	No.	M	SD
1	98	62·21	8·78	46	62·76	10·09
2	93	60·81	10·58	38	59·89	10·79
3	61	59·27	10·87	30	58·90	14·20
4	42	57·31	8·84	17	56·88	
5	20	53·40	8·29			
6	3	54·67				

$r = T_1 : T_2, T_1 : T_3, T_1 : T_4 = 0·01$ $r = T_1 : T_2, T_1 : T_3 = 0·01$

$t = M_1 : M_2 = 0·05$

$M_1 : M_3, M_1 : M_4, M_1 : M_5 = 0·01$

$F = 0$ $F = 0$

There is one statistically significant difference between the experimental and control groups in the standard deviations ($F_3 = 2·815$, significant at a 0·01 level)

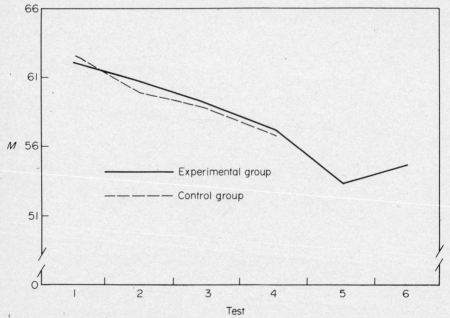

Note: Both groups show a positive trend. The experimental group is more homogeneous than the control group.

Test	Experimental group			Control group		
	No.	*M*	*SD*	No.	*M*	*SD*
1	98	65·54	12·18	46	69·29	9·35
2	93	65·62	10·21	38	66·83	10·79
3	61	64·16	9·78	30	66·93	10·01
4	42	61·17	9·29	17	69·02	
5	20	63·30	9·48			
6	3	66·67				

$r = T_1 : T_2, T_1 : T_4 = 0·01$
$\quad T_1 : T_3, T_1 : T_5 = 0·05$

$t = M_1 : M_4 = 0·01$

$F = SD_1 : SD_2, SD_1 : SD_3 = 0·05$

$r = T_1 : T_2, T_1 : T_3 = 0·05$

$t = M_1 : M_2, M_1 : M_3 = 0·05$

$F = 0$

There are two statistically significant differences between the experimental and control groups: one in arithmetic means, and one in standard deviations, both for T_1 (t_1 = 2·935, significant at a 0·01 level, F_1 = 2·004, significant at a 0·05 level).

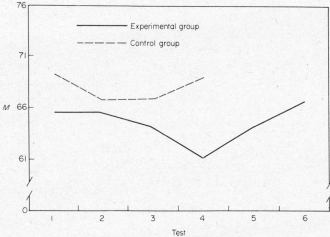

Note: We may consider the trend of attitudes to be generally positive if we disregard the last results (invalid because of the small number); this holds for both the experimental and control groups. However, on a dynamic time scale the results of the experimental group are consistently more positive than those of the control group. The experimental group is less homogeneous than the control group at the first testing.

It is one of the exceptional statistically significant differences between arithmetic means within both groups that, however, could be argued to have a more important meaning. Some authors are of the opinion that the level of immaturity is correlated with the level of social maladjustment.

Test	Experimental groups			Control groups		
	No.	*M*	*SD*	No.	*M*	*SD*
1	98	57·27	9·40	46	56·22	10·32
2	93	55·53	12·59	38	54·19	11·99
3	61	54·07	12·29	30	55·50	15·20
4	42	52·71	9·49	17	53·44	
5	20	51·30	9·18			
6	3	42·00				

$$r = T_1 : T_2, T_1 : T_3, T_1 : T_5 = 0·01 \qquad r = T_1 : T_2, T_1 : T_3 = 0·05$$
$$t = M_1 : M_3, M_1 : M_4 = 0·01 \qquad\qquad t = 0$$
$$\quad M_1 : M_2, M_1 : M_5 = 0·05 \qquad\qquad F = 0$$
$$F = SD_1 : SD_2 = 0·01; SD_1 : SD_3, SD_1 : SD_5 = 0·05$$

There is a statistically significant difference between the experimental and control groups in the arithmetic mean for T_1 (t = 2·148, significant on a 0·01 level). The other differences are not statistically significant.

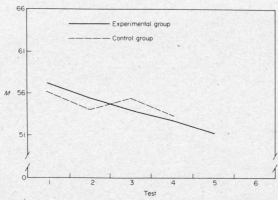

Note: The graphic and numerical trends do not confirm the statistically significant differences between the groups and within the groups that we found in our statistical calculations. The trends are found with the complete numbers. The positive trend from greater towards lesser aggressiveness is more marked and consistent for the experimental group. To a greater extent than seen in the graph, the more positive position of the experimental group can be seen in the numerous statistically significant differences that were found in favour of the experimental group.

5 Asocialisation (general category)

Test	Experimental group			Control group		
	No.	M	SD	No.	M	SD
1	98	63·67	9·38	46	63·89	11·04
2	93	63·70	9·64	38	62·87	11·70
3	61	60·01	9·60	30	62·13	10·24
4	42	59·33	7·49	17	62·48	
5	20	60·00	9·96			
6	3	61·33				

$r = T_1 : T_2, T_1 : T_3 = 0·05$ $\qquad r = T_1 : T_2 = 0·01$

$t = M_1 : M_4 = 0·05$ $\qquad\qquad t = 0$

$F = 0$ $\qquad\qquad\qquad\qquad\quad F = 0$

There are no statistically significant differences between the groups.

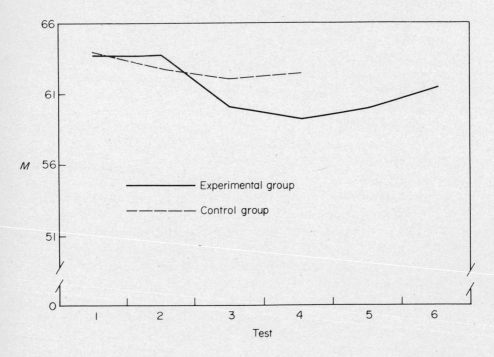

Note: The trend of attitudes is more pronounced for the experimental group than for the control group (the result of the last test is invalid), though the trend is generally positive for both groups.

Summary

In the summary we shall consider all the findings, and not only those which arise from the selected categories and which we showed in the results.

We found some statistically significant differences between the experimental and control groups in standard deviations and the arithmetic means. Significant differences in the standard deviations are found for the categories 'social maladjustment' (T_3), 'value orientation' (T_3), 'alienation' (T_1), 'denial' (T_3), and 'repression' (T_1). All the differences, except for the last one, indicate a greater dispersion or lesser homogeneity of the control group; the difference for the category 'repression' indicates a greater dispersion for the experimental group for T_1.

We found significant differences between the groups in the arithmetic means for the categories 'immaturity' (T_1) and 'repression' (T_1, T_3). In both cases the experimental group has a more favourable position than the control group. However, for the category 'manifest aggression' the significant difference in the arithmetic mean for T_1 shows a more favourable position for the control group.

The experimental group is less prone to the mechanism of repression and thus manifests more aggression than the control group; in addition the experimental group is on the average more mature than the control group.

Despite the small differences between the experimental and the control groups (ou of sixty-six possible variations we found only nine statistically significant differences: four in arithmetic means and five in standard deviations), which do not allow the conclusion that there are statistically significant differences between the experimental and control groups, we find markedly different dynamics and differing characteristics within the experimental and control groups on a temporally dynamic scale.

In the experimental group there are seven categories for which the positive trend is confirmed by statistically significant differences in the arithmetic means; for three categories the trends are less marked but globally are still positive; only for the category 'denial' is the trend negative.

For the control group, a positive trend with statistically significant differences between the arithmetic means is found for three categories; for seven categories there is no clear trend, but rather a fluctuation in a positive and negative direction. As for the experimental group, the trend for the category 'denial' is negative.

There are more statistically significant differences in the standard deviations for the experimental group than for the control group. For the experimental group we find marked differences in five categories. In all cases the group increases its dispersion with successive testings. This means that educational influences and the circumstances of institutional life caused the group to become increasingly differentiated.

The correlations for the relations $T_1 : T_2$ and $T_1 : T_3$ are statistically significant for both the experimental and the control groups. With subsequent testings the experimental group showed a decreasing number of statistically significant correlations, which indicates that the inmates changed their attitudes.

We may conclude that the dynamics of attitudes on a temporal scale is more favourable for the experimental than for the control group. The differences, for the most part in favour of the experimental group, can be ascribed to the permissive atmosphere in the experimental institution, which can be supposed to have accelerated socialisation more than the atmosphere prevailing in the control institutions.

19   Inmates (III)

Vinko SKALAR

RESULTS OF THE PERSONALITY TESTS GIVEN TO THE POPULATION OF INMATES

During the experimental period we gave the inmates of the experimental and control institutions a series of personality tests. There were two purposes for these tests:

1   To measure possible changes in some personality dimensions of the inmates of the experimental institution during their stay there.
2   To measure possible differences in personality structure between the experimental and control groups.

Explanation

Purpose 1. Inmates who were admitted to the experimental institution via the observation centre were already personally diagnosed. In the autumn of 1968 we arranged with the psychologist of the observation centre to administer a well-established series of test instruments. We arranged for the following tests: progressive matrices[1] (intelligence test), Bender Gestalt test,[2] MMQ[3] (questionnaire for the discovery of neuroses), the Mooney list of personal problems,[4] Sachs projective sentences[5] and 0–I[6] (personal interest test). We soon abandoned the 0–I test because it was too difficult for our population. The psychologist of the observation centre also tested the inmates with the same series of tests upon their release from the experimental institution. The number of inmates for whom we carried out the comparison between the initial and final testings was different for different tests and on the whole small, since many inmates rejected the testing either in parts or entirely, or completed the tests so that they were unusable.

Purpose 2. The small number of statistically significant differences between the experimental and control groups for the Jesness inventory, in particular the frequent identity of the results of the first testing, especially for the asocial index, supports the hypothesis that there are no essential

195

differences in the personalities of the populations of inmates which the courts or the social service bodies direct to the different institutions, with their régimes of differing severity. We wanted to test this hypothesis with personality tests.

For the population of inmates that we had selected, from both control institutions, as a control group for the testing of attitudes, we applied the same series of personality tests as was used in the experimental institution. Since we did not conduct the personality test immediately upon selection of the control group, we do not have results for the entire number (forty-six) for whom we have results for the initial testing with the Jesness inventory.

The numbers of inmates in the experimental institution that were compared for the initial and final testings were as follows:

Test:	Progressive matrices	Mooney	Bender	MMQ
No.:	42	24	42	27

The numbers of inmates that were compared between the experimental and the control groups were as follows:

Test:	Progressive matrices	Mooney	Bender	MMQ
Experimental group:	55	38	58	41
Control group:	39	40	40	40

The results of the Sachs projective sentences are not included in the statistical analysis here, since in the experimental period they were not evaluated quantitatively, but rather only qualitatively. Additional quantitative analysis would have been too time-consuming, especially since we received a large number of the protocols from the observation centre only recently.

Hypotheses

1   We assume that there are no statistically significant differences for the experimental group between the initial testing and the testing upon release from the institution.

The length of stay of the inmates in the institution was too short (an average of 18·9 months) and the educational influence of insufficient intensity to bring about changes in personality dimensions.

2   We assume that at the first testing there are no statistically significant differences in individual personality dimensions between the experimental and control groups, since the two populations of inmates are presumably similar in personality structure at the time of admission to the institution.

Results of individual personality tests

For the purposes of comparison we have included (except for the MMQ test) data from several special groups and from groups of the general population[7]. For determination of differences between the groups we used the same statistical methods as for the Jesness inventory.

Results of the tests are given in Tables 19.1 to 19.9.

Table 19.1
Progressive matrices

	Non-delinquent population (1957)	Delinquent population (1957)	Experimental group First test	Last test	Control group
No.	405	86	42(55)	42	40
M	39·30	28·17	37·19(36·95)	41·72	35·98
SD	8·29	9·71	7·01(7·84)	6·79	9·45

Experimental group – initial testing: last testing

$r = 0.01$
$t = 0.01$ (the group had greater success at the second testing)
$F = 0$
Experimental group: control group

$t = 0$
$F = 0$

Note:. The numbers in parentheses for the experimental group for the first testing refer to the entire number in the experimental group which we compared with the control group. For comparison between the first and last tests of the experimental group we used equalised groups – i.e., equalised numbers.

Table 19.2

Bender Gestalt test (raw scores)

High school students		Industrial workers	Experimental group		Control group
			First test	Last test	
No.	216	314	42(58)	42	40
M	7·08	14·63	30·36(29·24)	26·72	21·43
SD	6·49	6·14	18·39(17·56)	14·85	12·91

Table 19.3

Distribution of results by classes

Class	Experimental group 1	Experimental group 2	Control group
0– 4	0	1	2
5– 9	6	0	2
10–14	6	8	9
15–19	7	6	10
20–24	6	7	5
25–29	9	2	2
30–34	3	3	4
35–39	5	7	2
40–44	5	3	2
45–49	4	2	1
50–54	0	2	0
55–59	3	0	0
60–64	1	0	1
65 and over	3	1	0

Experimental group — initial testing: last testing

$r = 0·01$
$t = 0$
$F = 0$

Experimental group: control group
$t = 0·05$ (the result is more negative for the experimental group)
$F = 0·05$ (the experimental group shows greater dispersion)

Table 19.4

MMQ (questionaire for the determination of neuroses). Detector of neuroses

| | Experimental group | | Control group |
	First testing	Last testing	
No.	27 (41)	27	40
M	13·37 (12·05)	13·19	13·60
SD	5·87 (6·05)	7·49	7·77

Table 19.5

Distribution by classes (clinical norms)

Class	Experimental group 1	Experimental group 2	Control group
0–14 (normal)	28	16	23
15–20 (suspected neurosis	9	6	8
21–26 (mild neurosis)	4	5	7
27–38 (severe neurosis)	0	0	2

Experimental group – initial testing: last testing

$r = 0·05$
$t = 0$
$F = 0$

Experimental group: control group

$t = 0$
$F = 0$

Table 19.6

MMQ (questionnaire for the determination of neuroses). Detector of lies

| | Experimental group | | Control group |
	First testing	Last testing	
No.	27 (41)	27	40
M	4·00 (4·78)	5·04	7·05
SD	2·48 (2·97)	3·13	3·77

Table 19.7
Distribution by grades (clinical norms)

Grade	Experimental group 1	Experimental group 2	Control group
0– 2 (dissimulation)	11	6	6
3– 9 (normal)	26	18	24
10–12 (suspicion of simulation)	3	3	6
13–18 (simulation)	1	0	4

Experimental group – initial testing: last testing

$r = 0{\cdot}01$
$t = 0$
$F = 0$

Experimental group: control group

$t = 0{\cdot}01$ (the control group was less sincere in its answers)
$F = 0$

Interpretation of results

1 We find no statistically significant differences between the experimental and control groups in intelligence level. The results for both groups are within the average range and approximate a non-delinquent population from the year 1957 more than a delinquent population. This phenomenon presumably results from at least the following factors:

– In 1957 tests were little known in Yugoslavia and used rarely. The generally poor results for both normal and special groups in all kinds of tests may be due to unfamiliarity with tests.

– Progressive matrices were first used in1957, whereas later this test was frequently used in schools, in vocational guidance and other applications. We assume that the majority of the inmates in the control and the experimental groups had already taken this test at least once.

– It is probable that the delinquent population in recent years has been selected otherwise than was the case in 1957. Delinquents are less exclusively recruited from the lowest social strata – a phenomenon that has been confirmed by numerous analyses in recent years.

Table 19.8: Mooney list of personal problems

| | Cadets | | Experimental group | | | | Control group | |
| | | | First testing | | Last testing | | | |
	M	SD	M	SD	M	SD	M	SD
1 Health problems	1·57	1·91	6·08 (5·61)	3·29 (3·43)	5·13	2·63	6·98	3·88
2 School problems	2·72	2·62	8·29 (7·32)	6·19 (5·69)	5·75	4·39	6·87	5·09
3 Family problems	2·36	2·83	11·96 (11·11)	4·49 (4·76)	11·08	5·07	10·64	5·36
4 Economic problems	4·89	3·68	11·67 (10·61)	5·96 (5·97)	9·75	4·78	9·95	4·89
5 Interpersonal relations	3·51	3·52	8·50 (8·08)	5·45 (5·98)	5·92	4·45	8·10	4·69
6 Problems of self-assertion	2·14	2·71	9·83 (9·24)	4·24 (4·72)	7·17	4·77	9·00	5·92
7 Personality problems	2·77	3·24	10·79 (10·05)	5·68 (5·69)	8·25	6·11	9·85	5·86
8 Total result	20·00	15·80	67·13 (62·24)	26·75 (27·54)	53·04	25·25	61·39	28·11
	No. = 314		No. = 24 (38)				No. = 39	

Experimental group – first testing: last testing

Health problems	$(r = 0.05; t = 0; F = 0)$
School problems	$(r = 0.01; t = 0.05; F = 0)$
Family problems	$(r = 0; t = 0; F = 0)$
Economic problems	$(r = 0; t = 0; F = 0)$
Interpersonal relations	$(r = 0.05; t = 0.05; F = 0)$
Problems of self-assertion	$(r = 0.05; t = 0.01; F = 0)$
Personality problems	$(r = 0; t = 0; F = 0)$
Total result	$(r = 0; t = 0.05; F = 0)$

Experimental group: control group
There are no statistically significant differences between the groups for any of the subtests.

2   We find a statistically significant difference for the experimental group in the first and last testing with the progressive matrices; on average the results are more favourable for the last testing. The results of the second testing are still within the range of the normal average, but none the less the change is obvious. This may be explained in terms of greater familiarity with the test, with more favourable motivation (prior to release) of the inmates, and a favourable institutional atmosphere which supported improvement.

3   In comparison with the normal population, the results of the Bender Gestalt test are less favourable for both the control and the experimental groups, and indicate personality deviation which is more pronounced for the experimental than for the control group. The standard deviation is markedly high for the experimental group, which supports the conclusion that this negative result can be ascribed to a sub group of inmates with a markedly pathological personality picture. This conclusion is supported with the frequency results by grades. If a group of seven inmates with the worst results were excluded from the experimental group, there would be no statistically significant differences between the groups.

There are no statistically significant differences between the first and last testings with the Bender test.

4   For the MMQ test we do not have the results of a comparison group from the normal population. The author's clinical norms can serve to orient us, as shown in the distribution of results by grades (tables on pages 199 and 200). These norms reveal that, for the most neurotic, symptoms are not appreciable for the experimental and control groups. There are no statistically significant differences between the experimental and control groups, nor are there statistically significant differences between the initial and final testings of the experimental group. This result is consistent with the theoretical findings — i.e., that neurotic symptoms are less characteristic of the delinquent population than is deviation in behaviour manifested in extroverted, aggressive forms.

Of interest are the differences between the experimental and control groups as revealed by the detector of lies. Specifically, the control group were significantly less honest in their answers than were the experimental groups. This difference can probably be explained as a result of the different institutional climate to which members of the control group were exposed.

5   The Mooney list of personal problems revealed that the experimental

group, as well as the control group, exhibited many more personal problems than did a population of candidates for a military school. For both groups problems in connection with the family, problems of a material nature, problems in connection with self-assertion and personal problems are particularly prominent. There are no statistically significant differences between the experimental and control groups for any of the sub-categories.

There are several differences between the first and last testings of the experimental group. These are primarily in the sub-categories of school problems, problems in connection with interpersonal relationships, and problems in connection with self-assertion. The group attained more favourable results in the last testing for all of these sub-categories. At the last testing the group showed fewer problems in areas in which the institutional atmosphere and the specific institutional possibilities could to some extent compensate for past deficits.

Summary

1   The hypothesis that there are no statistically significant differences between the experimental and control groups was confirmed. It was apparently contradicted by the results of the Bender test, which showed a greater number of problems in the experimental group, as well as by the results of the detector of lies in the MMQ test, which showed that the control group were less honest than the experimental group. The differences in the MMQ test are presumably a result of the situation, whereas the results of the Bender test show a difference in favour of the control group because of a subgroup of seven inmates with pronounced pathological results in the test.

The results of the Jesness inventory relevant to the question of maturity contradicted the hypothesis (see the section concerning the dynamic development of the inmates). Maturity, which is defined in several different ways in the literature, was not included in the personality tests that we used. However, the literature ascribes considerable importance to maturity, with reference to the possiblity of successful treatment and the prognostic possibilities of institutional education. In Warren's opinion, as well as that of others, successful treatment is more likely with more mature inmates. Thus it would be necessary to treat inmates in groups arranged according to level of maturity, and to adapt treatment methods to the various levels of maturity.

If we take this point of view, then, despite the finding that there are no personality differences between the inmates that the courts and social welfare offices send to various institutions, we assume that there are differences in the level of maturity, and that the inmates sent to Radeče are less mature.

This factor is worthy of special attention in future research. It is interesting that Jesness does not consider maturity in the global score—asocial index.

2   The hypothesis that no differences exist between the first and last testings of the experimental group was partly confirmed and partly rejected. It was confirmed by the tests that measure complex aspects of the personality, and contradicted by the tests that measure specific personality dimensions that are more sensitive to situational influences.

Notes

[1]   Progressive matrices, non-verbal intelligence test. L.S. Penrose and J.C. Raven, Great Britain 1938.
[2]   Bender Gestalt test, L. Bender, USA 1938.
[3]   MMQ (questionnaire for determination of the degree of neuroticism), Maudsley hospital, Great Britain 1948.
[4]   Mooney list for survey of personal problems, Ross L. Mooney, Office for the study of education, Ohio 1950.
[5]   Sachs, J. M., and Levy, S., 'The sentence completion test' in Abt., L.E., and Bellak, L., *Projective Psychology*, A. A. Knopf, New York 1952, p. 370–97.
[6]   O–I (personality and interest test) adaptation and standardisation of the Vienna version of the MMPI.
[7]   See Chapter 7.

20 Inmates: Some Special Observations

Milica BERGANT, Franc HOČEVAR, Bronislav SKABERNE

SCHOOLING AND INTERESTS OF THE INMATES

A high percentage of the inmates had no definite life of professional goals (62 per cent). Only a quarter of them expressed a wish to learn a trade and thus become self-supporting. That this professional goal was also somewhat remote for our inmates is shown by the fact that only 13 per cent of them achieved it by successfully completing a part of the trade school while they were in the institution. Their low level of aspiration is rather realistic, since their efforts to become qualified were also hindered by incomplete elementary schooling.

The data concerning the interests and activities of the inmates are more favourable (30 per cent are involved in sports, 20 per cent with popular music, and 13 per cent with both activities. Only 17 per cent of the inmates showed no interest in free-time activities). Comparison with research done ten years ago shows improvement in this area. The number of Logatec inmates that are interested in independent activities is considerably higher than was the case ten years ago among our dyssocial juveniles. This fact is important because it was with recreational activities that some of the most difficult juveniles, who at first completely rejected the institution, were drawn into institutional life.

In our research we tried to survey the course of the inmates' compulsory education and to determine when and why school difficulties began to accumulate.

We found that our inmates began the first grade without difficulties and that pronounced drop-out did not occur before the fourth grade (15 per cent). Poor school success continued in the fifth grade and reached its maximum in the sixth grade, with 30 per cent. From the fourth to the sixth grades the drop-out rate totalled 66 per cent, whereas in the second and third grades it was only 5 per cent. Only a minority of the inmates reached the seventh and eighth grades and finished elementary school. The reasons given by the teachers for this poor school success were: laziness and disorderliness (58 per cent), educational neglect and poor psychological development (30·2 per cent), and problems of discipline involving truancy, fighting and stealing (8·7 per cent).

Conflicts over discipline between students and with the school appeared earlier in our group than did school failure. In this respect the first grade was also free from particular difficulties. But by the second grade the percentage of inmates who had disciplinary problems rapidly rose to 23 per cent and remained high in subsequent grades. The reasons for the disciplinary problems were: stealing, lying (44·7 per cent), unauthorised absence from and disturbance of instruction (32·7 per cent), and general educational neglect (22·9 per cent). Potential dyssocial disturbances in our inmates thus were clearly visible during the elementary school years and before puberty. This leads to the conclusion that in the future it will be necessary to organise preventive and resocialisation measures at this early time, though these measures should not result in stigmatisation and prosecution in the courts.

Schooling in the institution

The institution organised instruction, intended to help the inmates complete elementary school, according to an elastic programme and system of education for adults. In general, the inmates did not show particular enthusiasm to prepare themselves and learn in school. Despite this resistance, the majority of inmates completed at least one grade of compulsory schooling in the institution (70 per cent), and some attempted to complete two years. The inmates who lacked only two years of elementary schooling were better motivated for school work. 24 per cent of the inmates actually completed two grades in the institution and thus completed their compulsory schooling, while 6·3 per cent failed to complete even a single grade in the institution and more or less openly rejected all instruction. All of the inmates were also involved in various trade workshops and schools in the institution and had the opportunity for learning a trade and for other more demanding learning. In general they were better motivated for learning a trade than for school work. None the less, they did not show as much success in this as they did in the completing of the grades they lacked. Some inmates were hindered in their learning of a trade by their incomplete elementary education, which in Yugoslavia is prerequisite for serious trade-school training. 68 per cent of the inmates were successfully apprenticed and only 13 per cent of the inmates passed all the practical and theoretical tests for the first year of trade school. 44 per cent of the inmates tried to become trained, but did not complete all of the necessary tests. There were also 8 per cent of inmates who did not undertake any kind of serious work or trade-school education.

We determined the school success and trades education of our inmates because these accomplishments belong to the area of so-called productivity, which can be realistically evaluated and measured. These results also relate to the work of the institution, particularly because we observed that the inmates could become seriously involved in school and learning a trade only after they had settled down and oriented themselves in the resocialisation process. In keeping with the school and trade successes of the inmates, the institution directed their employment or schooling after release from the institution.

M.B.

RELATIONS BETWEEN PARENTS AND INMATES[1]

Problem

For adolescents, particularly those in late adolescence, there is a decreased need for establishing ties with parents. Maintenance of ties is influenced by social factors and the atmosphere of the family environment. Adolescents seek basic models of behaviour outside the family circle; but it is probable that the basis for these role models is established in the family. Adolescents tend towards independence and, at least outwardly, the least possible emotional and social attachment to the family.

The possibility of maintaining ties with the family is reduced when the development of the child takes place under constant emotional and social pressures. None the less, it is important to the adolescent in general (including behaviourally and personally disturbed juveniles) to maintain ties with parents and family, not only because of economic dependence, but also because of the feeling of relative security which the family environment offers.

In the everyday functioning of institutional education it is a question of knowing in which cases it is necessary to encourage relations between inmates and their families, and in which cases intensification of these ties is contra-indicated.

Population and research methods

The data were gathered for inmates who lived in the educational institution at Logatec from December 1970 to April 1971. During this time it was possible to observe the contacts of thirty-seven inmates with their families. At that time there were six other inmates in the institution, but one had escaped, two were at trade schools outside the institution, and three were released from the institution during this time.

The sources of data for our analysis were:

— records of the inmates (social histories, psychological tests and psychological observations, pedagogic reports, opinions of psychiatrists, paediatricians and other experts, elementary school records, minutes of professional meetings in the institution, teachers' reports, court decisions)
— questionnaire concerning inmates' visits home
— questionnaire concerning visits by family members to the institution

– supplemental interviews with inmates and teachers
– observation of inmates' moods upon their return from a visit home or during a visit by family members to the institution
– participation in the meetings of the institutional staff during the time of the author's practical training in the institution.

A large amount of data was gathered in this way. Unfortunately the observed population was too small to allow detailed comparisons between the various sources of information. Therefore the study remains on the level of a description of the individual factors, though together these give such similar results that certain general conclusions about the observed population can be made.

Results

Twenty-four (65 per cent) of the inmates were between seventeen and twenty years of age (late adolescence), and thirteen were from fifteen to sixteen years of age (early adolescence). The inmates orginated as follows:

– fifteen (41) per cent came from complete families (before coming to the institution they lived with both parents and the other family members);
– sixteen (43) per cent came from incomplete families (before coming to the institution they lived with one of the parents – usually the mother, but sometimes with a step father or step mother);
– six (16 per cent) came from substitute families (before coming to the institution they lived with foster parents or relatives).

The data permitted construction of a summary of the family and social problems into eighteen categories.

The average number of different problems was:[2]

– inmates from complete families   3·13 problems
– inmates from incomplete families   4·12 problems
– inmates from substitute families   6·25 problems

It was not possible to measure the intensity of individual problems. We found emotional disturbances in early childhood in all the inmates.

We tried to determine (see Table 20.1) which of the parents had good relations with the inmates by reviewing things the inmates had written, with the teachers' opinions adding to and correcting the information we obtained in this manner.

Table 20.1

Acceptance of the inmates

Which of the parents accepts the inmate	Number of inmates
Mother and father	6
Mother only	14
Neither father or mother	12
Not known	5
Total	37

In most cases the half-brothers and half-sisters were much younger than the inmates. Some of the inmates were emotionally attached to them, but in all cases there was rivalry with the brothers and sisters, or half-brothers and half-sisters.

The Sachs sentence completion test was available for determining the relationships of the inmates to their families (thirty-three inmates took the test). See Table 20.2.

Table 20.2

Relationship of inmates to their families

Relationship	to mothers	to fathers	to family
Positive	22	10	13
Undecided	8	8	5
Negative	3	15	15

From 19 December 1970, to 16 April 1971 we followed the contacts of inmates with their families by means of special questionnaires. During this time thirty-five inmates had 254 contacts (for two inmates the records are incomplete).

During this period of approximately four months the inmates from different types of families had the following numbers of contacts:

— inmates from complete families   9·8 contacts
— inmates from incomplete families   6·3 contacts
— inmates from substitute families   4·3 contacts

Seventeen inmates were visited in the institution by parents and others (twelve inmates once to twice; five inmates three times and more). Except in two cases, the visits of parents to the institution lasted less than one hour. During their visits, all the parents also spoke with teachers, the social worker and the principal of the institution. These people report that the parents were interested and participated in discussion. It is interesting that many of the parents did not talk with the inmates at all. Most of the contacts between parents and inmates in the institution were short, on average less than fifteen minutes. These visits usually took place within the institution. In only seven out of thirty-seven visits did the parents and the inmate go on a short outing or visit a restaurant (even though the staff encouraged this kind of visiting and did not hinder it for any of the inmates).

Inmates who had been in this or other institutions for a longer time had less contact with their families than those who had been in an institution for a shorter time. Longer institutionalisation is also correlated with a greater number of problems in the family and poor interpersonal relationships.

We evaluated the moods of the inmates upon return to the institution from home as follows:

- normal mood (no observable significant   157 occasions
  differences in behaviour)
- spoke about the visit   59 occasions
- had been given something at home   44 occasions
- inmate was in a bad mood on returning   18 occasions
- inmate was subdued   9 occasions
- inmate was drunk   5 occasions
- mood could not be determined   22 occasions

Inmates that had a greater number of contacts with their families were generally in a good mood on their return. Inmates with less frequent contacts did not show significant changes when they returned. We conclude that the positive effect is also influenced by the frequency or continuity of the contacts.

On the basis of all these findings we conclude:

- that during the observation period about 30 per cent of the inmates had the opportunity of returning to their families after their release from the institution;
- that 70 per cent of the parents (one or both) could participate in the educational process;
- and that it would be necessary to prepare about 30 per cent of the inmates for a completely independent life after release from the institution — i.e., a life independent of the family group.

Evaluation of work in the institution

Contacts of inmates with their families were left to the daily schedule rather than purposely included in the educational programme. The possibilities of including these contacts in the educational programme remained unexploited. On the other hand the absence of the inmates from the institution meant a welcome reduction in work for the staff, and on the other hand the visits of the parents to the institution meant an unwelcome addition to their work.[3]

On average, nearly every inmate had two contacts per month with his parents. Our evalution shows that inmates from other, similar institutions in Slovenia do not have as frequent contacts with members of their families. The reasons for the relatively large number of contacts must be sought in the openness of the institution and the work principles adopted by the staff (based on the relatively greater permissiveness and democracy than the other institutions). The teachers encourage the inmates to intensify their contacts with their families.

F.H.

FOLLOW-UP DATA

Method of gathering personal history data

In May 1972 the professional team agreed to gather information about inmates who were released from the educational institution during the experiment.

First we found out from the institution which inmates had been released. Then, in July 1972, we sent forms containing the basic information about the inmates to the social welfare offices in the communities, requesting that they gather information concerning:

— with whom the inmate is at present living
— what he is doing
— whether and how he is employed
— jobs held since release from the institution
— whether he is attending school, and if so, what grade
— whether he had been involved with the courts since his release from the institution.

Finally, the social welfare office was also to give its opinion of the degree of success with which the inmate had become a part of society following his release.

We gathered this data, concerning sixty-five inmates, from twenty-six social welfare offices in Slovenia. In analysing the data we considered the findings for only fifty-eight inmates (those who had been released at least one year previously — i.e., before July 1971). Thus we ignored data for the seven inmates who were released after 1 July 1971.

Since the data were gathered by social welfare offices, which also deal with the social problems of dyssocial youth, we considered the data quite reliable and able to give an impression of the problems, or lack of them, for former inmates after their release from the institution. For financial reasons we had to forego the determination, with psychological techniques, of the problematical or adjusted nature of these inmates.

Results

From the data gathered for fifty-eight inmates we initially excluded three inmates who had since died (one in a motor accident, another in a parachuting accident in the military, and a third by committing suicide when abroad). In addition we had to drop six more inmates from the study, because the social welfare offices were not able to gather data about them due either to their place of residence being unknown or to the fact that they had been in the army for the entire time since their release from the institution. Thus our group was reduced to forty-nine inmates.

We classified the inmates in three groups: 'not problematical', 'problematical' and 'probably problematical'.

As 'not problematical' we included inmates who had a permanent place of residence, steady employment, did not come before the courts again, and who, in the opinion of the social welfare agencies, had become well-integrated into their environment.

We considered as 'problematical' those inmates who had appeared before the courts again after leaving the institution. For the most part, they did not get jobs after release and, in the opinion of the social welfare agencies, their re-education in the educational institution was not a success.

In the group 'probably problematical' we included inmates who did not settle down after release, got only odd jobs, and caused further disturbance in their environment, even though they did not come before the courts.

According to these criteria, the individual groups contained the following numbers of released inmates:

not problematical	29
problematical	14
probably problematical	6

We compared these personal characteristics with the prognostic asocial index of Jesness. We calculated the arithmetic means of the last asocial indices before release from the institution, with the results shown in Table 20.3.

Table 20.3

	Number	Arithmetic means of the asocial indices
Not problematical	27*	56·7
Problematical	12*	63·5
Probably problematical	6	66·8

* Four inmates were not considered because they did not complete the last test.

214

If we consider that the norm according to Jesness is fifty points and that scores in excess of fifty indicate an increased degree of asocial inclinations, we see that the arithmetic mean of the asocial index is less favourable for the 'probably problematical' inmates than the 'problematical' ones. Therefore we grouped the group of 'probably problematical' inmates with the 'problematical' ones for comparison with the 'not problematical' group.

Table 20.4

Prognosis and personal data

Prognosis according to the asocial index of Jesness	Personal data			
	Number of inmates		Percentage	
	Not problematical	Problematical	Not problematical	Problematical
44–49	4	–		
50–54	6	2	37	[11]
55–59	7	4	55·5	44·5
60–64	8	4		
65–69	–	2		
70–74	2	3	[7·5]	44·5
75–79	–	1		
80–84	–	2		
Total	27	18	100	100

$Chi^2 = 9.66$; significant at the $p = 0.01$ level

Our results (see Table 20.4) indicate that the Jesness Asociability Index is also a good prognostic measure for our situation,[4] even though the test has not been standardised for Slovenia. It is possible that the standardisation of the test here would show a lower average for behaviourally average youth than Jesness found for the United States, this being due to the differences in the degree of urbanisation (smaller cities in Slovenia) and differences in the social and cultural conditions.

Finally, in 1969 and 1970 we twice compared the prognoses derived from the Jesness test with the prognoses given by the teachers. We found no correlation.

B.S.

Notes

[1] During the experiment the author — as a student at the Defectological High School in Zagreb — practised in the educational home at Logatec. This contribution is a summary of his diploma work 'Development of relationships among inmates and their parents, and the possibilities of returning home after release from the institution' submitted to the school authorities in December 1972.

[2] The results of the Mooney test (210 items) were also available to determine the family problems. For the analysis thirty-three items were considered which relate to the family situation. On average the inmates listed nine items (problems). According to the results of this test, there is no difference between inmates from variously structured families.

[3] For the institution's social worker, this was the first job after graduation. She was young and, due to family circumstances, was often absent from her working place. She was responsible for many administrative matters in the institution: for instance the compilation of dossiers, care of money for the inmates, the writing of reports for the courts; she also took part in court proceedings and had dealings with the social services and so on. In 1970 the Institute of Criminology suggested to the responsible office that the Institution should be given another social workers. The suggestion was not accepted.

[4] Similar results have been found by:
— Davies, Martin, *The use of the Jesness Inventory on a Sample of British Probationers*, Home Office publ. 12, Her Majesty's Stationery Office, London 1967;
— Mott, Joy, *The Jesness Inventory: application to Approved School boys*, Home Office publ. 13, HMSO, London 1969;
— Weychick, T. James, 'Asociability, index scores relationship to adjustment of youthful offenders' *The Journal of Correctional Education,* vol. XXII, no. 2, 1970, p. 12.

21 Social Climate in the Experimental and Control Institutions

Vinko SKALAR

Introduction

The behaviour of the individual is determined by ecological, social and situational factors (which can be included in the concept of climate), together with personality factors. This thesis is based on the theoretical principles proposed by Kurt Lewin (field theory), and in addition has adequate support from a great deal of research, including the studies of Raush, Barker, Moos, Zinner and Cressey.[1] If we consider climate as one of the factors that contribute to and determine the behaviour of the individual, then it must also be understood as a dynamic factor that is at once both a cause and effect of the behaviour of people (who on the one hand create climate, but on the other are its product as expressed in their behaviour). The climate changes as those who create it change, and the changes in people are again partly determined by the established climate.

If we consider climate in this light, we may consider various hypotheses for any of the points of the dynamic circle of climate—behaviour. For example:

— From the climate determined for a given institution it is possible to infer the quality of the interactions among people in the institution, the relation of superiors to subordinates, the quantity and quality of conflict situations, and so on.

— A more favourable climate reflects favourable interpersonal relationships on all levels; it reflects the conditions for more acceptable behaviour and, indirectly, for social instruction of people.

— Favourable relationships in the institution reflect a favourable climate as perceived by all of the inhabitants of the institution.

These three hypotheses led us to evaluate the climate in the experimental and two control institutions. In this way we could indirectly confirm or refute the results reflected in the trends of attitudes of the staff and inmates (Chapters 16 and 18).

In light of the way that the courts and social welfare offices which send youths to institutions view all three of the institutions (the experimental and both controls), we should expect that the climate would be least favourable in the educational correction home in Radeče (a control institution), which has the status of (and is perceived as) the most strict and closed institution; and that the climate would be most favourable in the educational institution at Slivnica (also a control institution), which has the status of the most open institution (the young people go to school exclusively outside the institution and are objectively least restricted and exposed to various control mechanisms). The experimental institution is perceived by the courts and social welfare offices to be somewhere between the two control institutions in its strictness, restrictiveness and quantity of control over the inmates. Thus we should expect that the inhabitants (inmates and staff) of the experimental institution would percieve the climate of the institution to be qualitatively somewhere between the climates of the two control institutions.

If we consider the continual advisory influences of the consulting team on the experimental institution, we can anticipate that comparison of all three institutions would show either that the experimental institution closely approximated the educational institution in Slivnica, or that the climate of the experimental institution would assume first place.

Methods and source of data

We have at our disposal three sources of data for the determination of the climates in the experimental and two control institutions:

1   Moos's questionnaire for determining the climate in educational institutions (Correctional Institutions Environment Scale, Form C).[2]

2   Records of the escapes of inmates from both control institutions and from the experimental institution for the period 15 September 1967 to 14 September 1972.[3]

3   Data concerning the turnover of personnel in the educational institutions during the period 1 September 1967 to 1 September 1971.[4]

218

1 Moos's questionnaire

Moos's questionnaire contains eighty-seven questions, which belong to nine categories that reveal various aspects of the institutional climate. The categories are as follows: (1) involvement, (2) support, (3) expressiveness, (4) autonomy, (5) practical orientation, (6) personal problem orientation, (7) order and organization, (8) clarity, and (9) staff control. Results obtained by use of the questionnaire are given in Tables 21.1, 21.2, 21.3, and Figure 21.1.

Table 21.1

Institutional climate as perceived by staff and inmates

		Staff		Inmates		
Elements of Climate		Radeče	Logatec	Radeče	Slivnica	Logatec
No.		28	18	94	54	38
1	Involvement	4·29	6·06	4·64	6·10	6·19
2	Support	6·31	8·56	5·68	7·02	7·81
3	Expressiveness	4·64	7·00	3·62	3·92	5·70
4	Autonomy	5·43	8·00	5·27	5·94	6·78
5	Practical orientation	7·32	8·19	6·51	6·74	7·39
6	Personal problem orientation	6·30	7·19	5·12	5·85	6·86
7	Order and organisation	3·70	2·53	5·25	5·72	5·37
8	Clarity	5·93	7·17	5·86	6·30	7·00
9	Staff control	4·89	1·89	5·60	4·77	3·75

Besides arithmetic means for particular categories we have computed also global scores for staff and inmates. Global scores are totals of arithmetic means for items (1), (2), (3), (4), (5), (6) and (8) minus items (7) and (9). We considered items (7) and (9) as negative characteristics since they relate to order and organisation as well as to staff control. Both characteristics are attributes of an authoritarian system and in contradiction with the remaining characteristics, as attributes of democratic guidance.

219

Table 21.2

Institutional climate as perceived by educators and instructors

Elements of climate	Educators			Instructors	
	Radeče	Slivnica	Logatec	Radeče	Logatec
No.	14	14	11	14	7
1 Involvement	4·93	8·78	5·91	3·65	6·33
2 Support	6·00	9·50	8·50	6·57	8·66
3 Expressiveness	4·86	5·36	7·00	4·43	7·00
4 Autonomy	5·36	7·35	7·73	5·50	8·50
5 Practical orientation	7·07	8·57	8·27	7·57	8·00
6 Personal problem orientation	5·86	8·36	7·18	6·77	7·20
7 Order and organisation	3·92	7·50	2·09	3·86	3·33
8 Clarity	6·43	8·07	6·82	5·43	7·71
9 Staff control	4·57	4·21	2·18	5·21	1·43

Note: EI Slivnika has no instructors.
Therefore, regarding instructors, we can compare only ECH Radeče and EI Logatec

Table 21.3

Global scores of climate

Population	ECH Radeče	EI Slivnica	EI Logatec
Staff	31·58	—	47·06
Educators	32·21	44·28	46·87
Instructors	30·62	—	47·46
Inmates	25·86	31·07	36·86
Educators + inmates	28·72	37·68	41·96

2 *Escape of inmates*

We defined escape as any departure of an inmate from the educational institution without permission, or unauthorised or approved absence if the inmate did not return to the institution before 6 a.m. Results of our analysis of escapes are given in Tables 21.4, 21.5 and 21.6.

220

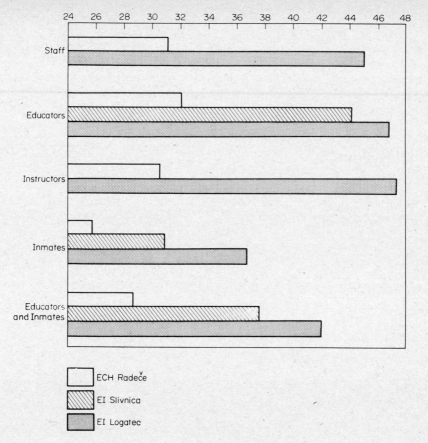

Fig. 21.1 Graph of climate total scores

Table 21.4

Number of escapes

Educational institution	Average capacity of the institution	Number of escapes	Average number of escapes per inmate
ECH Radeče	123	146	1·2
EI Slivnica	76	30	0·4
EI Logatec	43	115	2·6

Table 21.5
Return of inmate to the institution

Educational institution	Returned by himself No.	%	Returned by the police No.	%	Other No.	%	Discharged while escaped No.	%
ECH Radeče	17	11·5	97	66·5	32	22·0	–	–
EI Slivnica	21	70·0	5	16·6	4	13·4	–	–
EI Logatec	92	80·0	6	5·2	15	13·0	2	1·8

Table 21.6
Punishable act committed

Educational institution	Yes	%	No	%	Unknown	%
ECH Radeče	34	23·2	69	47·3	43	29·3
EI Slivnica	2	6·7	6	20·0	22	73·3
EI Logatec	9	7·9	80	69·5	26	22·6

3 *Turnover of personnel from 1 September 1967 to 1 September 1971*
The results of our analysis are given in Tables 21.7, 21.8, 21.9.

Table 21.7
Number and age of the staff members

Educational institution	Number of professional staff	Age range	Average age
ECH Radeče	48	24–56	33
EI Slivnica	21	23–62	30
EI Logatec	22	21–38	27

Table 21.8

Number of staff members who left the institution during the observation period

Educational institution	Departed from the institution	Percentage
ECH Radeče	11	22·9
EI Slivnica	6	28·6
EI Logatec	4	18·2

Table 21.9

Number of educational staff members who left the institution during the observation period

Educational institution	Number of educators	Left the institution	Percentage
ECH Radeče	15	6	40·0
EI Slivnica	15	6	40·0
EI Logatec	9	2	(22·2)

Interpretation of results

1 Moos's questionnaire

The staff of the experimental institution in Logatec perceived and reflected a more favourable institutional climate than did the staff at the ECH in Radeče. The differences are particularly pronounced for categories 2 (support), 3 (expressiveness), and 4 (autonomy). There is also a marked difference in the negative category 9 (staff control), in favour of the experimental institution.

The educators of the ECH in Radeče have the least favourable results for all categories. There are no large differences between the EI Slivnica and the EI Logatec for the individual categories except for the first category (involvement), in which the EI at Slivnica has a better result than the experimental institution. The experimental institution has a decided advantage in the negative categories 7 and 9, with the result that the global index of the climate is more favourable for the experimental institution than for the educational institution at Slivnica.

However, the results for the educators at the educational institution at Slivnica are questionable for the following reasons:

- the positive categories are in contradiction with the negative ones (7 and 9), something we did not find for the other two institutions;
- the difference between the perceptions of the climate by the teachers and inmates is bigger in this institution than it was for the other two.

The instructors in the experimental institution perceived the climate as being more favourable than did the instructors at the ECH in Radeče.

There is no obvious difference between the instructors and educators of both institutions. But it is worthwhile mentioning that globally the instructors in the experimental institution reflect a more favourable climate than do the educators, but that in the ECH at Radeče the more positive climate is reflected by the educators.

The inmates of the experimental and both control institutions perceive and reflect a poorer, less favourable climate than do their educators. The differences in the perception of the climate between the educators and inmates is smaller in the experimental institution and the ECH at Radeče than at the EI at Slivnica.

The least favourable climate was perceived by the staff at the ECH at Radeče, followed by the EI at Slivnica; the staff of the EI at Logatec perceived and reflected the most favourable global climate. The institutions can be ranked in the same order if we compare the results for the inmates, or the grouped result for the inmates and educators for all three institutions.

2   Escapes of inmates

Escapes of inmates during the observation period were most numerous for the experimental institution. The next most numerous escapes were from the ECH in Radeče, while the EI in Slivnica had by far the fewest escapes.

The favourable number of escapes of inmates from the EI in Slivnica can be explained by the fact that the inmates in this institution are employed outside of the institution, which reduces the subjective feeling of imprisonment.

Table 21.5 shows that at the institution at Logatec the inmates for the most part return themselves, and are only in exceptional cases returned by the police, whereas return of an inmate by the police is nearly always the rule for the ECH at Radeče; it is also a more frequent event at the EI at Slivnica than at the EI at Logatec.

The inmates from the experimental institution and the institution at Slivnica rarely commit punishable acts while at large, but the dark field for the inmates from the EI at Slivnica is quite high in comparison with the experimental institution.

The escapes of inmates from the experimental institution are thus the most frequent, but on average they do not have the same meaning as escapes of inmates from the two control institutions. They are more an expression of a permissive (and perhaps somewhat too loose) institutional atmosphere, and cannot be ascribed to defensive behaviour by the inmates.

3 Turnover of staff

The turnover of staff in the experimental institution during the time of the experiment was smaller than for either of the control institutions. The favourable position of the experimental institution in this regard is most clear in Table 21.8, which shows the turnover of teachers during the experimental period.

Conclusion

The climate in the experimental institution is presumably due to a systematic factor — the efforts of the consulting team. The results of the testing of the institutional climates confirm the results of the measuring of attitudes of the staff and inmates.

Notes

[1] After Moos, R. H., 'The assessment of the social climates of correctional institutions', *Journal of Research in Crime and Delinquency*, July 1968.

[2] Moos, R. H., 'The assessment of the social climates of correctional institutions', *Journal of Research in Crime and Delinquency*, July 1968. (The questionnaire was sent to us by the author personally.)

The questionnaire was translated into Slovene by the psychologist of the Educational Institution at Logatec, Janez Bečaj. It was adapted by Dr Alenka Šelih, scientific co-worker of the Institute of Criminology. Dr Alenka Šelih, with the help of the psychologist Brejc Anton, and the criminologist Dr Skaberne, also conducted the testing with the questionnaire in all three institutions.

[3] The data are taken from the study of the Institute of Criminology entitled 'Escape of inmates from educational institutions'. The leader of the research is the scientific adviser of the Institute of Criminology in Ljubljana, Dr Bronislav Skaberne. The research, which is still in progress, is financed by the Boris Kidrič Fund in Ljubljana.

[4] The data were gathered by Dr Bronislav Skaberne, Scientific adviser of the Institute of Criminology in Ljubljana.

22 The Institution in its Local Setting

Bronislav SKABERNE

Number of registered interactions with the environment

Public opinion is generally negative and repressive towards personally and behaviourally disturbed youth. These attitudes are particularly evident in a provincial town such as Logatec. Both the inmates and the staff were aware of this situation from the very beginning. Therefore the entire institutional collective made efforts to establish positive contacts with the townspeople. Thus both positive and negative contacts with the environment arose during the experiment.

We gathered information about these interactions primarily from the staff's diaries, and to a much smaller degree, either day-to-day or retrospectively. The institutional staff was not specifically instructed to record such interactions systematically in their diaries. Because of this we cannot evaluate the dynamics of the interaction for the four-year period. The percentage of entries concerning the relationships between the institution and its environment relative to the number of entries made by the educator and instructors are as follows:

1967/68	10 per cent
1968/69	7 per cent
1969/70	6 per cent
1970/71	17 per cent

However, we can evaluate the relation between the positive and negative interactions during that time (see Table 22.1)

In addition, co-operation with the environment was often discussed at the community therapy meetings, which were not in operation until the end of the spring semester, 1970. The staff suggested most of the themes for discussion at these group meetings. In this context the staff concentrated on those problems which they felt to be most pressing. Thus it is not surprising that the minutes of the therapy groups contain sixteen discussions of the relations of the institution with the environment, ten of which concerned conflict situations. It is of importance to ask to what extent such discussions motivate the inmates, and what kind

227

of success can be expected from this kind of community therapy meeting. But a more detailed consideration of this question is beyond the scope of this section.

Although the minutes of the community therapy meetings cannot be taken as representative indicators of the relations between the institution and its environment, we feel that Table 22.1 is a quite accurate reflection of the true situation. The percentage of conflicts with the environment is less than the percentage of positive contacts for all years, and the percentages remain relatively constant. This may also indicate that the permissive atmosphere cultivated in the institution also reflects (at least in part) on the institution's surroundings.

Table 22.1

Number of registered interactions with the environment

School year	Number of registered interactions	Number of negative interactions	%
1967/68	102	44	43
1968/69	82	36	44
1969/70	61	26	43
1970/71*	(21)	(13)	
Total	266	119	45

* The data for 1970/71 are biased. In this year only four educators and instructors kept diaries. There was a total of 124 entries 56 or 45 per cent of which were made by one person. Most of the situations mentioned in these diaries are conflicts.

Examples of conflicts

Aggression of local residents against the inmates

Soon after the institution opened, in September 1967, a local resident called out to a group of inmates walking along the street, 'Are you going stealing in Logatec?'. The inmates were incensed and only the intervention of a teacher prevented an incident.

The local residents sometimes accused the inmates of crimes they did not commit. The first such case occurred in September 1967, several days after the inmates arrived in the institution. A local resident insisted that the inmates has stolen three bicycles – an accusation which proved to be unfounded. In May 1969 a local resident came to the institution with the accusation that an inmate had fired on him with an air rifle. The police determined that the guilty party was not an inmate from the institution. The local residents also accused the inmates of breaking a grapevine trellis, a mailbox and street lights, and of conspicuously hanging up a pig's head. In the end it was found that all these things were done by local boys. In 1968 the local residents accused the inmates of causing a disturbance at the celebration of national holiday. Investigation of the matter revealed that the disturbance was caused by young men of the community.

Some of the local residents could not accept the inmates with long hair. In October 1968 a man confronted an inmate in a pub, saying that a hooligan with long hair had no business being there. A similar confrontation took place in December 1969. A man grabbed an inmate by the arm, called the waitress and asked for a scissors. The boy was angry and afraid, but nothing happened.

In April 1970 a local resident provoked an inmate at a bus station by saying, 'You castle thief, out of my way – we should string you all up'. The inmate could not restrain himself and hit the man. For this the police reported him to the court for misdemeanours.

Aggression of inmates against the local residents

Soon after the institution began to function in 1967 the inmates began to commit punishable acts. As early as October 1967 an inmate stole a bottle of whisky from a self-service market. A salesgirl caught him in the act. In 1968 the punishable acts began to increase. They began with instances of fishing without a licence. When the teachers discovered some theft, they prepared the inmates to go with the teacher to the shop or home-owner to pay for the stolen goods or to return what had been stolen.

In August of the same year, while eight inmates were employed in the installation of central heating in the elementary school, the inmates stole some money and a number of things of smaller value. For the most part they compensated for the damages later on.

A theft of a large amount of alcoholic drinks by fourteen inmates was very poorly received in Logatec. In 1970 a few inmates broke into a hotel and a close neighbour's. Two were caught in the act, and three got away.

The inmates also stole motor vehicles from the local residents – everything from motorised bicycles to cars — and damaged some of them. On several occasions inmates took motorised bicycles in order to return the vehicle to the police themselves when the police inquired about it. There was great indignation when some inmates stole and damaged cars in the autumn of 1970. As a results of these offences two inmates were sent to the educational correction home in Radeče, and two were sent to juvenile prison in Celje.

Besides these offences, the inmates were involved in fights on a number of occasions, usually as a result of provocation, but at times also their own initiative. It is clear that the inmates did not endear themselves to the local residents by stealing from the fields (apples, corn, turnips) and throwing snowballs into houses.

In the beginning of 1971 the inmates invented a very dangerous game with the cars that drove in front of the institution. They put a burning piece of wood on the street, and then stood in a group at the side, holding their ears as if something was about to explode. Bets were made as to how the passing motorist would react. The teachers soon terminated this dangerous sport, thus preventing any accidents.

Inmates and police

The inmates were indignant when the police repeatedly came to the institution to ask if the inmates had committed some punishable act. This also resulted in the inmates' developing a generally negative attitude towards the police. Thus it happened that an inmate put a board full of nails under the tyres of a police car that had come to the institution. No damage was caused because the policeman backed his car away from the nails. But another inmate did cause serious damage by slashing the tyres of a policeman's motorcycle.

The inmates were also offended when, once each year, policemen came to the institution to take their pictures and finger prints. In 1969 they obstructed this procedure by short-circuiting the institution's electrical circuits.

Alcohol

Some inmates became repeatedly drunk and caused disturbances in pubs or on the street while intoxicated. On two occasions a car struck a drunken inmate on the street. Drunkenness and inappropriate behaviour on the street were problems with the teachers had to deal frequently.

The institution's administration tried to deal with the drinking problem in various ways. In 1968 and 1969 the administration wrote to the pub managers in Logatec requesting them not to serve alcoholic beverages to inmates. In some of the pubs this letter was displayed in a prominent place. Following each such letter some of the pubs informed the inmates that they could no longer serve them alcoholic drinks. As a result the inmates began buying alcoholic beverages in stores. The inmates were angry at this rule and embarrassed by it, especially when they went to a pub with someone who had visited them in the institution.

The institution's administration asked for help from the police in some cases. Individual teachers also spoke personally to the pub managers. Finally the institutional administration informed the municipal council's division for general administration of the social services about this problem.

All these measures had only short-lived effects. The diaries of the teachers bear witness to the fact that drinking among the inmates was one of the most significant problems that they were unable to master. We should note that the problem for the most part involved only a few inmates. But though the drinking and trouble-making was limited to a few inmates, the local residents blamed them all. And some residents themselves created the situation in which an inmate would get drunk. When inmates had done some work for them, they served them drinks, and in addition sometimes bought drinks for them in the pubs.

Relationships with girls

In the buying of drinks for the inmates a special role was played by some Logatec girls. These were girls who had bad reputations and thus were not able to establish ties with the local residents. The teachers related that these girls would even come to beneath the windows of the institution and invite the inmates to the pub. This also happened after the cinema.

The local residents were scandalised by the socialising between the inmates and these girls. The girls lived in such family circumstances as made intervention by the institution's social services quite ineffectual. The inmates knew that the girls they were with had bad reputations. They said that they wanted to meet others, but that that had not been possible. The local residents avoided them to the point of insult. Some inmates judged that 'we're hooligans and belong with them'.

In July 1968 the local council wrote a letter complaining that the inmates were not behaving properly at the swimming pool. As it turned out, the offenders were local residents. But some of the local residents did not like it that the inmates tried to make acquaintances with the Logatec girls at the swimming pool. In November of that year a mother forcibly broke off the relationship of her daughter with an inmate, saying, 'It is true that we are not rich, but it shames us if our daughter goes with a boy from an institution. That is a shame for the entire family'.

Negative perception of the relationship with the local residents

The inmates often discussed among themselves the relation of the environment to them. They imagined that the local residents held a negative opinion of them. For example, on one occasion some inmates were employed near the institution and a local resident was watching them work. One of the inmates said to a teacher, 'Comrade, I know what they are thinking — look how the criminals work'.

The educational staff also found, in conservations and meetings, that the inmates were not welcomed in Logatec, and that no one wanted to associate with them, except girls of bad reputation.

Upon publication in the newspaper *Youth*, from March to May 1971, of an article that attempted to describe objectively the life of inmates in Slovene correctional institutions, the inmates expressed their indignation at community therapy meetings (24 March 1971) as follows: 'People outside of the institution think that we are hooligans, and that because of this we live in impossible conditions, that we are beaten, that our rooms have bars on the windows and so on. It isn't true and it is necessary to emphasise that we live well and that in fact we don't feel like most people imagine'. The inmates experienced the public's conception of the institution as a personal discomfort, and consequently desired that the public be better informed.

At one of the community therapy meetings one of the inmates said, 'I know that the local residents point fingers at us and consider us to be common hoods. They all think that we are still the same as we were, and that we are just waiting to steal something'. Another added, 'Those that think that they can get anywhere with force are kidding themselves. For myself I know that nobody could convert me with force'. Another inmate said, 'If you know that there is a staff over your head, you are good only so long as you need fear it. Later nothing is changed. You remain as you were before'. (See *Youth* no. 17, 4 May 1971.) Thus the inmates experience fears in connection with public opinion.

Co-operation of the institution with the environment

Help given to the local residents

The inmates keep up the grounds and care for the memorials to fallen war heroes in the area. One of these is next to the institution; the other is in another village. The local council bought the inmates a football in June 1970, in thanks for keeping up the grounds of these memorials. In addition the inmates took over cleaning of the local swimming pool. In September 1969 the inmates helped for several days to build the gymnasium for the elementary school.

Some of the local residents came to like the inmates because they helped with the work, in particular the building of houses, field work and jobs. In 1968 the inmates helped a farmers' co-operative for several days in the drying of hay. In 1970 they helped the biggest firm in Logatec with the installation of doors and windows in an eighteen-storey building in Ljubljana and a six-storey apartment house in Jesenice. In this way the firm was able to avoid paying a penalty for missing their deadline, and the work was done to their general satisfaction.

The institution also does other favours for the local residents in its workshops, and also offers telephone services to them and help to those who are building or repairing houses. From this it is clear that the local residents are free of prejudice when seeking the inmates' help.

Co-operation with local forums

In the discussions of various local offices, as well as at many meetings of the local residents, there was discussion of the inmates and the institution. The participants made no attempt to hide their displeasure at having the educational institution in their midst. When an employee from the institution was present at such meetings he would give some clarification, and thus to some extent succeed in quieting the aroused emotions. In December 1967 a delegate to a local youth conference maligned the inmates. An inmate who was present refuted the attack so successfully with his explanations that he was applauded and later received an apology from the maligner.

In February 1971, because of the unflattering rumours about the institution that were circulating, the director presented both assemblies of the municipal council with a report of the work and conditions in the institution. In a report in the newspaper *Work* it stated that 'the councillors gave their support to the current work in the institution'. Unfortunately many of these meetings had no institution staff or inmate present, with the result that dissatisfactions accumulated, instead of being dealt with immediately.

The inmates held sport and cultural events in the institution on various holidays, and invited local representatives and other guests. These events were well-organised and were praised by the guests. On these occasions some of the inmates showed the ability to express their deeper feelings and inner life with poems and prose. These talents also came to light in contributions to the institution's newspaper *Our Truth,* which unfortunately only came out twice.

In November 1969 the inmates, together with the youth of Logatec, successfully organised a dance at which the institution's beat orchestra played. The inmates also played some of their own numbers at performances in the girls' school in Višnja gora and the observation centre in Ljubljana. They were well-received wherever they played.

Co-operation with the police

The institution's administration attempted to establish closer ties with the police station in Logatec. To that purpose a conference was organised in March 1969 for representatives from the institution and the Logatec police, together with the chief of police in Ljubljana. At this conference it was agreed that one policeman from the station at Logatec would have closer ties with the administration of the correctional institution and help with the problems connected with the inmates. In addition the police were to hold a driving course in the institution. The police made three motorised bicycles available for this purpose. For a while the policeman carried out a part of this agreement and the inmates had good relationships with him. He went with the inmates to the academy in Ljubljana on the holiday for workers in internal affairs, and expressed his satisfaction with his experiences with the inmates. Unfortunately the contacts ceased when the policeman was transferred to another station, and no replacement was named.

The driving course never came about, because no one came to give the lectures. However, the police loaned shortwave radios to the inmates for use on their excursions on several occasions.

The response of the police station to requests for co-operation were greatly dependent on the manner in which the teachers asked for it. There were cases in which the police refused to help, particularly when it was a matter of escaped or drunken inmates, arguing that the teachers should take care of it themselves. Teachers who knew how to ask for help more

234

appropriately in such cases usually were not refused. Recently the institution began to help the police by accepting in temporary custody juveniles who had run away from home or escaped from other correctional institutions.

Sports and other recreational activities

The correctional institution had the most contacts with the environment in the form of sports. In September 1967 the administration of the institution arranged with the local sportclub to have the inmates' team join the local football league. The inmates also competed with the local residents in other sports, especially basketball, handball, athletics and table tennis. The inmates were well received by their local peers in sport activities.

There were practically no conflicts with the local residents at sport activities. The local boys were glad to play with the inmates, since in such a small town there were few boys interested in playing a given sport.

At first the inmates were severely affected by losing at games, but later learned to lose in a sportsmanlike way.

The teachers succeeded in recruiting the boys from Logatec to help the inmates in setting up a basketball court. The institution's playing fields (for basketball, football, tennis and skating) were often the scene of sports involving both the inmates and the local boys. For these boys the playing fields became a great attraction, and they made use of them by themselves for recreation and entertainment.

On the other hand, the inmates also helped the local boys in the work involved in sporting events in the area (for instance, in preparing ski runs, removing snow from ski jumps, measuring the length of ski jumps, and so on). The staff also actively participated in the local society for physical culture and helped in the organisation of sport activities in the area.

Finally, we should note that there were no complaints against the inmates at sport competitions outside Logatec (for instance, at Žiri, Planina, Slivnica and Ljubljana).

Group excursions from the institution

When the teachers took the inmates on outings (to exhibitions, on holiday, and so on) or to take part in various outdoor activities (such as skiing, swimming and rowing) the inmates did not make themselves conspicious by their behaviour. For the most part they behaved respectably and caused no incidents. However, it did happen that they did not all return to the institution at the same time, but rather arrived with greater

235

or lesser delays, occasionally drunk.

The teachers frequently took the inmates on shopping trips for clothing in the city (Ljubljana, Kranj, Vrhnika). In the shops the inmates behaved in a relaxed way and did not attract attention. Some of them made their purchases quickly, others were more particular and took longer to decide, at times visiting several shops. The inmates helped each other with advice when buying, and often asked the teachers for their opinions. Once the inmates were very upset when the shopgirls found out from the cheque that they were dealing with inmates. After that, the teachers took care not to let it happen again. On such shopping trips the teachers often allowed the inmates to make a quick visit, or went with them as a group to a film or a coffee shop. The teachers record in their diaries that on such occasions the inmates would gather at a prearranged site and return to the institution together.

Inmates and the members of the experimental team

The members of the experimental team frequently visited the correctional institution. They were there at least twice a week, sometimes more frequently. During those visits the members of the team regularly came in contact with the inmates and talked with them. The inmates were polite in all of these contacts and there were no instances of vandalism concerning the team members' cars.

The inmates accepted the members of the team at the community therapy meetings in a manner similar to the way in which they accepted the teachers, albeit with somewhat greater reserve.

Conclusion

Katja VODOPIVEC,[1]

The four-year experiment was conducted in an educational institution of the partially open type with a relatively small capacity (between forty and fifty inmates of fifteen to twenty years of age), located in the country about thirty kilometres from the city. We shall limit our conclusions primarily to similar kinds of institutions. Judgement of the applicability of the results of the experiment to other kinds of institutions is left to our readers.

Verification of hypotheses

The hypotheses can be seen in Chapter 2. Verification of the hypotheses on the basis of the experiment is as follows:

1 Because of the nature of educational work in the institutional environment (exposure to continual pressure from the inmates, impossibility of verifying work success, insufficient rewards), the staff must be screened before acceptance in the institution. The selection committee was forced to reject 56 per cent of the applicants on the basis of relatively modest acceptance criteria; that is, relatively suitable psychological and physical health, relative personal stability and maturity, at least average intelligence, and suitable motivation for work. Without prior screening, most of the 56 per cent of rejected candidates would have been accepted, since they were among the first to apply (before the selection criteria were known to the public and before the staff that had already been selected began to suggest other candidates), and since most of the personality weaknesses for this kind of work were not evident either from previous work curricula, and even less from first impressions.

2 We no longer accept, at least not entirely, the hypothesis that the institution should be staffed by workers with varying basic education in order to create a microcosm of the variegated life outside the institution. An increasing proportion of personally disturbed young people who come to the educational institution require therapeutic treatment (this increase is due to an expansion of extra-institutional measures). They remain in the institution for a relatively short time (a year and a half to two years), which hardly suffices for therapeutic influence. Therefore a special basic

237

education and training of the staff would be needed.

Our initial hypothesis would be acceptable only if a basically hetero-geneously educated staff could be additionally trained over an extended period before and after acceptance into the institution.

3   The changes that we were able to effect with the inmates confirm the hypothesis that it is possible, with intensive professional co-operation, to help staff of average capability and motivation to enjoy greater success in their work. Since these successes are not usually immediately obvious, and the staff themselves could not compare them with the successes of other methods of work with the inmates, it is difficult to answer the question of whether the satisfactions that the staff experienced during the experiment were greater than those obtainable with other work methods. An indirect answer to this question can perhaps be found in the relatively small number of staff who left during the time of the experiment, and in the staff's evalua-tion of the institutional climate (Chapter 21).

4   The hypothesis that the permissive educational methods of the staff did not represent a greater threat to the society than repressive methods[2] was confirmed by the findings concerning changes in inmates' attitudes and concerning inmate escapes (Chapter 21). The number of escapes from the educational institution in Logatec was large (in light of the permissive educational atmosphere), but compared with other institutions the in-mates committed relatively few crimes while outside, and for the most part returned to the institution without police intervention.

Although the inmates did show positive changes in their attitudes, they rarely obtained the average for their age group (according to the Jesness standards for the USA),[3] which means that this and other educational institutions are releasing inmates who are still personally disturbed , and who, without intensive additional help, are unable to become part of life on the outside, a life which regards them with distrust equal to or greater than before, and which therefore will be a renewed source of frustration.

5   Group counselling of the staff was, in our case, an appropriate work method which contributed to the reduction of antagonism between theory and practice, and which helped to apply theoretical knowledge in practice. During the experiment the kind of group counselling was changed repeatedly, and we also made use of other work methods (group con-ferences, training, individual tutoring). We are still of the opinion that for an experiment of this kind, group counselling (as our present level of understanding conceives it) is the basic work method for reaching the goals we set. But the consulting team must be flexible enough to supple-

ment this method with all the other forms of work that each individual situation requires. Some members of the professional team are convinced that if this had not been done during the experiment, reliance on group counselling as the sole work method would in all probability have resulted in a failure to establish suitable communication with the staff of the institution.

6   The hypothesis that a single institution cannot deal with inmates with greatly varied kinds of disturbances is in our opinion supported, but not yet confirmed. Despite the limited criteria that we set for the acceptance of inmates, during the experiment the institution also accepted two inmates who did not meet these criteria: one personally and behaviourally disturbed invalid, and one inmate who was so personally disturbed that no other institution in Slovenia had been able to keep him for more than a short time. The results of work with both of these inmates were negative, and they had to be released from the institution after several months.

7   During the experiment three groups mutually influenced each other: the consultants from the institute, the institutional staff and the inmates. Experience confirmed our expectation that the beginning of the experiment would bring some unfavourable interactions between the three groups, in particular mutual distrust, aggressiveness and partial servility. Our expectation that these interactions would change during the experiment to more understanding and friendly co-operation was similarly confirmed. The groups of inmates, staff and consultants made a transition from an initial state of rigidity, authoritarianism and fixed attitudes, to a more flexible and fluid solution of problem situations.

The dynamics of development in this direction were different for each of the above groups. We feel that the greater flexibility and fluidity was first attained by the staff (in about the third year of the experiment), followed by the inmates (especially after the introduction of community therapy groups), and last of all the group of consultants. The group of consultants cannot be criticised for not reacting to situations arising out of mutual interactions with sufficient flexibility from the very beginning. However, the group achieved this primarily through pressure of the majority upon the minority, rather than as an homogeneous whole. This allowed the individual consultants rigidly to persist in their initial attitudes and viewpoints. It was only after the last conflict (end of the third year of the experiment) that the members of the consulting group began to accept each other's views with greater tolerance and thus begin to undergo personal change. In the writing of this report we discovered for the first time that we had all changed some of our views during the experiment, but

239

only with difficulty and relatively late.

Thus through the experiment we attained the following goals:

- We were able to encourage a more permissive and understanding relationship between the staff and the inmates.
- We succeeded in varying degree to resolve conflict situations on all levels and between all work groups.
- We succeeded in raising the level of tolerance for the staff and for ourselves (the consultants).

We did not succeed in training the staff for enlightened, planned leadership of the inmates, particularly in the therapeutic and socialisation sense (Chapter 9 and Chapter 20, Hočevar's article). The obstacles that prevented attainment of this goal as well are as follows:

- Insufficient special educational preparation of the staff for work with this kind of young people.

- An excessive burdening of the staff with a great variety of tasks, and the persistent question of whether only highly qualified staff should work with these young people, or whether highly qualified staff should work together with less qualified staff (such as assistants for routine tasks like waking the inmates, maintaining their personal hygiene and external appearance, running the food supply, and so on).

- Lack of developed models for the democratic and pedagogic leadership of institutions of this type (see Chapter 15, final section).

- Perhaps also the personal inclinations of the university and high-school educated staff who decide from personal motives to work with emotionally and behaviourally disturbed youth. Several members of the consulting team favour the hypothesis that this kind of work attracts people who dislike bureaucratic orderliness and office work, and instead wish to test their own responsiveness in varied and initially unknown situations and interactions. This is one of several hypotheses which need to be tested in the future. If this hypothesis is confirmed, then it would have to be taken into account as one of the factors that can significantly interact with the theoretical requirement that it is necessary systematically to guide and follow up the development of inmates. It is questionable whether such a requirement can be met in practice.

We also realised goals of the experiment by achieving equal or better educational results than those of the institutions we used for comparison; by the fact that inmates in our institution did not pose a greater threat to the environment during their stay than inmates in other institutions; and because in our opinion the inmates' stay in the institution did not signify a greater hindrance to the development of their personalities than staying in similar existing institutions.

The experiment was expensive and required exceptional efforts on the part of at least two groups: the consulting team and the educational staff. Was the experiment worth it, in light of the results?

A first answer to this question is that we are accustomed in the natural sciences to accepting as perfectly normal the fact that a large number of experiments is necessary before there is a significant change in people's knowledge and work methods. Also in this area, results can only be achieved by a series of experiments, which together with the necessary laboratory materials entail considerable expense. In the social sciences we expect each individual experiment to yield decisive discoveries.

We showed in the experiment the possibility of direct communication between theory and practice in pursuit of the goal of changes in attitudes. This implies that theory can influence practice in the social sciences as well, and that this influence is beneficial in practice and can aid in the attainment of practical goals. The benefits of the experiment will be even greater if the institutional staff develop the accepted methods of work with personally and behaviourally disturbed youth in future, and attempt to achieve a higher level of work than was obtained by the end of the experiment.

Immediately after the end of the experiment the staff of the experimental institution showed only a relatively modest willingness to continue working with the consulting team, even though the staff and the institution's administration gave assurances that they intended to continue with the work methods that had been initiated and to develop them further. Efforts in this direction were expressed as follows:

— In the school year 1971/72 the staff asked both consultants (the psychiatrist and the psychologist Mlinarič) to continue the consulting group meetings. The psychiatrist responded to the request immediately, the psychologist only towards the end of the spring semester, 1972.

— The institution retained the practice of having community therapy groups and other group meetings with the inmates. The consultants of the institute, who visited the community therapy sessions and the related staff meetings, felt that the level of these meetings was higher than had been the case during the experiment.

On the other hand, in the first year after the close of the experiment we also found the following:

— the staff did not express the wish to continue the educational seminars, even though the team of mentors offered this opportunity.

— The institution did not accept an initiative to establish it as a training base for interns or students as well as teachers from other institutions.

— Three teachers and two shopmasters left the institution shortly after conclusion of the experiment.

— Beginning with the school year 1972/73, the staff no longer involved the team of consultants in further co-operative work.

One may conclude that the institution wanted to retain in part methods of working with the inmates which had been developed during the experiment, but that some signs of vacillation were also evident.

In 1972 the psychologist Skalar decided, with the agreement of the other members of the team of consultants, to transmit the team's theoretical principles and findings from this experiment to staff from other institutions in Slovenia. This was to be done in seminars. The series of seminars began with a selected group (two representatives from each of the Republic's institutions), with the later addition of a group of institutional principals and pedagogic leaders.

These seminars had two effects:

1 The staff people, including the administrators of educational institutions, considered the permissive orientation of the experimental institution acceptable and appropriate for the treatment of behaviourally disturbed and delinquent youth (results of a questionnaire). Most of the educational institutions showed a willingness gradually to accept a therapeutically oriented conception and incorporate in their work the methods that had been shown to be successful in the experimental institution (community therapy groups, group work with the inmates).

2 The positive evaluation of the experiment in Logatec on the part of other educational institutions had a reciprocal influence on the experimental institution. The staff of the experimental institution no longer felt isolated from other institutions, and began to get public recognition for their efforts during the experiment. Work which had been previously experienced as an exceptional stress acquired, in the new context, a primary motivating value. This state of affairs was reflected in the following:

242

- The staff again expressed the wish for continuation of the training seminars.

- The staff requested weekly consultation meetings with several members of the team.

- The administration of the institution sent a letter to all of the institutions in Slovenia stating that the staff of the experimental institution were prepared to function as consultants to the staff of other institutions. The letter noted that the institution was open to active co-operation in community therapy groups for all those interested, and the institution was prepared to accept teachers from other institutions for extended practical training.

- The administration of the institution took several measures to strengthen the organisational structure and function of the institution (the position of pedagogic chief was filled, greater discipline was required of the staff, an agreement was reached on the documentation of the educational process).

- The staff began to popularise their work in appearances at various meetings and conferences. The principal of the institution accepted the position of lecturer at the teachers' college, which trains, among others, educators for work with maladjusted youth.

- The institution began on its own initiative to translate the foreign professional literature.

Problems and new hypotheses

In man's continuing search for knowledge, no result is final. Every result creates new problems and new hypotheses. In connection with our research the problems outlined below press upon us.

Staff

Some character traits are probably shared by people who are motivated for work with personally and behaviourally disturbed youth. It is necessary that these traits be determined and reckoned with as a reality to which theoretical aspirations must be adapted. The goals of theoreticians who would ignore this factor are unrealistic and unobtainable.

We find ourselves in a dilemma about whether only staff with university or college education should be employed in the educational institution, or

243

whether, in addition to them, staff with elementary or secondary school education should be employed, to help with routine tasks. Our experiment did not answer this question. We only found that the more educated staff resented, in varying degrees, assignment to these tasks. On the other hand, we recognise that the educational process is a whole, comprised of many small and apparently insignificant duties. We do not know if it is realistic to expect highly qualified staff ever to see their role in the institution in this light.

We consider the hypothesis confirmed that the staff in the educational institution is exposed to frequent and severe pressure, together with strong guilt feelings for some of their reactions. We also feel that these burdens are greater in an institutional climate which does not allow the staff to react spontaneously and aggressively to these pressures as is the case in authoritarian institutions. Thus we are convinced that the institutional staff itself (and not just inmates) requires consultation help, particularly in the form of support.

During our experiment we consultants were intensely involved in the dynamics of events in the institution. A part-time consultant who could not be so involved in events in the institution could not represent such support for the staff. Thus we feel that each institution must find at least one adviser within its own ranks.

In our opinion the director of an institution cannot successfully play this role, since among other things he is also a disciplinary factor and decisively influences the promotion of the personnel.

As possible consultants we consider either a special pedagogic adviser or an institution psychologist (the opinion of several members of the consulting team).

We attach a number of considerations to the idea that a psychologist could act as a consultant for the institutional staff. The current duties of a psychologist in an institution are the diagnostic testings and possible treatment of the inmates. Institutional psychologists are in conflict with the rest of the staff in institutions nearly everywhere in the world — including our institutions. We presume that direct attempts at taking over therapy increase conflicts with the rest of the staff, particularly if the therapy is successful. No one is grateful for someone else being more successful than himself. But we are probably and quite readily grateful to someone who helps us to succeed. The only question is whether psychologists can accept the role of someone who does not himself achieve successes; that is, whether the teachers' satisfaction in work carried out with the psychologist's help is sufficient motivation for a psychologist to work in an educational institution. Of course psychologists in Yugoslavia who would want to assume such a role would have to be specially trained for it, since the training of psychologists here has been primarily of a diagnostic nature.

As we have mentioned, the psychic and work stress on the personnel is unusually severe. Because of this turnover of staff is normally high in all educational institutions. In light of this fact, it should be taken into account in the education of staff, in organisational schemes and in a planned allowance of staff turnover. This implies at least the following two points:

1 It is necessary to educate staff in such a way as to enable them to work both in an institutional environment as well as elsewhere. We would consider to be an appropriate combination the training of staff for work with behaviourally and personally disturbed youth and, for example, work with young people generally, in the area of recreational activities (young people's clubs, and so on).[4]

2 Since in Yugoslavia each institution is run on a self-government system, there would have to be an agreement among such institutions for the partial gradual exchange of staff (we should anticipate that this would be on a four-yearly basis). This implies that educational institutions would have to be located in cities where recreational activities for young people are well-developed.

We feel that changes in employment of this kind (including alternating contacts with disturbed and 'normal' youth) would contribute to a lessening of professional failings on the one hand, and on the other to an increase in the mental hygiene of the staff.

Institution

The efforts of the staff in the re-educational process of inmates in the institution at Logatec brings us again to the question of the goals of institutional education of personally and behaviourally disturbed youth. In Yugoslavia, as well as elsewhere, increasing numbers of personally disturbed young people are entering educational institutions, and these youngsters are disturbed primarily because of the conditions in which they lived before coming to the institutions. The important character deficiencies that we can rely on finding in them are: deficient emotionality (together with a feeling of insecurity), insufficient development of positive dispositions and abilities, and an inability to achieve success in a socially acceptable way. These young persons are alienated from adults

(Redl) and have not had a chance to follow normally the path of the primary and secondary socialisation process (Bergant, Chapter 17). These last two defects are usually referred to as 'insufficiently developed work habits' and are usually ascribed to so-called 'educational neglect'. But especially for inmates, these two externally observable forms of disturbance are more a consequence of deeper disturbances in the relationships between adults and children, and of the environment's denial of ideals from earliest childhood onward – and not a primary cause of behavioural deviations.

Institutional education, as currently conceived, combats these two disturbances primarily with the help of conditioning methods, and only exceptionally with treatment of their causes.

In the experiment at Logatec our goal was to reach into all of these areas with therapy, teaching and accustoming the inmates to work. Several members of the professional team repeatedly asked during the experiment, and are still questioning, whether such attempts and the accompanying expectations are at all realistic.

The inmates live in the institution for one and a half to two years. Their age on admission averages sixteen to seventeen years. Is it at all possible or justified to attempt in a short time to replace practically all that had been missed ot at times irrevocably lost? Is it not possible that the lack of success in institutional education, and our scepticism towards it in general, can be ascribed in part to excessive demands and unrealistic expectations from those who direct their demands and expectations – however well-intentioned – towards personally disturbed youth? We must at least consider that such demands can be handled successfully only by a juvenile who is strongly motivated towards furthering his personal development. But our juveniles are anything else but motivated in this way. The exceeding of human capabilities with unrealistic and unattainable demands can be an additional formidable obstacle which reinforces the experience of failure. If in this context the young person perceives the educational institution as his last chance, then by failure he obviously loses that as well.

Acceptance of the concept that the essential problem for personally and behaviourally disturbed inmates is insufficiently developed work and study habits, without penetrating to basic causes, implies an acceptance of concepts of institutional education from bygone times (forced work and forced learning – Skaberne, Chapter 1) with the modest addition of therapeutic efforts in recent times.

Perhaps it is still necessary to turn the concept of institutional education to face the opposite direction: to place first among the goals of institutional education in general the mitigation of developmental disturbances and the motivation of young people towards realistically attainable life goals.

If, as we anticipate, the general educational system becomes more flexible than it is at present, and if the institution is only one of many episodes in the development of the young person, then it would perhaps be sufficient if our efforts were aimed at releasing a juvenile who has reduced disturbances and burdens, and a higher level of motivation for future education and work.

With this I do not want to imply that teaching and work in the workshops should be eliminated from educational institutions. But it seems probable that both of these processes need to be organised differently from the usual educational process, with greater attention paid to a search for and encouragement of motivation, and less attention to the acquisition of grades and qualifications.

Let me cite the problem of reading as an example. It is well known that many inmates read poorly. Training of the inmates to read, think and enjoy reading would probably awaken interest in new things (popular scientific literature, and so on). At the same time it would be possible to instil motivation for writing letters, applications, short articles for the young people's press, and the like. In book-keeping the inmates could calculate their earnings, interest from deposits, changes in the value of money, the relations of the various currencies and so on.

Workshops of a more polytechnic nature, furnished with a greater variety of materials and fewer machines would serve to determine the interests and capabilities of the inmates. Together with creative recreational activities this would allow the inmates to open a wider spectrum of their own inclinations. Such motivation, encouraged and tested in practical work, could serve as a starting point for the inmates to become involved in correspondence schools or in schools for commercial apprentices outside the institution.

The goal of institutional education, defined differently from the way it has been to date, could be as follows: therapeutic guidance, and a seeking and encouragement of motivation (A.S. Neil) for realistically attainable life goals. I am personally convinced that this approach would not neglect the developmental process of the inmates, and could in fact accelerate it. Of course this would only be true if release from the institution followed upon intensive help in the incorporation of the juvenile into a suitable environment, learning situation and work. Thus institutional education seems to us to be only one of the phases in the developmental process for the juvenile, and not a final 'last chance'.

In Chapter 15 we explained that the problems of suitable organisation and democratic management of educational institutions with permissive educational methods remain unsolved, and require special attention in the future. The pedagogic part of institutional training also remains unperfected.

Inmates

The basic problem which arises out of all we have said so far is that we are releasing from all educational institutions young people who are still personally and behaviourally disturbed. Any other expectation would be unrealistic, and criticisms due to this fact that are directed against institutional staff are unjustified. Institutional education is only a part of the re-education process, and not its conclusion. If the embryonic experience in communication with adults is not purposely reinforced with leadership and help after release from the institution, then, no matter how positive the efforts of the institutional staff may be, these efforts will eventuate in nothing, and may even remain as the single positive life experience of the young person.

Our findings about the family circumstances (and about interpersonal relationships within the families) and the personality structures of the inmates (see Chapters 19 and 20) show that the inmates in the educational institution at Logatec were not a homogeneous population. Because of this they would require differentiated treatment.

In our work with the staff we attempted to develop their personally determined and therefore varied identities. The institution has not yet accepted our suggestion that the inmates be divided into educational groups appropriate to the individual teacher's personality.

Since we feel that differentiated treatment of different groups of inmates (also adapted to the personal characteristics of the educator) could result in better educational results than undifferentiated treatment (Warren; Folkard, Lyon, Carver), we are of the opinion that classification of inmates according to the personality traits of the educator, as well as other relevant variables, should be one of the first duties of experimental and other educational institutions in the future. At the same time it would be necessary to devote special attention to preventing repetition in the educational group of a negative role that the inmate might have had in his family.

In the light of the purposes that the two control institutions and the experimental institution are supposed to serve, we expected that the inmates would be least personally disturbed at the time of their admission in the institution at Slivnica (open institution), more disturbed in the experimental institution at Logatec (partially open institution), and most disturbed in the educational correction home in Radeče (the most closed educational system of the three institutions). We found no significant differences at the time of admission in the personality traits and the levels of asocial inclination of inmates entering these three institutions (this is also supported by comparisons between the individual institutions, and not only by comparison between the two control institutions taken together and the experimental institution). Contrary to our expectations, we also found no significant differences in the levels of outwardly directed aggressiveness. But we did find a statistically significant difference at the time of admission in the level of maturity of the inmates, a difference which also appears in later testings (although the difference is no longer statistically significant, probably because of the small number of cases).

Inmates are sent to the experimental institution in Logatec and the institution in Slivnica by the social welfare offices and the courts, and to the educational correction home in Radeče by the courts alone.

Since the courts rarely make use of the observation centres for the assignment of inmates to the various kinds of institutions, but do, in most cases in Slovenia, have access to social histories, we assume that the courts' main criteria for the assignment of inmates are still: the severity of the punishable act, to some extent also recidivism (which is poorly registered and documented in Yugoslavia), and the juvenile's family situation.

The question of whether there is a connection between these manifest labels and the level of maturity of inmates (according to Warren's definition) remains open. Although there are other possibilities, we hypothesise that less mature offenders are more frequently involved in penal proceedings than more mature ones (who because of their other behavioural disturbances are more frequently treated only by the social welfare offices).[5]

Although we feel that our system for sending inmates to various educational institutions is quite flexible in comparison with systems in some other countries, we are of the opinion that the system should be made even more flexible in the future. For in practice it happens that an inmate cannot be transferred from an educational institution to the educational correction home without committing a new punishable act in the educational institution.

Our records show that juveniles who are not found to commit additional punishable acts after release from institutions can be more asocial and anti-social than those who are (Chapter 20).

Thus in Yugoslavia there are two formal differences between educational institutions and educational correction homes:

1 The social welfare offices cannot send a juvenile to an educational correction home.

2 If an educational institution (because of being open, and due to special lodging characteristics) is not equal to dealing with an inmate, the court will not transfer the inmate to an educational correction home until he commits a new punishable act, even though the court sent the inmate to the educational institution in the first place, and has the legal power to transfer him.

In order to make the entire system of institutional education more flexible and adapted to the personality structures of inmates (and less dependent on the externally visible behavioural disturbance) one should:

— develop a well-thought-out system of institutional treatment of juveniles in general, with reference to the personal disturbance they have;

— attempt to avoid establishing any institution as a 'dumping ground' for the most disturbed inmates from other institutions;

— make the educational methods and institutional climate in the educational correction homes more like the methods and climate of the educational institutions:

— consistently and professionally diagnose the juvenile before sending him to an institution or transferring him to another one.[6]

In conclusion we want to add that we are aware that the comparisons we made between the two control institutions as a group and the experimental institution were not entirely accurate. For if the experimental institution in Logatec lies between the two control institutions in the severity of disturbance of its inmates, then the average for two control institutions would have to approach the results we found for the experimental institution. It is possible that this could also be the reason why we found so few statistically significant differences between the two groups. Unfortunately the small numbers, particularly in the later testings of inmates and staff in both of the control institutions did not permit more detailed and specific comparisons.

Since we were primarily interested in determining trends in the developmental dynamics for two populations, one of which was exposed to experimental influence, the other not, we feel that we were justified in making such comparisons (considering the objective difficulties), for in this way we did find differences in trends in the dynamic development of the staff and inmates in the great majority of observed parameters. We may hypothesise that a more specific comparison between larger populations would cause these differences between the three institutions to become greater, and not less.

Notes

[1] Vinko Skalar contributed an evaluation of the work after the end of the experiment (pp. 241–3).
[2] Lerman pointed out such a working hypothesis in January 1968.
[3] We were not able to standardise the test for Slovene youth during the experiment.
[4] In France, for example, some teachers are educated for work with personally and behaviourally disturbed youth both inside and outside institutions.
[5] We found no statistically significant differences in the level of maturity of inmates at the time of their admission to the educational institutions at Slivnica and Logatec, but the differences were significant between the educational institution at Logatec and the educational correction home in Radeče (with a higher level of immaturity for the inmates at Radeče) and remained so through all testings.
[6] For further discussion of the problem of flexibility in the commitment of inmates to various educational institutions see Hood and Sparks.

References

Hood, R. G., and Sparks, R. F., 'Community homes and the approved school system', Introduction to *Papers Presented to the Cropwood Round Table Conference*, Institute of Criminology, University of Cambridge, 1969, pp. 7–13.
Lerman, Paul, 'Evaluative studies of institutions for delinquents: implications for research and social policy', *Social Work Journal* of the National Association of Social Workers, USA, no. 3, 1968, pp. 55–64.
Neil, A. S., *Theorie und Praxis der antiautoritären Erziehung*, Rowohlt, Reinbek bei Hamburg, 1969.
Summerhill, *Pro und Contra*, Rowohlt, 1971.
Redl, Fritz, *The Aggressive Child*, The Free Press, New York and London 1966.

Warren, Q. Marguerite, 'Correctional treatment in community settings', a report of current research at the Sixth International Congress on Criminology, Madrid 21–27 September 1970, manuscript.

Folkard, Steven; Lyon, Kate; Carver, Margaret M., *Probation Research, A preliminary report*, Home Office, London 1966.

Appendix I

EVALUATION OF THE INSTITUTION STAFF'S EXPERIENCE OF THE CONSULTING TEAM

In April 1973 an anonymous opinion poll of the staff engaged in the experiment at the Logatec educational institution was carried out. A retrospective evaluation of the staff's experience of the consulting team through the entire period of the experiment was sought. Twenty questionnaires were sent out; nineteen were returned.

Results of answers to questions

1 When you applied for the post in the Logatec institution were you informed of the co-operation with the consulting team of the Institute of Criminology?

2a Have your expectations been fulfilled? [Results in Table 1A.1]

Table 1A.1

Expectations of staff

Expectations	Expectations fulfilled?				
	Yes	No	In part	No answer	Total
1 Professional and theoretical help	6	5	0	0	11
2 Concrete help in work	2	3	0	0	5
3 Both professional, theoretical and concrete help in work	0	0	1	0	1
4 No answer	1	0	0	1	2
Total	9	8	1	1	19

Table 1A.2 How do you evaluate the consulting team today, if you try to think of the entire period of the experiment?

Staff-member	Consulting group (+)	Group wishing to help (+)	Group contributing to personal and professional strength (+)	Supervisory group (−)	Group imposing their own view points (−)	Group opening new dilemmas and increasing personal uncertainty (−)	Group adding additional loads on staff (0)
1	×	×	×			×	×
2		×					
3	×	×	×				
4		×	×				
5	×	×	×			×	×
6	×	×	×				
7	×	×	×				
8		×	×				
9	×	×	×				
10	×	×	×				
11		×	×	×		×	
12		×	×			×	×
13	×			×		×	
14	×	×	×				
15		×	×		×		
16			×		×	×	
17		×	×		×	×	
18	×	×					
19	×	×	×				
Total	11	17	16	2	3	7	3

2b Explain your viewpoints concerning expectations:

Answers of those whose expectations were fulfilled

- I realised what team counselling means   1
- I increased my knowledge   3
- I acquired more knowledge and personal stability   1
- I experienced it as a help   1
- I experienced it as an intensive search for new forms of work together with the team   1
- In the situation as it was nothing more could be expected from the team   1
- No explanation   1

Answers of those whose expectations were not fulfilled

- Co-operation with the team was on a professional level which was too high   1
- Permissiveness and its use in practice was not explained clearly enough   1
- Not enough concrete, direct help was given   3
- The team did not offer concrete help for work in the workshops   1
- The team was not sufficiently sure when giving advice   1
- The team imposed their own viewpoints   1

The answer of one whose expectations have only partially been fulfilled

- The problems that arose in the group to which I belonged occupied me emotionally so much that I was unable to devote myself to an analytic study of the problems

3 How do you evaluate the consulting team today, if you try to think of the entire period of the experiment? [Results in Table 1A.2]

4 How did the consulting team interfere with the work of the staff? [Results in Table 1A.3]

5 What in your opinion was disturbing in the operation of the counselling team in the institution?

Table 1A.3

A combination of answers to question 4 (How did the consulting team interfere with your work?) and to question 7 (If the experiment was restarted would you wish to co-operate with the consulting team under the same conditions?)

Interference with work	Readiness for repeated co-operation		
	Yes	No	Total
Too great	1	2	3
Adequate	2	–	2
Too small	10	4	14
Total	13	6	19

Answers of those who would be willing to repeat co-operation

— Disagreements in the team	5
— An unequal engagement of team members in the experiment and too pronounced ambitions of individual members	1
— Too much theory	1
— The wishes of the team were too distant and owing to fear of additional burdens we did not want to understand them	1
— Impossibility of translating advice into practice	2
— The team's insufficient co-operation with the inmates	1
— No answer	2

Answers of those who would not be willing to repeat co-operation

— Disagreements in the team	2
— Uncertainty of the team in connection with the aims of the experiment	1
— Inability of some members of the team to stand criticism	1
— Too great demands on the part of the team	1
— Too little concrete advice	1

6 What was in your opinion useful and acceptable in the functioning of the consulting team?

Answers of those who would be willing to repeat co-operation

- Offering help in the moments of uncertainty 2
- Prevailing of the human approach over the expert approach in team members 1
- Tolerating the expression of opinions 1
- Team contributing to the cohesiveness of the staff 1
- Delegating initiative to the staff 1
- Equal evaluation of contributions regardless of vocabulary 1
- New suggestions and ideas that team members were initiating 1
- Handing down of expert knowledge 1
- Degree of engagement of team members 1
- Group counselling 1
- No answer 2

Answers of those who would not be willing to repeat co-operation

- Expert help 4
- Expert help and help in crisis situations 1
- Provision for dialogue and support 1

7 If the experiment was restarted would you wish to co-operatewith the consulting team again under the same conditions? Explain your viewpoint. [See also results in Table 1A.3]

Viewpoints of those willing to co-operate again

- I would like further to improve my professional knowledge 3
- Only now do I realise how much I learnt — I would wish for more co-operation 2
- I should accept any conditions just to have co-operation 1
- The entire experiment was an intense experience for me 1
- It would be useful 1
- Team members ought to devote more time to happenings in the institution 1
- I would wish to co-operate but not under the same conditions 1
- No answer 3

Viewpoints of those not willing to co-operate again

The following conditions would have to be changed:

257

- The consulting team's professional views ought to be integrated   2
- Personalities and capabilities of the institutional staff ought to be more justly taken into account   1
- The team's co-operation with small groups of inmates and their educator ought to become the rule   1
- Successful co-operation between inexperienced staff and a team who only give advice is impossible   1
- I don't wish to work in an educational institution under any conditions   1

(Compiled by Vinko Skalar)

Appendix II

Eugene S. JONES*

CONSULTATION REPORT

Introduction

The study covered by this report was carried out in response to a request for consultation in connection with a five-year research project currently under way at the correctional institution at Gorenji Logatec. The research project title is 'Changes in Educational Methods in an Institution for Maladjusted Youth' and has recently entered upon its fifth year.

The present report is based on daily observation of the institution rehabilitation programme at Gorenji Logatec for the past two months and attendance at weekly meetings during the same period with the research team of the Institute of Criminology.

The writer feels compelled to preface this report by stating that in his experience, the programme at Gorenji Logatec is unsurpassed in its overall therapeutic community climate and humanitarian approach to the treatment of delinquent youth. The reader is cautioned that if this report at times appears to be overly critical, it should be remembered that the recommendations are submitted on the premise that the best of human social institutions is subject to improvement.

Evaluation

1   Staff—youth relationships

Interpersonal relationships between adults and boys at the institution are generally characterised by mutual respect and healthy, constructive interaction. The staff demonstrate an understanding and permissive attitude in their treatment approach. (Initial staff selection and continuing support from clinical research staff consultants appear to be major contributing factors here.)

* Superintendent, Northern Reception Center Clinic, Sacramento, California.

It is suggested that the permissive attitude of staff should be linked to an emphasis on the personal responsibility of the boy for his behaviour; the boy should learn not only to understand his impulses but also to control his behaviour (including respect for the rights and possessions of others, care of personal living quarters, personal hygiene, table manners, etc.). (See Recommendations 1 and 2, below.)

2 Staff communication

Day-by-day communication between staff in connection with critical events, behaviour and programme participation of individual boys, off-campus visits, and so on, is generally very good. This type of communication is maintained by daily written entries in logs (diaries) which are required reading for all programme staff, as well as by face-to-face communication.

Communication on long-term treatment planning and follow-through on individual cases, however, needs to be improved in order to eliminate the not infrequent, arbitrary, last-minute decisions on case management and placement which now occur. (See Recommendation 3.)

3 Institution–local community relationships

The permissive treatment philosophy of the institution clashes inevitably with the prevailing authoritarian–repressive attitudes toward delinquent youth in the surrounding community. This creates a serious problem for staff whose homes and families are located in this small, rural setting, and who are therefore exposed to conflicting pressures regarding approaches to delinquency. (See Recommendation 4.)

4 Training and treatment programme elements

The programme elements which demonstrate better-than-average effectiveness are large group therapeutic community meetings, the vocational shop work training programme, and the recreation and leisure time programme.

Those programme elements which need strengthening are small group counselling, individual treatment planning and follow-through, and academic instruction.

(a) *Large group therapeutic community meetings.* Participation is regular and generally active and constructive for both boys and staff: attempts should be made to encourage greater individual and group responsibility on the part of boys. (See Recommendation 1.)

260

(b) *Small group counselling.* Staff—boy relationships are generally healthy and constructive, but more effectively planned interaction is needed. (See Recommendation 5.)

(c) *Individual treatment planning and follow-through.* Case conferences should be held with greater regularity, with better advance preparation of progress reports by participants, and with more emphasis upon consistent follow-through on agreed-upon treatment goals and objectives for individual cases. (See Recommendation 3.)

(d) *Recreation and leisure time programme.* Small institution size combined with staff imagination and flexibility make this element a strong programme feature.

(e) *Vocational training (work shops).* Shopmasters are developing good motivation for learning through constructive work training assignments and pay incentives; this is also a strong programme element.

(f) *Academic training.* Formal academic training is currently being provided on an irregular basis without a sufficient number of trained staff. (See Recommendation 6.)

5 *Custodial security coverage*

A vulnerability has been demonstrated here in connection with coverage at night by a single duty officer. (See Recommendation 7.)

6 *Organisation and Co-ordination*

It is predictable that any new organisation which must function during its first year of existence without a director, with totally inexperienced staff who receive guidance primarily from a newly formed research team composed of various professional disciplines representing different points of view, will experience initial organisational problems. While the institution organisation at Gorenji Logatec has survived remarkably well despite this initial handicap, serious organisational problems are currently apparent. Partly because the organisation is small, top managers are performing supervisory functions which should be delegated to subordinate middle managers in order to free top management for more effective overall programme planning and evaluation. A related organisational problem is that direction of major programme elements is divided between two top managers at present, rather than being provided by co-ordinated direction from a single manager. This situation renders it difficult, if not impossible, to clarify lines of authority and areas of responsibility. (See Recommendation 8.)

261

Recommendations

1 Experiment with youth leadership in large group therapeutic community meetings (possibly by rotating chairmanship from a committee selected democratically by small groups).

2 Develop youth participation in social self-government by including students as members of the Workers' Institution Council.

3 Utilise the skills and knowledge of the psychologist and social worker as a resource to educators and shopmasters by means of the case conference method on selected problem cases, in addition to regularly scheduled individual case progress reviews.

4 Continue to develop public relations through community education. Relocation of the institution to a metropolitan setting as currently planned will probably alleviate this problem considerably.

5 Educator work styles should be matched so far as possible to interpersonal maturity (l-level) of small group membership composition in order to permit development of more effective treatment strategies. (Reference material forwarded by consultant.)

6 Strengthen programme element of academic instruction by acquiring an additional trained staff position for a teacher-coordinator or by reclassifying one of the existing shopmaster positions when a vacancy occurs.

7 Provide regularly scheduled standby coverage for night duty officer.

8 Reorganise administratively along lines depicted in attached organisational charts. Designate a supervising educator from existing educators and a supervising shopmaster from existing shopmasters, providing economic incentive of 5 or 10 per cent salary differential. [In discussing Recommendation no. 8 with Mr Skoflek and Dr Vodopivec after this report was submitted, an additional alternative was considered; namely, centralisation of administrative control of the major programme elements (educators and shopmasters and clinical staff) through creating a new position of clinical director or treatment team supervisor which would report to the director.]

Note: The preceding recommendations are not listed in any order of priority; the final recommendation (no. 8), however, probably deserves the most urgent consideration.

12 July 1971

Appendix III

Dr Vojin MATIĆ*

A REPORT ON A PSYCHOLOGICAL ESTIMATE OF THE TEAM TAKING PART IN THE RESEARCH AND THEIR INTERACTIONS IN THE COURSE OF WORK

Because the aim of the research was to establish a mode of communication, two types of tasks can be distinguished:

1 One part of the team worked predominantly as counsellors to the people in charge of the inmates, that is of shopmasters and educators.

2 The other part was mainly preoccupied with establishing the research policy, contributing information from their particular fields of knowledge, and integrating relationships among team members as well as between the team and the educational staff of the institution.

Although basic directions for work had already been laid down in the project itself, they underwent gradual changes. The concepts underwent changes, too, partly in connection with the filling of new work places and the one-year leave of the psychologist Skalar, and partly owing to differing viewpoints existing at the very beginning and the appearance, in the course of work, of new unforeseen problems.

Differences in theory manifested themselves in the practical problem of how to reduce everyday conflicts and disciplinary infringements in the institution. Rooted in the professional background of the team members, two different viewpoints regarding this problem emerged. The question was whether disciplinary difficulties could be solved without pedagogic restrictions and only by means of such forms and channels of non-directive group work as were gradually introduced.

Such a solution was pursued by project leaders at team meetings and in work with shopmasters and educators, and later in the therapeutic communities. The need for a certain active psychological intervention, which is essential in the process of re-education, emerged only much later. In the

* Psychiatrist, Professor at the Faculty of Philosophy, Belgrade University.

course of 1967 the consulting team experienced an emotional progress in their interactions, which led to a general enthusiasm both of the management and the educational staff of the institution. This optimism was particularly evident in the educators, but also in some members of the consulting team, because it helped many people to solve certain problems of self-confidence.

The educators and shopmasters apparently gained most by being freed from the fear and tension that are usually aroused in them by traditional repressive education, which demands great responsibilities, brings little satisfaction, and generally creates a feeling of mistrust among them behind which they try to cover up their mistakes. In the course of group-work they gradually began to understand the motives of the youths' behaviour, to see their own share in the conflicts, and to think of the ways and means of dealing successfully with undesirable behaviour. They stopped fearing that they might be accused of inefficiency. A major, perhaps the greatest, relief was the transformation of their group into a structured and differentiated collective, which included both the managing personnel and the educators; all these were aware of being in the same situation, in which seeking help was not a shameful act. Thus in addition to receiving aid from counsellors they gave one another enormous help in this phase of the development of their relationships.

In this way the responsibility of the managing personnel, the educators and shopmasters became a collective one. Thus individuals felt less need to settle their personal reckonings with colleagues and inmates, and could dedicate their efforts to the common goal. In addition, the attention paid to shopmasters, who represent a subculture that is often considered inferior, with their educational influence also being underestimated, brought about an atmosphere of greater confidence and better communication with the other professionals, as well as the possibility of seeking mutual advice. In this atmosphere of open communication on all levels, many problems arising from unadmitted conflicts among the educators themselves, and among the educators and their charges, disappeared. In this way the atmosphere was cleared of the constant, sometimes even paranoiac caution that often prevails in such institutions. Thus the educational staff, liberated from their tensions and some of the conflicts on one hand, and learning new facts and techniques on the other, were happily welcoming the new knowledge they were offered. They also showed interest in further self-education, in order to improve their knowledge and techniques and the treatment of their charges.

However, conflicts duly arose both from rational and from emotional, unconscious sources. After the first optimism, which had boosted the morale of all the participants in the research and work, certain daily problems of institutional discipline increasingly came to be noted. They had to be resolved, but were rooted in such conflicts as could not be resolved on the spot by group work. They disturbed not only orderly life in the institution, but also the relationships among educators, and those among educators and the inmates who were not involved in the conflicts. These incidents increased the tension and led to some sort of 'flight from freedom' in those who were not willing to bear the consequences of aggressiveness against offenders by the other inmates, or by people in the neighbourhood of the institution. The conflicts arising in the neighbourhood led to aggressiveness on the part of the citizens both against the management and the inmates of the institution. This is a normal reaction, because all the members of the educational staff could not operate on the same level in group work so as to liberate their charges of conflicts immediately on their occurrence. On the other hand, in certain structures of asocial behaviour of individual inmates, resolving the problem of inner conflicts presents an extremely difficult task even for highly trained experts in group therapy of any kind.

This state of affairs led to perceptions which differed according to the professional training of the team members: the psychiatrist with experience in non-directive group work, came to the conclusion that it was necessary to deepen the educational staff's understanding of the hidden motives of the inmates' behaviour, while the pedagogue and the psychologist concluded that a way of resolving immediate interpersonal conflicts had to be found either within, or without regard to, the general course of re-education.

Clashes in the team increased. They were partly overcome, but they also obstructed and demobilised individual members, causing a certain restructuring of the dynamics of relationships in the team. The psychiatrist, who in spite of everything continued to instruct the educators, among whom he had won some enthusiastic followers, became increasingly isolated. We are sorry to state that his work sometimes curtailed the participation of other team members, notwithstanding their open or concealed disapproval of it before the educational management of the institution. Therefore a conflict arose among team members, based on the differing approaches of their professions; i.e., between the therapist and psychologist, and between the psychologist and the pedagogue. Finally aggression turned towards the leader of the project, who, according to her role, took the stand of the mediator.

The initial belief that 'we will all learn something' created a certain optimism and a sufficiently high motivation for work. It brought about an

265

almost unbelievable readiness in the educational staff for overcoming the usual resistance and misgivings towards other professionals. The shifting of their interest from the worry about other people's evaluation of their efficiency to the happenings in the group, made them sensitive to the motivation behind their charges' behaviour and to the goals of re-education. This greatly improved their ability to establish contacts with their charges and created a true therapeutic atmosphere. On the other hand, their judgement of an educator's abilities underwent a basic change.

A good educator was no longer a person who maintained discipline by repression or fraud or cover up, but was he who, at staff meetings, succeeded in communicating to his colleagues that understanding which is necessary in order to comprehend the inmates' behaviour. 'Let's consider the problem together' became heard far more frequently in their discussions, instead of the competitive 'You haven't done this well. It should be done this way ...'. Naturally, this attitude has its drawbacks, too. On the one hand the educators could not free themselves from the responsibility for the behaviour of their charges, and were ready to retreat to repressive positions, thus relieving the inmates of the responsibility while they themselves felt guilty towards their colleagues. On the other hand no account was taken of the need for punishment of certain youths; this need increased due to the permissive attitude and the lack of awareness of this need.

In spite of the permissive concept of work with the youths, the fact that preliminary diagnostic classification was not a rule, and that diagnostic meetings did not deal with the development of all individuals, revealed itself in the course of work as a shortcoming. It could be said that in these conditions the youths had a substitute mother, but lacked a father. Regardless of the fact that the father image in the institution would have a democratic and not a repressive character, it has to be present as a figure of identification with love.

Although at the beginning a lot was left open in the belief that in the course of work it would become clear what path should be followed, it is obvious that the father figure ought to have been postulated at once. Relief from the fear of criticism for indulgence on the part of colleagues and superiors, and the pleasure in discovering new phenomena in the youths' and in their own work, accounted for the fact that disciplinary problems seemed of minor importance. Therefore the relevant members of the team, in the first place the psychologist and the pedagogue, tried to introduce this principle too into the work. If the respective roles of those who re-educate by group work and those who resolve current problems had been established, together with their co-operation, at the very beginning, the many bitter hours in the life of the managing team, and the numerous uncertainties of the educators, whom the conflicts deprived of courage and self-confidence, could have been avoided. There is no doubt that a certain standard of success and social behaviour, of knowledge and skills existed in the institution, because it cannot be absent from any community; but not enough attention was paid to it, with the result that it became a hidden and unconscious source of conflict. The level of success and behaviour could not be the same as in regular schools and workshops, but whether we want it or not, this level − whatever it is − presupposes certain criteria of behaviour which should be taken account of. A certain degree of aggressiveness of educators reveals itself in a more or less concealed way through these criteria, and this aggressiveness always stood in contrast to the permissive stand of the group therapist. It came to the fore both in the groups of inmates and in the therapeutic community, and structured the relationships among the inmates, as well as between them and the educators. The permissive stand which lasts twenty-four hours every day, and which exposes the educator in numerous unforeseen situations, when he is unable altogether to control his own therapeutic attitude and think of the hidden impulses, also makes work difficult at particular meetings dedicated to group therapy. The neglect of all more or less concealed aggressive attitudes of the educational staff during the entire working day creates, whether we want it or not, a certain confusion in relationships as well as in the therapeutic meetings. This is bound to arise if the same technique of work is applied on all levels and in all groups. The inmates are unable to accept the same relationships on all levels, and the educators are unable to control themselves to the same degree as in therapeutic meetings throughout their working day.

Therefore, instead of neglecting this structuring repressive aspect of education, which cannot be avoided despite all efforts, it ought to have been considered and assigned a role and way of operating right at the beginning, or at least in the course of work. If this is not done an unacceptable mode of communication between the various structures involved in the therapy is created, and this is bound to lead to warped communication on all levels.

Such a structuring repressive role, in relation to certain persons and also to group meetings (for example when decisions are made), would have given greater strength both to groups in cases of conflicts, and to educators when they felt lost. It would also have been necessary to introduce meetings different from the therapeutic ones, both with regard to group members and with regard to leaders. These should have been organised on the basis of some institutional aspect, such as that of workshops or dormitories, and they should have dealt with everyday questions. Moreover, the possibility of individual counselling, in other words psychotherapy, ought probably to have been introduced. This could have been included in group work and in the therapeutic unit, thus removing the possibility of misunderstanding and a break in communication.

It goes without saying that it is easier to see the causes of misunderstanding afterwards than to foresee them, and it is certain that from our present perspective each member of the team could make constructive suggestions regarding both his own work and that of the other team members. My role of an unbiased observer who has not involved in any definite concept affords me the opportunity of saying things that make it appear I know much more than I actually do.

In addition, it could be foreseen what kind of information would circulate among the participants. Conflicts that are concealed for understandable human and professional reasons can constantly disturb the circulation of information, but can also improve it, if brought into the open. This circulation in institutions is disturbed anyhow, because of the psychological disturbances of the inmates, their mistrust, their need to provoke others, and the compulsory repetition of offences. Therefore the channels of communication ought to be even wider and smoother than in other working units. In order to obtain a comparison between what is taking place in the consulting team, the group of educators and the inmates' groups, it would be a good plan to organise a sociological registration of everything taking place on all the previously mentioned levels by means of a formal, and possibly also informal, exchange of information both horizontally and vertically. Excellent ideas, decisions, solutions and suggestions could be conducted along these channels and recommended or proposed for discussion and observance. Making and adhering to decisions is a major factor influencing the relationships in the institution. Paying attention to what has been decided should be bound up with certain rewards, while disregard of it should not necessarily entail punishment.

All these modes of indirectly influencing people are nowadays used in psychiatric and educational institutions, and they yield good results. However, the best structuring or relationships in an institution, and the best techniques of work, can go to pieces through the inability of individuals to communicate, which prevents them, on one hand, from translating their knowledge into practice, and, on the other, from giving accurate information on the inmates. Therefore, for the educational staff to have high professional qualifications is not a guarantee of the best results. It is necessary constantly to control the ability of the educators to transmit information and use the techniques they acquire at group meetings. It is well known that the ability to transmit information and techniques correctly is not realised equally on all levels of interaction; i.e., in individual, group and mass work, in work with children and grown-ups, in work with neurotic and psychotic persons, and so on. Educators themselves often behave differently towards their equals, their superiors and the youngsters. In the course of time these psychological and sociological findings enable us better to assign each educator his role and to transfer inmates to the groups they are best suited for. Moreover, in non-directive therapy, which is the most acceptable for many reasons, it is absolutely necessary to introduce — at least, in the course of time if not at the very beginning — meetings at which personalities of individual youths are evaluated, a measure not foreseen by non-directive therapy, but the lack of which poses difficulties for the composition of groups. In these meetings the character of the disturbance of individual youths would be discussed, and additional individual treatment, as well as any change in the choice of the most suitable group, would be suggested.

Perhaps it would be a good plan to organise some kind of temporary group — they already exist in some institutions — in which the inmates would undergo observation until it was decided, in a common meeting, to which group they properly belonged.

Everything that has been pointed out in this report would probably ease the relationships in the group and result, not in the avoidance of conflicts, which is undesirable, but in a better exploitation of them with the aim further to structure and develop the relationships in the group. All this would contribute to a more efficient work with educators and their charges.

Belgrade, 12 August 1972.

Index